Interpretation and Construction

New Directions in Aesthetics

Blackwell's New Directions in Aesthetics series highlights ambitious single and multiple-author books that confront the most intriguing and pressing problems in aesthetics and the philosophy of art today. Each book advances understanding of the subject at hand, written in a way that is accessible to advanced undergraduate and graduate students.

Interpretation and Construction

Art, Speech, and the Law

ROBERT STECKER

Blackwell
Publishing

350 Main Street, Malden, MA 02148-5018, USA
108 Cowley Road, Oxford OX4 1JF, UK
530 Swanston Street, Carlton South, Melbourne, Victoria 3053, Australia
Kurfürstendamm 57, 10707 Berlin, Germany

First published 2003 by Blackwell Publishing Ltd

Library of Congress Cataloging-in-Publication Data

Stecker, Robert, 1947–
    Interpretation and construction : art, speech, and the law / Robert Stecker.
        p. cm. — (New directions in aesthetics)
    Includes bibliographical references and index.
    ISBN 1–40510–174–1 (alk. paper) — ISBN 1–40510–175–X
(pbk. : alk. paper)
    1. Hermeneutics. 2. Constructivism (Philosophy). 3. Art—Philosophy.
4. Law — Interpretation and construction. I. Title. II. Series.
BD241 .S78 2003
121′.68—dc21

2002006134

A catalogue record for this title is available from the British Library.

Set in 10 on 12.5 pt Galliard
by Ace Filmsetting Ltd, Frome, Somerset
Printed and bound in the United Kingdom
by MPG Books Ltd, Bodmin, Cornwall

For further information on
Blackwell Publishing, visit our website:
http://www.blackwellpublishing.com

*To the instigators: Michael Krausz, Joseph Margolis, and Philip Percival;
and the agitators: Sonia and Nadia*

Contents

Preface

I began to write this book with two ideas in mind. The first was to refine and ramify a theory of interpretation that has been developing for at least ten years. This theory identifies the issues under debate more clearly than its rivals and provides solutions to these issues that find some truth in most of the competing positions. The ramification of the theory involved applying it beyond art and literary interpretation, where it has been confined in my earlier writings, to such everyday things as conversations or instruction manuals and to other extraordinary things such as the law. It also meant exploring the theory's implications for various conceptual and ontological issues, as well as what my favored resolution of those issues implies for the theory.

The other idea was to explore the various constructivist conceptions of interpretation. The basic thought behind constructivism is that interpretations contribute to the making of their objects either by altering their meaning or creating new objects outright. This is one of the large-scale ways of approaching the topic of interpretation that is an alternative to my own. I wanted to set out the various versions of constructivism, the numerous arguments for these versions, and give them their due, which by and large meant showing why the arguments were bad and constructivist views implausible. I trust that I have carried out this project.

However, along the way I discovered a few things that I did not expect. The first thing I discovered was that under the right conditions constructivism, or a particular version of it, can be true. The fact is that in the case of art the conditions typically are not right despite what the constructivists think. At least this is one of the theses I will argue in the following pages. However, I also will argue that in the realm of law the conditions are right, and a good theory of legal interpretation should have a fairly strong constructivist component.

The other thing I discovered unexpectedly was that this solves an intellectual problem that I never set out to solve. This is the dilemma of the liberal humanist. Being a humanist, this type of character does not buy into claims about the death of the author, the irrelevance of origins, or the relativism of interpretive truth. Rather, an encounter with a work of literature ought to have the potential of being an encounter with its author speaking to us through the work (or at least the best historically grounded hypothesis about what this author is saying). An interpretation ought to be capable of revealing this. In fact, the humanist thinks, if we are interested in the meaning of a work, this is what we should try to grasp. On the other hand, being a liberal, this fellow cannot bear those politicians who claim that only considerations of original intent, or of the text as would be taken in its original context, are relevant to the judicial interpretation of the law. That, the liberal thinks, is a smoke screen for maintaining the status quo. A document like the United States Constitution needs to be reinterpreted anew as times change. Hence, a certain amount of judicial "activism" is both desirable and unavoidable.

The problem is that being both a humanist and a liberal my character also seems to be inconsistent, claiming what is good interpretation for literature is bad, indeed hopeless, interpretation for law. The liberal humanist faces many problems, and is attacked these days on fronts both from the left and from the right. However, if the first discovery mentioned above is correct, this apparent inconsistency is not a real one. We should not suppose that law is to be interpreted in the same way as literature – or so I will argue in what follows.

This result reflects one of the larger themes of this book. Interpretation is not one thing. It is not, because there is not one, but several interpretive questions we can ask. It is not, because there is not one but several interpretive aims we pursue. Finally, interpretation is not one thing, because the questions we ask and the aims we pursue are in part a function of the practice we are interpreting.

This book was written during 2000–2001 by virtue of a sabbatical, extended to a full year by a Research Professorship. I am grateful to Central Michigan University for granting a year off from teaching to pursue research. Many of the thoughts, however, began to develop in earlier papers and in my book *Artworks: Definition, Meaning, Value* (Pennsylvania State University Press, 1997). A shorter version of chapter 2 appeared as "Interpretation," in the *Routledge Companion to Aesthetics*, edited by Berys Gaut and Dominic Lopez (Routledge, 2000), 229–51. A paper, "Interpretation and the Ontology of Art," in *Is There the Single Right Interpretation?*, edited by Michael Krausz (Pennsylvania State University Press, forthcoming), is now a scattered object to be found in chapters 3, 5, and 6. Chapter 6 also includes some parts of my "The Constructivist's Dilemma" and a slightly revised version of the discussion piece "Is the Constructivist's Dilemma Flawed?" both published in the *Journal of Aesthetics and Art Criticism* (1997, 55:43–52, and 2002, 60:81–2, respectively). Chapter 8 contains "Relativism," which first appeared in the *Encyclopedia of Aesthetics*, edited by Michael Kelly (Oxford University Press, 1998), 120–4. I am grateful to all of the above for permission to reprint.

I have received helpful comments from many people. Stephen Davies and two anonymous reviewers for Blackwell Publishing read chapters 2–6 and have provided invaluable advice. Philip Percival has engaged in extremely helpful discussion with me on the material in chapters 5 and 6, and I am most appreciative for his criticisms and suggestions. Maite Ezcurdia, Gary Fuller, William Irwin and Jonathan McKeown-Green helped a lot with chapter 1, as did Dom Lopez with the Routledge *Companion* version of chapter 2. I received very helpful comments on chapter 5 from Sherri Irvin. Alan Goldman, Michael Krausz, and Joseph Margolis commented on earlier versions of chapter 6. I am especially grateful to Steve Manley, Jonathan Neufeldt, and Dennis Patterson for their comments on chapter 7, since I was most in need of help on the topic of legal interpretation. Parts of the book were discussed at colloquiums at the University of Auckland, University of Canterbury, Central Michigan University, Georgia State University, and the University of Miami, and I express gratitude to the philosophy departments at these institutions for their invitations and comments, and most especially those of Andrew Altman, Alan Casebier, Tim Dare, Gary Fuller, Cynthia Macdonald, Barbara Montero, Steve Reiber, and David Weberman.

Interpreting the Everyday

I begin with something that I constantly need to interpret: instruction manuals. I have before me instructions for installing a ceiling fan and light kit. It is full of expressions the meanings of which are elusive to me. For example, what is a clevis pin? Fortunately, I do not have to *figure out* the answer to this question, because there is an assembly diagram that clearly identifies a clevis pin (at least if I can find a definite match in my kit). However, then I come across this: "Inspect locating ridge in hanger bracket to insure positive location in hanger ball." I can identify hanger ball and bracket from the diagram, but nothing indicates what a locating ridge is, and the instructions are completely silent about what I should do with ball and bracket if I succeed in making the inspection. As I look down the list of steps, I find no further illumination, but I do come to some fine print that contains warnings. They tell me that failure to follow instructions or mistakes in assembly are likely to result in my maiming or killing myself as well as voiding the warranty.

I return to ball and bracket. What I am trying to figure out is what the author of the manual is intending to tell me to do. My object is not simply to identify what he does tell me to do, because I know I have to do more than make an inspection to complete the assembly, and making an inspection is all I am actually told to do with the items in question. My first step is to see what the instruction *could* mean. Taken literally, it seems to say that I should see how the bracket could fit in the ball. But brackets do not fit in balls; it is the other way round. So the literal meaning is not the right one. I notice that the bracket contains a semicircular region where a ball could fit. I reach a conclusion: What the instruction is trying to tell me to do is to see how the ball fits in the semicircular region and then to fit it in there. The significance of all this to me is (in order of importance): preservation of life and limb versus death or injury, success or failure in completing the project, keeping warranty intact.

The questions raised by the instruction manual are the basic interpretive questions in one of the central domains where interpretation occurs. This domain includes not only instructions, recipes, ordinary linguistic and nonlinguistic behavior, but also art, literature, the law, and human thought and its expression in writing of all kinds. I proceed by saying something more about this domain and the basic questions just alluded to. This chapter will then focus on one of the everyday items in the domain: utterances made in ordinary conversation.

The Intentional Domain

This book is about interpreting what we do and make. For this reason, it is not concerned with every application of the word "interpretation," and it is not concerned with every domain in which interpretation occurs. It is concerned with the interpretation of intentional human behavior and its products – the things made as an intended consequence of the behavior.

I choose this domain (the intentional domain) for several reasons. First, it is central, because it is at least one of the domains where "interpretation" has primary application. Second, it is the right size. It is sufficiently large that it leaves room to compare the nature of interpretation in various subdomains, which in turn helps us to test the adequacy of our theory. It is reasonable to expect all interpretations in this domain to have some things in common, while other things are determined by the character of the subdomain. One way we can test our theory is to see if it meets this expectation. However, the expectation would not be reasonable if we attempt to account for everything that gets called "interpretation," and it could not be tested in this way if we confined ourselves to a fairly narrow subdomain such as literary interpretation. Third, it is a common view that the object of interpretation is an intentional object or an object with intentional properties. We will see in subsequent chapters that people who hold this view mean many different things by "intentional object" and that the view should be resisted given many of things that are meant. However, one reasonable notion of intentional object is an object in the domain I specified above as forming a single coherent, if diverse, subject matter for interpretation.

Just to avoid any possibility of confusion, let me distinguish "intentional," in the sense I am here using it from one other sense it commonly has in philosophical writing. As I am using it, "intentional" is, in the first place, a property of actions. Actions have this property, as a result of their coming into existence and their being "guided" by certain mental states: intentions. Of course, some intentions do not result in action at all, and some do not result in the intended action. These are intentions that fail in some way. "Intentional" in the sense used here carries over to the products of action. If I intentionally make a clock with a second hand, then having a second hand is an intended (intentional) property of the clock, just as installing a second hand is something I intentionally do. On the other hand, I may have no intention regarding the color of the second hand. The fact that the second hand is bronze in color is not an intended property of the clock.

This sense of "intentional" should be distinguished from another, alluded to above. On this second sense, "intentional" refers to the property of aboutness had by our thoughts, among other things. A thought of Yellowstone National Park may arise in my mind. It may arise nonvoluntarily without my intending to think about the park. If so, the thought has the property of being intentional in the second sense, since it is about something, but not in the first, since I did not intend to think about the park. Many things that are intentional in the first sense are also intentional in the second, which is the chief reason the two could be confused. For example, discourse of all kinds is intentional in both senses. However, just as there are things which are not intentional in the first sense but are intentional in the second (e.g., certain thoughts), so there are things which are intentional in the first sense, but not the second. These include many artifacts. Consider ceiling fans. They intentionally have many properties and parts, but fans are not about anything.

While in the business of avoiding confusions, let me clarify one other thing. I use "intentional" to characterize the domain of objects I am concerned with. This is not meant to imply that all interpretation of these objects is necessarily concerned with identifying the intention with which they are done or made. As we will soon see, this is only one interpretive issue among others.

Although I am concerned with the whole intentional domain, not all the items in it will receive equal treatment. Chapters 2–4 are concerned with art and literature, which is also the primary, if not the exclusive, concern in chapters 5 and 6. Chapter 7 is concerned with legal interpretation. The reason for this special attention is that these are areas where interpretation occurs on an elaborate scale, self-consciously executed by people (though not only by them) whose training and profession it is do so. These are also areas where there are well worked out, competing theories of interpretation. In addition, I believe the differences between these two important subdomains provide considerable illumination about one of the chief issues with which this book will be concerned: whether interpretation discovers truths or constructs something new (in addition to the interpretation itself).

This chapter, on the other hand, will be concerned with interpretation in the intentional domain in general and in everyday situations where we encounter talk, behavior, or discourse of which sense needs to be made.

Four Questions

What all objects of interpretation in our domain have in common is that, of each of them, four basic questions can be asked: (1) What is the object intended to mean (be, do)? (2) What could it mean (be, be doing)? (3) What does it mean (what it is; what it is doing)? (4) What is its significance to me (group g)? These are the basic interpretive questions. When we interpret objects in our domain, we answer at least one of these four questions, though not every answer to them is an interpretation, and there are other interpretive questions we might answer as well. Even at its most basic, interpretation is not simple. There is not a single question all interpretations are trying to answer.

The example with which I began this chapter is not only a good example of interpretation, but it is one where all the basic interpretive questions come into play. I had to ask what the instructions could mean in order to figure out what they mean in order to determine what they were intended to mean. I also had to figure the significance of the instructions to me, which turned out to be greater than I initially believed.

Situations requiring interpretation do not always raise all four basic questions. Here is an example. We are conversing. You say, "Your last paper was magnificent. It contained distinctions I could never have noticed." I know what you said. I am not sure what you intended by it. Is it a genuine compliment or a backhanded one? Is it said in passing or as an implicit critique of a tendency to make too many fine distinctions? These are the main interpretive issues other then the significance I should give to your opinion.

Notice a few further things about our basic questions. I did not know what either "clevis pin" or "locating ridge" referred to when I started to install the ceiling fan. However, finding out the referent of the former expression did not require interpretation, because I was able to identify it straightaway by looking at the diagram, just as, if I find out the meaning of a word by looking it up in a dictionary, I am not interpreting. (If you do want to claim this is interpretation, you would need to give an argument why it has crucial similarities to clearer cases.) My figuring out what was meant by "locating ridge" in the manual (viz., the semicircular region) is much more a matter of interpretation. Second, just as I can ask essentially the same question, and be interpreting on one occasion, but not on another, different people who come up with the same answer may be such that one is interpreting and the other is not. Unlike me, an experienced electrician who has installed countless ceiling fans may not have to interpret to find out what "locating ridge" means. He may just know. Third, while some claim we interpret only when there is no definite fact to be discovered, notice that whether I interpret or not in the cases just mentioned does not depend on whether there is a fact of the matter. I take it there is a fact of the matter as to whether "locating ridge" (was intended to) refer to the semicircular region and as to whether you meant nothing but praise in your remark to me about my paper. Whether we have an instance of interpretation has more to do with the steps I need to take to figure out an answer to the relevant question(s) than whether my question(s) have answers that are true.

Special Aims

So far I have said that all interpretations in the intentional domain are answers to at least one of the four basic "interpretive" questions. We have looked at a couple of examples of this as well as an example of a case (of the clevis pin) where we can answer one of these questions without interpreting, or at least, without it being obvious that we are.

I also said that we should expect that some aspects of interpretation are determined by the subdomain in which they arise. In future chapters, we will see how this gets worked out in detail in the cases of art, literary, and legal interpretation. For now, let me express the basic thought underlying the expectation. It is that we interpret with specific aims shaped not only by the four questions but by the character or point of the subdomain. So in the case of the instructions for assembling and installing a ceiling fan, my ultimate aim is to use the instruction to infer what I *should* do to accomplish the assembly so that I end up with a working fan, while life, limb, and warranty remain intact. Questions about what the instructions could mean, do mean, or even are intended to mean ultimately serve this aim.

What I have just said about the special aim of instruction manual interpretation is an instance of an interpretive aim being shaped by values, which gives point to a subdomain of the intentional domain. Such manuals have purely instrumental, noninherent, nonintrinsic, value.[1] They are means to ends that are means to further ends. The special aim I attributed to instruction manual interpretation is simply the aim of arriving at an understanding of a manual so that it optimally fulfills its function of being such a means.

When we are dealing with complex practices such as those found in the art or legal worlds, it is unrealistic to suppose there is such a thing as *the* point or aim of the practice.[2] In such cases, there are multiple values which give rise to distinct special aims, which either have to be pursued separately by different interpretations or jointly in a single interpretation.

Though this is largely a topic for later chapters, I will give one example here of an aim of art interpretation being shaped by artistic values. Among the things we value in artworks themselves is the satisfaction of aesthetic interest – the desire to have intrinsically valuable aesthetic experiences. Something else we value both in artworks and the practice of art is the free exploration of an area of interest even where the directions this takes one are found shocking by many. Both of these values, and others as well, influence not just the practice of creating art but also of interpreting it. The way this happens (as I see it) is to redirect the point of asking one of our four basic interpretive questions, namely, "What could it mean?" Normally (e.g., in conversational contexts) this question is a preliminary to finding what we really want to know: what something does mean or is intended to mean. In these contexts, if we know what something does (is intended to) mean, we would never go back and ask what (else) it could mean. In the realm of art interpretation, however, although we sometimes ask, "What could it mean?" (or "How can it be taken?") for precisely the same reason, we do not always do so. We sometimes ask it for its own sake, because doing so enhances the aesthetic interest of a work or because it allows us to explore possible ways of taking the work that happen to interest us. This leads to multiple conceptions of works, many of which are not required by what a work does mean. This sort of interpretive exploration is something we tend not to allow ourselves in many other contexts. The reason we allow it in the art context is that it is done in pursuit of things highly valued in art practice in general.

Sometimes the realization of what we value in a subdomain is pretty happily captured by one or more of the four basic questions in their standard employment. This is the case in the conversational contexts alluded to in the previous paragraph. Even some who are anti-intentionalists, when it comes to the interpretation of literature or law (S. Davies 1991, Dworkin 1986, Levinson 1996, Moore 1996), claim that our ultimate interpretive aim in conversational contexts is to recover an interlocutor's intention(s). My own view is that the case is a bit more complicated than that. We often have to balance an equal interest in what is said or conveyed (what an utterance does mean) and what someone intends to say or convey (what the utterance is intended to mean).[3] For example, consider a context where someone's speech expresses an official position of some sort. One can think of many cases: a politician at a press conference, a department chair explaining tenure requirements to a new hire, a person presenting a paper at a conference, or an employee of an airline announcing a new departure time. In cases like these, the question we tend to ask first is "What was said?" We may go on to ask, "Is that what was intended?" We may ask this of the politician if what he says seems to depart from long-held positions, but is passed without the fanfare such a departure would be expected to elicit. Did he really mean to express such a departure or was what he said more like a slip of some sort that will receive subsequent "clarification"? In these situations, we are in fact on the lookout both for what is actually said and what is intended. Caring about both, we are ready to notice disparities.

There are other conversational situations, where one attends to words just as a means to figuring out what someone intends to say or do with them. Suppose you say to me, "Let's meet at the bistro on Main and High at eight." I know there is no bistro at that location, but that there is a cafe, and I also know you tend to ignore distinctions like those between bistros and cafes. I may just say, "Sure." Instantly forgetting what you actually said, I am secure in my knowledge that we have a date to meet at the cafe just as you intended.

Utterances

The centerpiece of interpretation in conversational situations is the utterance issued by a speaker and addressed to a hearer or hearers (the audience). However, we just noted that many assume that the hearer's main interest in conversation is understanding what the speaker intends to say or do with the utterance. We also noted that there can be a discrepancy between this and what the utterance says or does, and that, at least sometimes, we are just as interested in this.

A linguistic utterance is the production of a sentence or sentences on a particular occasion. The meaning of a linguistic utterance is what someone says or does in making it on that occasion. When we use a sentence to make an assertive utterance, the utterance says something, and what it says is (at least part of) the meaning of the utterance. Sometimes we use a sentence to make an utterance, but not an assertive one. Then the utterance does not say something but (among other things) asks, commands, make believes, considers, assumes, or suggests something. In these cases, the meaning of the utterance is (at least in part) what it asks, commands, or whatever else it does. In this section, I investigate how we can specify further this notion of the meaning of an utterance and how it is to be distinguished from what the speaker intends or means in making the utterance, as well as from the meaning of a sentence used in making it. It is standard to make both of these distinctions, but this does not mean that everyone makes them in the same way.

Sentences

Before turning to the sentence/utterance distinction, something should be said about the meaning of sentences because there are at least two different ways to think about this. Consider the sentence "Joe met Sam at the bank." Many people, myself included, think of this sentence as ambiguous, that is, as having two or more meanings. This is because "bank" can refer to a type of financial institution, a building housing a branch of such an institution, or land abutting a river, among other things. Sentences containing "bank," on the present view, inherit the multiplicity of meanings possessed by the word. When we use a sentence containing the word "bank," we often wish to express a proposition by selecting just one of the meanings of "bank." We intend to say something strictly about a building, or about a stretch of land along a river, but not both. If our intention is successful, we do this. However, the sentence itself that we use to do this is still ambiguous. It is our utterance that is not.[4]

The alternative possibility is that there only seems to be one ambiguous sentence type: "Joe met Sam at the bank." In reality, there are at least two perceptually indistinguishable sentences, one in which "bank" unambiguously refers to a branch of a financial institution, the other in which "bank" unambiguously refers to land abutting a river.

Is there a way to choose between these views about the individuation of sentences? Ultimately this will be a question of what fits with the best theory of language (if there is a best theory). That is a matter I certainly cannot address here. I can, however, explain my preference for the first view in the context of a theory of interpretation.

First, it seems hard to deny that there are ambiguous sentences. If there are not, how can we explain what is going on when, as we would normally put it, ambiguity is being intentionally exploited, say in a line of a poem? We would have to say the poet has intentionally left it unclear whether she has written one line (sentence) or another. However, that does not describe the situation correctly, because what we want to say is that we have something that actually has two or more meanings.

Second, even if we say that *sentences* aren't semantically ambiguous, there would still be linguistic items, individuated by syntax or phonetics, that are. So we haven't done away with ambiguous linguistic items. We have just created another layer of items that imperceptibly avoids this ambiguity.

Third, when we are engaged in utterance interpretation, there would be an analogous extra layer added by the second view, which gives it an unattractive complexity. Since natural language sentences do not have subscripts or other perceptible markers that distinguish "Joe met Sam at the bank" from "Joe met Sam at the bank," where the first sentence refers to a branch of a financial institution and the second to land along a river, utterance interpretation would require at least three stages. First, we have to identify the syntactic item that is common to various sentences. Then we have to pick out the sentence uttered, from all the perceptually indistinguishable sentences that were not uttered, and assign the correct meaning to that sentence. Finally we have to identify the utterance. Whereas on the first view, there are just two steps: identifying the sentence and figuring out what utterance it is used to make.

In what follows, I assume the first view of sentence meaning. Much of what I say could be translated into the second view, for those who insist on it.

The sentence/utterance distinction

In distinguishing between utterances and the sentences used to make them, it is usual to point out that the same sentence can be used on different occasions to say different things, and that different sentences can be used on the same occasion to say the same thing. To illustrate the first conjunct, consider that "John doesn't have a heart" predicates "doesn't have a heart" of different individuals on different occasions of utterance. It can also say different things of the individual in question: that he is callous and uncaring, that he lacks the organ than pumps blood, that he has the organ but it is barely functioning, that he did not receive a Valentine's Day card, that he did not receive the item he is supposed to dissect today, that he does not have a single member of a certain card suit, that he cannot trump his opponent's ace, and so on. To illustrate the second conjunct, consider that on a given occasion "he doesn't have it" or "that guy is heartless" can say exactly the same thing as "John doesn't have a heart."

All this shows that one cannot identify sentences and utterances. It is less clear what this shows about the *meaning* of utterances as compared to the meaning of sentences. When it comes to the predicate part of sentences it seems plausible to say that when we use it to say something of an individual *it is common that* the meaning the predicate has in the utterance is *one* of the linguistic meanings of the predicate. Being callous and uncaring, being without the organ that pumps blood, being without a single member of a certain suit of cards are all literal meanings of the words "doesn't have a heart." However, it looks like it is not always true that the meaning of the uttered predicate is one of the predicate's literal meanings. It is a stretch to suppose that being without a Valentine's Day card is one of the literal meanings of "doesn't have a heart," but when Sally approaches her kindergarten teacher and, pointing to a weepy John, says "he doesn't have a heart," it is quite clear that she is saying (her utterance means) that John does not have such a card. Certainly if I can say that he cannot trump his opponent's ace by uttering the words "John doesn't have a heart," then I can certainly say things that the sentence I use does not literally mean. Whether or not one is willing to admit that one *says* such things, one sometimes conveys them, and to do so may be the main point of the utterance. Where one is able to exploit the context of utterance to extend the literal meaning of one's words in order to convey a piece of information, this will be sufficient (though not necessary) to make such information part of the meaning of the utterance.

When it comes to the referring expressions in a sentence, like "John," it is quite common for their meaning in an utterance and their meaning in a sentence to *differ*. In an utterance, the meaning of "John" is John, that is, the person my words refer to on the occasion in question. But in the sentence "John doesn't have a heart," "John" does not refer to any particular person, and so the linguistic meaning of "John" could not be a John. Perhaps it does not have a definite meaning but functions something like a variable. If it does have a definite meaning, it must be one that allows different utterances of sentences containing the word "John" to refer to different items.

There is at least one other respect in which the meaning of utterances differs from the meaning of the sentences used to make them. While indicative sentences tend to be used to make assertive utterances and interrogative ones tend to be used to make utterances that ask questions, this need not and does not always happen. It is not part of the meaning of a sentence that it is used to assert something. However, I take it to be part of the meaning of an utterance that it is asserting the proposition that p rather than asking the question whether p is true or making believe that p. The reason I take this to be so is that one cannot understand what the speaker is doing in making the utterance unless one knows this sort of thing. A more cautious way to put this point is to say one has to know what speech act is being performed to understand the utterance. If you feel queasy about making the speech act part of the meaning of an utterance, you may put things in the more cautious way. What is important is that when we are interpreting utterances, the speech act performed, or the propositional attitude expressed, is something we need to identify.

The utterance meaning / intended meaning distinction

Let us now turn to the distinction between the meaning of an utterance and intended meaning. Very often these coincide; for example, if I utter, "Do you want to go for a walk?" intending – and succeeding in – asking you whether you want to go for a walk. So the situation is different than it is with sentences and utterances, where their meanings typically do not coincide. The question is: When does utterance meaning and intended meaning fail to coincide?

Let us return to the case where someone utters, "John doesn't have a heart," where the point is to convey that John cannot trump his opponent's ace. That is the intended meaning. I claimed that it could also be the meaning of the utterance. Some might not agree. They might agree that someone could intend to convey this, reasonably expect to succeed, and in fact succeed, but still deny that the utterance means that John cannot trump his opponent's ace, because *the words* do not mean that. The objector is proposing, as a necessary condition on utterance meaning, that an utterance means what the utterer intends to convey only if the utterer's words mean this. This implies that the meaning of the utterance has to conform to one of the literal meanings of the predicate part of the sentence. The referent(s) picked out by the utterance has (have) to be a function of one of the literal meanings of the subject expression(s) and the context.

This proposal should be rejected. Suppose I say, "John is heartless," meaning this ironically. John has just gone out of his way to help someone. I am trying to convey the idea that John is big-hearted – kind and generous. I expect to succeed, the expectation is reasonable, and I do succeed. The sentence I use means (among other things) that John is heartless, but my utterance means that John is big-hearted. One would need to understand that I am saying the latter to understand or correctly interpret my utterance.

If we say this, we still have to answer the question "Where do we draw the line between cases in which my utterance means what I intend and cases in which it does not?" This occurs when I *fail* to do what I intend. There are two relevant intentions: intentions to say something, and intentions to communicate something. Slips of the tongue, malapropisms, and other misuses of words, as well as syntactic blunders, and unclear or inaccurate formulations of our thoughts, are cases where we intend to say something, but end up saying something else. I fail to say what I intended to say, because it is neither among the literal meanings of the words that come out of my mouth nor has a context been established that give the words an extended meaning. In cases where I fail to say what I intend to say I may nevertheless communicate what I intend to communicate. Sometimes, even this does not happen. The audience is unable is identify the intended communication. Whether communication occurs or fails is partly due to a matter of luck. It depends in part on whether the speaker has an audience that is attentive, perceptive, and has the desire to understand the speaker.

Here are some examples of the sorts of success and failure sketched above. If there is a local convention (holding in a classroom rather than in the language or dialect) according to which "heart" means Valentine's Day card, then Sally can utter, "John doesn't have a heart," and thereby *say* that John does not have a card. Suppose, however, there is no such convention. Sally can make the utterance and still easily convey that John does not have a card, because she can take advantage of a context in which all the Valentine's cards are heart-shaped. Whether or not she *says* it, she is able to effectively *convey* it. For this reason, I would say her utterance still means that John does not have a card. These are both cases where Sally's intentions are successful. Now consider some cases where they are not. If the words "John doesn't have a cart," come out of Sally's mouth, either because she makes a slip of the tongue or because she does not realize that "cart" and "card" are different words, then she does not say that John does not have a card (heart). She does not say what she intends to say, and her utterance does not mean that John does not have a card. However, with some luck, her teacher may figure out what she intends to say, so that it gets communicated. Suppose now that Sally decides to attempt to convey John's situation by indirect means, saying, "We are all looking at our hearts but John is not, and I think he looks sad." Here she may fail altogether to communicate, much less say, what she intends. Perhaps later, after a visit to John, her teacher may figure out what Sally had intended, but if Sally had succeeded in communicating this, her teacher would have understood her intention before, not after, the visit to John.

I am taking here a somewhat different line than does Donald Davidson when he addressed a similar topic in "A Nice Derangement of Epitaphs" (Davidson 1986: 433–46). In this paper, Davidson does not distinguish between intended meaning and utterance meaning, or between saying and communicating. He seems to hold the view that if Sally can "get away with" communicating to her teacher that John does not have a card by saying, "John doesn't have a cart," then on this occasion "cart" means card. ("Someone who grasps the fact that Mrs. Malaprop means 'epithet' when she says 'epitaph' must give 'epithet' all the powers 'epitaph' has for many other people," 443.) Her teacher will have a prior theory that predicts that Sally will say "card" (or perhaps "heart") when she means card, but (if Sally gets away with it) the teacher will construct a passing theory in which "cart" means card.

"Getting away with it" means managing to communicate what one intends to communicate. To do this, a hearer or audience needs to formulate a hypothesis about what the speaker is trying to say or do in making the utterance. The hypothesis can be correct and a high degree of understanding achieved, but this understanding does not imply that the speaker has said what she intends to say or that her utterance means what she intends to communicate. A successful hypothesis about an intended communication may be based on a perceived gap between performance and intention that the hypothesis is trying to explain.

The reason that Davidson and I give different accounts here turns on the different conceptions we have of the object of understanding/interpretation. For Davidson, it is sentences/utterances that belong to an idiolect or something even more narrowly circumscribed such as an individual's speech disposition on a given occasion (as Dummett points out in Dummett 1986: 459–76). Every time we encounter a new person, or a new set of speech dispositions, we encounter a new "language," and so comprehension is always a matter of "radical interpretation." Given this, there is less room to distinguish between what I mean by making an utterance and what my utterance means. Whereas for me (as for Dummett), the utterance is made in a public language (a natural language or dialect), and there is a shared, social practice of using that language to say or do things. This leaves more room for discrepancies between intended meaning and utterance meaning and the formulation of hypotheses about where the discrepancies lie.

These reflections (and preferences) point to the following inexact distinction between intended (speaker's/utterer's) meaning and utterance meaning. A speaker, using a language L, means something by uttering x in L, only if she intends to do A by uttering x and intends the audience to recognize this, in part because of conventional meanings of x or contextually supported extensions of those meanings. For example, a speaker, using L, means to *assert that p* by uttering x if she intends to say or convey that p by uttering x, and intends her audience to recognize this, in part because of the conventional meaning of x or a contextually supported extension of that meaning. An utterance does mean what a speaker intends if the intention is apt to be recognized in part because of the conventional meaning of the words used, or of a context that extends those meanings. I will say an intention is successful if it is apt to be recognized on the basis just mentioned, and otherwise unsuccessful or failed. The meaning of an utterance is the meaning successfully intended by the speaker or, if the speaker's intention is not successful, the meaning is determined by convention and context at the time of utterance.

Comparison with Grice

The view just stated is usefully compared with Grice's well-known account of nonnatural meaning (Grice 1957). Grice's primary focus is on utterer's meaning (intended meaning). Grice's views underwent many revisions but, for our purposes, all we need is the basic, original account, which states that a person means something by uttering x if and only if:

1. The person intends to produce in his audience a particular response r.
2. He intends that the audience recognize the first intention.
3. He intends to fulfill 1, in part, on the basis of fulfilling 2. (He intends to produce the response by getting the audience to recognize the intention to produce the response.)

The first thing to point out about Grice's account is that it is in the service of doing something far more ambitious than I am doing. Grice is trying to give a "bottom up" account of meaning based on a set of nested intentions. I am trying to distinguish two different objects of understanding and interpretation: utterances in a language, and speakers' intentions in making those utterances, where these take place under normal circumstances. Unlike Davidson, I take such circumstances to be those in which a common shared language provides conventional meanings for sentences uttered, which conventional meanings are relied upon in our attempts to understand or interpret. Grice agrees that common shared languages do provide such conventional meanings for sentences uttered, and that we rely on this, but, because of what he is trying to do, he has to eschew appealing to such facts.[5]

Second, the sort of meaning that Grice is intending to account for is not confined to a natural language and so cannot be analyzed in terms that refer to such a language. Hand signals devised on the spot to help a driver back into a tight space are also examples of nonnatural meaning. As we will see in the next section, I too want to extend my account of intended and utterance meaning beyond the case of natural languages, but given my aims, I can do this in stages rather than all at once.

Third, Grice hopes to run his account by means of an intention to produce an effect on or response from an audience. It is not clear this will work, because it is not clear that an utterance always has such an intended effect. To take one of Grice's primary cases, suppose I utter x assertively, meaning that p. Grice tended to take the intended audience response to be forming the belief that p. Sometimes I may have this intention, but I may often mean that p but lack the intention to get my audience to believe that p. When Sally told her teacher that John does not have a card (heart), she intended to get the teacher to believe this because she intended the teacher to remedy the situation, and this would not happen unless the teacher believed that there was a situation to remedy. However, consider the following case. You stop me to ask directions to a nearby apple orchard. I tell you that it is 5 miles down the road. I take your request for information seriously, and want to truthfully convey what I believe is the correct information. However, whether you go on to believe that the orchard is 5 miles down the road, or even whether you come to believe that I believe this, does not matter to me in the least and is not an effect that I intend. For this reason, it seems to me that the "first" intention characteristic of utterer's meaning is the intention to say or do something rather than bring about a certain response in an audience, other than the recognition of what I am saying or doing. Although what I intend to do may sometimes essentially involve a further audience response, there is good reason to suppose this is not always the case.

So what seems to characterize utterances made in a natural language is that

a.   They are made with the intention to say that p or do some action A in part on the basis of the conventional meaning of words used or the contextually supported extension of that meaning.
b.   They are made with the intention that an audience recognizes the proposition said or the action done in part, on the same basis.

   It is at least often true that

c.   Utterances are made with the intention to bring about the recognition that utterer intends to say that p or do A, in part on the basis of recognizing that he says that p or does A.

It is not *unusual* for me to figure out what you intend to say or do in making an utterance in part by first figuring out what you do say or do (by recognizing a conventional meaning of your words or a contextually supported extension of that meaning). Speakers are aware of this, and it is plausible they intend it. For example, I make the utterance "The orchard is 5 miles down the road," with the intention that you recognize that I intend to say that the orchard is 5 miles down the road, partly on the basis of recognizing that I do say that the orchard is 5 miles down the road.

Should we also say that I *mean* that the orchard is 5 miles down the road *only if* I intend you to recognize that I intend to say this in part on the basis of recognizing that I do say this?

No. If we were to answer in the affirmative and regiment this into a Gricean style analysis, we would say that a person means something by uttering x in L if and only if

1′.   The person intends to say or do something in part in virtue of the conventional meaning in L of the words used or the contextually supported extension of that meaning.
2′.   The person intends his audience to recognize what he says or does in part in virtue of the same considerations.
3′.   The person intends his audience to recognize 1′ in part on the basis of recognizing 2′.

1′–3′ imply that I mean that the orchard is 5 miles down the road, only if I intend that you recognize that I intend to say this, in part on the basis of your recognizing that I say this. But 3′ is not a necessary condition for a speaker to mean something, since the holding of 1′ and 2′ is sufficient. (Even if such an analysis were correct, it would turn out to be very different from Grice's, despite the appearance of similarity. I do not do what I set out to do on the basis of getting you to recognize that I intend to do this. Rather, you recognize my intention on the basis of recognizing what I do.) What is true, however, is that, we do have to recognize certain intentions right at the start, though ones more general than the intention to say some specific thing or produce a specific response. One has to recognize the background intention to use language to say *something* in part in virtue of the conventional meaning of words, in part relying on context to disambiguate and extend those conventional meanings.

In everything I have said above, I have helped myself to the notion of conventional meaning. How this notion is to be analyzed is left here as a completely open question. I have not given a bottom-up account of meaning.

Semantics and Pragmatics

Some readers may wonder how the account of utterance meaning given in the previous section stands in relation to the distinction between semantics and pragmatics. As I understand this distinction, semantics concerns what we strictly and literally say (ask, command, etc.). Pragmatics concerns what we convey in context over and above what we say, or how we can expect our words to be taken when this is not something they strictly say.[6]

What I am calling utterance meaning covers both semantic and pragmatic meaning. I spoke earlier of someone asserting that p if they say *or* convey that p. I pointed out that the meaning of an utterance may be due to the conventional meaning of one's words or an extended meaning licensed by context.

Many writers confine utterance meaning to semantic meaning. That would not work here simply because more often than not when we are engaged in the interpretation of utterances, we are not just interested in, or in need of understanding, semantic content. Part of what we need to understand is the point of the utterance, and this is often what is pragmatically conveyed. What properties of the utterance are the important ones to grasp for the purpose of understanding it varies greatly with context and kind of utterance in question. This will come out even more clearly in the section that follows.

Extending the Utterance Model

A previous section discussed the meaning of speakers and of spoken utterances in the context of conversing with others using a natural language. That is a fairly specific context. We communicate using other means in different contexts. Other than speech, we produce many meaningful objects and mean things by them. There is obviously writing, there are gestures and signals, there is art, among many other things.

I am with Grice in wanting to think of all these things as utterances or on the model of utterances. This will be especially important when we turn to art interpretation in the chapters that follow. So here I will explain what is involved in extending the model and justify doing so.

Let us begin with what looks like an easy sell: writing. Writing, like speech, is in a language, normally in a natural language, so we are still dealing with someone's utterance of x in L. One is still relying on the conventional meaning of the words used. A difference between conversational utterances and writing is that the former tends to come in bits, while the latter often comes in blocks. It is easier to select a bit and ask, "What does that mean?" For example, what did you mean when you said, "John doesn't have a heart"? It looks a bit odder, and it is certainly harder to answer, if you point to a 300-page block of writing (a book) and ask, "What does that mean?" However, those 300 pages are composed of sentences, and of each sentence we can ask what it is saying or doing, as well as what the writer is intending to say or do. From that we should be able to work to an answer of what various parts of the book are doing, and from that to the book as a whole. (This is not to say that the best strategy for understanding a book length piece of writing is always to *self-consciously* build up one's understanding, sentence by sentence.)

When it comes to understanding or interpreting writing, a more serious issue is whether the identification of utterance meaning gives us the sort of meaning we are interested in. For example, if we are interpreting a work of philosophy, it may be unproblematic what a certain sentence says. The issue may be what its role is in the work as a whole or a section of the work. Is it expressing a central thesis, or rather expressing a position that will later be undermined or rejected? Similarly, it may be unproblematic what a sentence or paragraph fictionally represents in a novel. The issue may be what the piece of writing is doing that has larger significance for the work. For example, the novel *Grüne Heinrich*, by Gottfried Keller (which was Wittgenstein's favorite novel), opens with an amazing description of the village where the title character is born. It begins with a thumbnail history of the village and ends in the local graveyard run wild with flowers. There is no problem in understanding what is said in this paragraph about the village. What one could easily not see, and what is significant about the paragraph, is that it symbolically unfolds in miniature the whole story to follow, while expressing a mood that is the predominant mood of the work.

Is the fact that a sentence in a philosophical work expresses a thesis that will be gradually undermined as the work proceeds part of its utterance meaning? Is the fact that a paragraph symbolically represents in miniature the plot of the novel, or that it expresses the predominant mood of the work, part of its utterance meaning? The meanings in question *are* properties of utterances, though they are not, strictly, semantic properties. In some cases they will be properties of utterances other than those made in the original sentence or passage in question. In some cases they will be properties of the original utterance.

In the case of the philosophical thesis, if the author is coy about its treatment in the work so that the *sentence* expresses the thesis but does not indicate that it will be undermined, then it is not part of *its* meaning that this will happen. It can still be part of the utterance meaning of the work that the thesis is undermined.

In the case of the novel, the paragraph can have symbolic and expressive properties as part of their utterance meaning, although they may not be available to a reader until the whole work is read or until a second reading is begun. These are things that the author does in the paragraph, of high literary significance, so in the context of literary interpretation, they are meaning characteristics of the utterance. Just as, to understand an utterance in ordinary conversation, one needs to know, not just the proposition expressed by an utterance but the attitude of the speaker toward the proposition or the speech act performed, so in a literary context, one needs to be able to identify important literary properties to understand it.[7]

Let us briefly turn to meaningful nonlinguistic items, such as gestures, on the one hand, and paintings on the other. Like sentences in a language, a gesture can have a perfectly conventional meaning. However, gestures do not belong to, or derive their meaning from a language. Rather, when they have a conventional meaning, this is simply the meaning they are generally taken to have in a given locale. Unlike the meaning of a word, one cannot expect the meaning a gesture has in one's own locale to be preserved in a different one, unless by luck it happens to be generally taken in the same way. So that upon arriving at a new place, it can easily happen that you mean one thing by a gesture, but your gesture means something else. In other words, your intended meaning diverges from your utterance meaning.

Gestures can also be meaningful while lacking a conventional meaning. Perhaps it is conventional that, when helping someone to back into tight space, holding one's hand apart a given distance indicates how much room the driver has to maneuver. However, the meaning of the gesture is clear enough apart from the convention. Here too we do not hesitate to talk about the meaning of the gesture and what someone means by it. Here too these can diverge. For example, someone may just be rather bad at conveying distance through hand signals so that the distances he intends to convey are never clearly expressed, like someone who can never express with precision what he is intending to say.

Turning to painting, we will sometimes ask what a work means when we do not understand its point. A painting can also have parts that have a meaning, as when figures it contains have symbolic significance. In general, however, it is far less natural to talk about the meaning of paintings than it is to talk about the meaning of words and gestures.

Nevertheless, we can make some of the same distinctions about paintings as we just made about gestures, only expressed in other terms. We can talk about what a painting does and what it is intended to do: what it represents, expresses, how its formal features interact among themselves and with representational features, and what the painting is intended to do along these lines.

Since these are the things we need to identify to understand and appreciate a painting, it is not an unreasonable extension of the word "meaning" to call these things aspects of the meaning of a painting, even though this is not our ordinary usage. It is analogous to utterance meaning, since it identifies things the artist "does" in the work (what is represented, expressed, etc.) just as utterance meaning identifies what a speaker does in using certain words.[8]

When Do We Interpret?

Ever since the section entitled "Utterances," we have been primarily concerned with the meaning and *understanding* of utterances and things like them. When we engage in interpretation, we are trying to understand something (or understand it better), by asking one or more of the four basic interpretive questions mentioned above. However, as we have seen, not all understanding requires interpretation. So far, I have been rather casual in distinguishing between cases where understanding is arrived at without interpretation from cases where it is interpretation that give us understanding. (Let us call the understanding in that latter case "U_i" and in the former "U_{wi}".)

When we understand straight away, no interpretation is needed. When answering the relevant interpretive question requires some figuring out, some formulating of hypotheses, interpretation occurs. I ask, "Do you want to go for a walk?" You understand straight away that I am asking you whether you want to go for a walk, and you answer accordingly. No interpretation is needed. I say, "John is without the organ that pumps blood." Since John is before us in perfect health, you may not understand straightaway what I am getting at. It may take some figuring out: you need to interpret my remark.

Is there a less casual, more precise way to make this distinction? To some extent, there is.[9] First, we should distinguish between interpreting something for oneself and interpreting it for someone else. If the meaning of some item is obvious to me at a given time, then at that time I grasp the meaning without interpreting. In this case, I am not interpreting the item for myself. When you uttered, "Do you want to go for a walk?" and I saw straightaway that you were asking whether I wanted to go for a walk, I did not need to interpret what you were saying because it was obvious to me. However, even if something is obvious to me, it may not be to someone else. They may be in need of an interpretation of an utterance, and I may provide it, even though the meaning of the utterance is obvious to me. Here, I am interpreting the utterance for them, though I understand it without needing to interpret it for myself.

Second, we should distinguish between something being obvious, and someone's taking it to be obvious, or its seeming so. In the latter case, one may be interpreting even though one may not be aware that one is doing so. In the former case, one is not interpreting.

Third, there are situations where something becomes evident after a process of interpretation has been completed. So, after a good deal of testing and analysis of a new archeological find, someone might say, "It is [now] obvious that these marks are to be interpreted as writing." When the interpreting was going on, it was not obvious that the marks are writing. For this reason, even if it is now obvious, the appropriateness of the comment is consistent with what I have just been saying. However, since what is now obvious to us was arrived at through a process of interpreting, it is perfectly correct to say that what we arrived at is an interpretation of the marks. Furthermore, this is an interpretation, not only for others, but for ourselves. So while we do not interpret the obvious, we can give an interpretation, where something has become obvious. This also reveals that sometimes interpretation can lead to knowledge, which in turn implies that some interpretations are true.

Although we can clarify, in these ways, our initial casual distinction between U_i, and U_{wi}, the distinction remains a rough one. Whether one's understanding is an interpretation depends on whether it was arrived at by interpreting, which in turn depends on one's epistemic position while arriving at the understanding. I have said (following Barnes 1988) that if the meaning of an utterance has always been obvious, one's understanding is not arrived at by interpreting the utterance. But there are many epistemic states one can be in with regard to the meaning of an utterance, other than its being obvious. Would understanding reached while in those other epistemic states always be interpretation? Clearly not. If I do not understand a word you used, and come to understand by looking the word up in a dictionary, I am not interpreting. If my epistemic state results from a brain tumor, that is, if the tumor somehow causes me to think, "By x, S meant that p," I am not interpreting. So a sharp line has not been drawn between the two kinds of understanding.

I am happy to leave this matter vague. Our usage is vague, and while we can invent a sharper usage, it will not be needed in what follows.

I would like, however, to distance myself from two alternative ways of understanding the distinction between understanding$_i$ and understanding$_{wi}$. 1. Some hold that one is interpreting only when one is not in a position to know whether or not one's interpretation is true. So, for example, one is interpreting x as meaning that p, only if one is not in a position to come to know that x means p. 2. Some hold that we are interpreting an object whenever our thoughts about the objects are mediated by something such as our concepts, historical location, or a culturally shaped point of view.

Someone could hold view 1 for a number of reasons. One might hold it because one holds that interpretations are never true, and, since what we know are truths, when we interpret, there is nothing to know. Our discussion of the interpretation of utterances belies this point of view. When someone makes an utterance, there is often a fact of the matter about what the utterance means, as well as what the speaker intends to say. For example, in one of the cases considered above, when Sally said to her kindergarten teacher, "John doesn't have a heart," it is a fact that she meant that John does not have a Valentine's Day card. Yet, her teacher may not know straightaway what Sally means; it may not be obvious to the teacher what she means. It is right to say that the teacher has to interpret Sally's words to figure out what she means. So if we are talking about interpretation in the intentional domain generally, this reason for holding 1, that interpretations are never true, is untenable.

A second reason one might have for holding 1 is that, although interpretive statements are capable of being true (or false), it is thought that if one is interpreting, one is necessarily in a situation where one's evidence is insufficient for knowing whether one's interpretation is true. If one's situation changes, so that one can know this, further inquiry just is not interpretation. However, this again appears to be belied by some of our examples. Sally's teacher is interpreting her meaning even if he has sufficient evidence to come to know that by "a heart" she means a Valentine's Day card. The archeologist was interpreting the marks, even though they found conclusive evidence that they are writing.

It is hard to deny that in the above examples, the use of the word "interpretation" is perfectly normal and natural. So it is hard to claim that I am begging the question in claiming that the examples are cases of interpretation. What someone could do in reply is stipulate that they use "interpretation" in a different sense. Alternatively, it might be claimed that the reasons given for accepting 1 apply to a restricted domain, such as the domain of art and literary interpretation. One cannot argue against a stipulation. We will return to claims about the nature of art interpretation in later chapters.

There are two ways to understand view 2, that, whenever our thoughts about objects are mediated in certain ways, we are interpreting those objects. One implies that all understanding is interpretive, and hence eliminates the need to distinguish between U_i and U_{wi}. The other maintains the distinction.

The first way understands 2 as asserting that thought or discourse that is mediated in any way is interpretive. All thought is mediated in some way. For example, all thought is mediated by concepts. It would follow that all thought is interpretive. The second way is to think of 2 as saying that only special types of mediation make a thought interpretive. For example, just because a thought is mediated by a concept shared across many points of view, cultures, or conceptual schemes, does not make the thought interpretive. The thought that Jane is walking uses concepts that are shared in this way, so it is not necessarily interpretive. A thought that is mediated by a uniquely cultural point of view would be interpretive.

On the first way to understand 2, if you ask, "Do you want to go for a walk?" and it is obvious to me what you are asking, I am nevertheless interpreting your words in reaching this understanding. I am interpreting because my understanding of those words is mediated, that is, depends on concepts: of a walk, of the referent of "you" (viz., myself), of wanting. Is there anything wrong with this view? What is wrong with it is that it conflates interpretation with thought of any kind, since all thought, as was just mentioned, is mediated by concepts. "Interpretation," then, just becomes an equivalent of "thought" or "cognition," while in normal usage, it is not. Of course, a technical or stipulated usage might improve on ordinary usage. However, the present suggestion is not an improvement, since it takes a useful, if vague, concept and replaces it with a much more general one for which we already have terminology.

The second way to understand 2 tells us that thought or understanding is interpretive if it is mediated in a special way. There is no threat here of conflating interpretation with thought in general, but there are equally serious problems with this approach. One is that it takes an already vague distinction and makes it more vague. Just when is thought mediated in the special way this view has in mind? That is going to be very hard to say. More important, while this view can distinguish U_i from U_{wi}, it does not draw the distinction in the right place. For example, very culturally specific concepts can be in question, but there may be no interpretation going on. Suppose I approach you on Valentine's Day with flowers in one hand, a card in the other and ask, "Will you be my Valentine?" I suppose that the concept of Valentine's Day is or was culturally specific. However, you may understand straightaway that I am asking you to be my Valentine. If so, it is implausible that your understanding is an instance of U_i, even though, a culturally specific concept is involved.

I conclude that interpretation is one thing, mediation another and that the former should not be defined in terms of the latter.

This completes the main argument of the chapter concerning the nature of utterance meaning and interpretation. In the remainder, I indicate some central themes and theses that will guide the discussion in the rest of the book. There are two main themes. One is the debate between the traditional historicist and constructivist conceptions of interpretation. The second is the relation of monism and pluralism to interpretation.

Conceptions of Interpretation

What I have said about interpretation in the intentional domain so far supports a certain general conception of interpretation. Call this conception *traditional historicism*. According to this view, the object we want to understand is there, already fully in existence. Further, what there is to understand about the object is also already there. There is something an utterance says or conveys, something an artifact is for, and a sense the artwork has before we inquire what these are. For a traditional historicist, the task of interpretation, at least when we are concerned with the meaning of the item is to *discover* what that meaning is.

We do this by turning to the situation in which the object of interpretation comes into existence. There are a number of features of this situation that jump out as relevant to discovering answers to interpretive questions. Among these are conventions in place that apply to the situation. For example, if one is attempting to figure out what an utterance says, one must know conventions of the language in which the utterance is made. Second, various contextual features can be relevant. In the case of utterances, they can disambiguate a sentence or gesture, or they can extend the meaning beyond a conventional one. Finally the intention with which an action is performed is relevant. In fact, one may think that appeal to convention or context is in the service of understanding intention or forming a plausible hypothesis about intention. For example, a classroom context suggests what someone might be intentionally doing with the gesture of raising one's hand.

Not everything we call "interpreting" works like this. Giving an interpretation to an uninterpreted formal language is quite different. We assign meaning to variables and constants, make rules, where there previously were none. Here we are creating or constructing rather than discovering. This provides a second model of what goes on when we interpret.

Some people believe that we should apply an element from this second model to the interpretation of such items as artworks, other artifacts, utterances, and behavior. The common element is in the idea that, when we interpret artworks, for example, there is something creative in the assignment of meaning. Meaning is to a greater or lesser extent constructed. We are not discovering something that is already there, at least not always.

Often associated with this idea is another: that the meaning of an object of interpretation changes. However, the relation between the former idea and the latter is complex. Someone might believe in the first idea: that meaning is constructed by a creative interpretive act, but not believe that there is one thing that previously had been assigned one meaning and now is being assigned another. Rather, the claim may be that each assignment of a new meaning creates a new object just as different uses of the same sentence makes different utterances. Such a person should not accept the second idea that the meaning of one and the same object changes. On the other hand, someone else may believe that assignments of the new meanings do precisely what the view just mentioned denies – it changes an object already in existence, changes it by giving it new meanings. There is also another route to the idea that the meaning of things can change. One may entirely reject the claim that interpretation is creative, that it constructs rather than discovers meaning. Rather, it may be denied that it is just the conventions, context and intentions that are instrumental in the *creation* of an item that determine its meaning. One may claim that the meaning of an object changes as it enters into new situations (new contexts, intentions, and conventions).

Three versions of constructivism

Because both of the ideas just mentioned – the idea that interpretation is creative and the idea that objects can change their meaning in the course of their history – are associated with the claim that the meaning of an object is constructed (subsequent to the activity of its original creator), there are actually three different views that are versions of constructivism. *Radical constructivism* claims that some (all) new interpretations create new objects. *Moderate constructivism* claims that some (all) new interpretations change (the meaning of) an object. *Historical constructivism* claims that the meaning of an object changes in the course of its history as it encounters new contexts, new conventions, new intentions, or any other relevant new developments. Moderate constructivism is actually a species historical constructivism, which claims that it is interpretations that an item encounters in the course of its history that change the meaning of the item.[10]

Traditional historicism and constructivism

Traditional historicism and constructivism are rivals. This rivalry will constitute one of the main themes of this book. In the next five chapters, I will be primarily concerned with competing conceptions of the interpretation of works of art and literature. After setting out the main controversies in this field of interpretation in chapter 2, chapters 3 and 4 will systematically set out my favored theory of art interpretation, a version of traditional historicism. Chapters 5 and 6 will attempt to arrive at a better understanding of the various constructivist views just set out, the arguments in their favor, and, finally, the reasons why these views should be rejected.

Chapter 7 will deal with the interpretation of the law, a complex interpretive enterprise that is in some important ways different from art interpretation. One of the most important differences is that legal interpretation fits a constructivist conception far better than art or literature. In seeing why the law is, of necessity, partly constructed by interpretation, it becomes easier to see the conditions that must hold for interpretive construction to occur. It also becomes easier to see that these conditions do not hold in the case of art interpretation.

Finally, chapter 8 will take up the issue of constructivism and relativism. Many proponents of constructivism accept some form of relativism. There is, however, no entailment from constructivism in general to relativism. This raises a question concerning the basis for the "attraction" between the two views. Whatever the basis of the attraction, I will argue that relativism is a coherent, but mistaken view. Instead of relativism, the view we should accept is pluralism.

Monism and Pluralism

The conversational utterances I have focused on in this chapter fit the traditional historicist model. They get their meaning from the intentions, context, and conventions from which they issue, and that meaning may be clarified but does not change in retrospect. However, even about these utterances, there is more then one interpretive question that can be asked, and there is more than one aim we may be pursuing in interpreting them. (Recall the four interpretive questions mentioned above and the special aims of interpretation in subdomains of the intentional domain.) This multiplicity of questions and aims of interpretation implies that there may be several acceptable interpretations of the same item. Call the thesis that there may be a multiplicity of acceptable interpretations of the same item *pluralism*. Notice also that pluralism is compatible with the fact that, for many utterances, there is such a thing as the meaning of the utterance. This is to say that there is a uniquely correct answer to the question "What is the meaning of the utterance?" Call the thesis that there is such a uniquely correct answer *monism*. What we have noticed is that the theses of monism and of pluralism are compatible. A second major theme of this book is the truth of pluralism, and its compatibility with monism as just defined.

Let us now turn to art interpretation and see how these issues get worked out in that large and complex arena.

NOTES

1 An item has intrinsic value if it is valuable for its own sake apart from any further good it is a means to. Something has inherent value if it creates intrinsically valuable states of consciousness. It has instrumental value if it is valuable as a means to other valuable things. Inherent value is a species of instrumental value, but one we have a tendency to set apart from other forms of that value.

2 Not everyone agrees that these practices lack a single dominant aim and that interpretation in these domains is not guided by that aim. For example, a number of people think of art and literature as practices guided by the aim of aesthetic appreciation (S. Davies 1991, Lamarque and Olsen 1994). This sort of view will be discussed in chapters 2 and 3.

3 In (partially) identifying what is said on an occasion of utterance with what the utterance means, I appear to be taking sides in a current controversy in the philosophy of language. Some (Bach 2001 is an excellent example) would argue that we should distinguish what is said, which is a purely semantic notion, from what an utterance means which is determined pragmatically depending, in part, on the speaker's communicative intention and broad features of context. Others (Recanati 2001 is an equally excellent example) argue that what is said is itself a pragmatic notion as just defined. To see how the difference in view plays out, consider an utterance of "I had breakfast," uttered in response to an offer of food at a morning meeting. On the pure semantic notion of what is said, on this occasion, this consists in saying that the speaker has had at least one breakfast (with no indication of when she had it). However, what the utterance states (means, communicates) is something more: that she had breakfast this morning (the morning of the meeting). On the alternative pragmatic conception, this is what she said.

It is true that my use of "what is said" aligns with the pragmatic conception. This, however, is more for convenience than because I have a settled view on the philosophy of language debate. When we interpret utterances in conversational contexts, we are typically concerned with the pragmatic notion of what is said. This is so even if there is a defensible distinction between what is said, understood in purely semantic terms, and what an utterance means. Even if such a distinction is viable, a looser conception of what is said serves our interpretive purposes better in conversational contexts.

4 This claim is complicated by the distinction between sentence types and to-

kens. All occurrences of "Joe met Sam at the bank" belong to a single sentence type. Each occurrence tokens the type. When I speak of the meaning of sentences, I am referring to sentence types. However, it might be said that a sentence token occurring in a particular context has, or may have, a disambiguated sense.

5   In later reworkings of his analysis, Grice refers to modes of correlation, one of which would be the sorts of conventions I have been discussing (1969: 163–4).

6   The distinction between semantic and pragmatic here is somewhat different from that found in note 3 above. Even if the "pragmatic" account of saying (as alluded to in note 3) is correct, we can still distinguish what is said from what is conveyed, though it will perhaps be a less sharp distinction than the one we would have on the "semantic" account of saying.

7   This issue will be discussed further in chapter 3 in connection with an objection to the utterance model.

8   This will also be argued for more extensively in chapter 3. Also see Stecker (1997a: 182–3).

9   The following discussion borrows heavily from Barnes (1988: 7–25).

10 Among constructivists, Stanley Fish (1980, 1989) is a good example of the radical camp. Joseph Margolis (1980, 1995a) is a moderate constructivist. Graham McFee (1980, 1995) is a historical constructivist. Others, such as Thom (1997, 2000a, 2000b) and Krausz (1993), are harder to classify, if the latter is a constructivist at all.

Art Interpretation: The Central Issues

When we interpret works of art and literature we are seeking to understand or to appreciate them or to improve on our current level of understanding or appreciation. We do this by attempting to discover or, at least, ascribe on *some* basis, a meaning in or to the work in question or to determine what significance the work has for us.

Around this feat of assigning a meaning or significance to a work of art, many controversies swirl. This chapter aims at giving an overview of several of these controversies, and some of the most important theories proposed to resolve them. Before doing this, it is worth mentioning why these issues have seemed important enough and uncertain enough to generate so much controversy.

Consider the poem "The Sick Rose" from William Blake's *Songs of Innocence and Experience*:

> *O Rose thou art sick.*
> *The invisible worm,*
> *That flies in the night*
> *In the howling storm:*
>
> *Has found out thy bed*
> *Of crimson joy:*
> *And his dark secret love*
> *Does thy life destroy.*

First note that there are aspects of the meaning of the poem that it would be natural to say we know prior to interpretation. We know that the poem is ostensibly about a rose that becomes infested with a worm that destroys it. We know the rose is red (crimson), the worm invisible and flies at night in a storm.

We know there is more to the poem than this. We know that we will appreciate the poem only if we can come to some understanding of what this more might be. We also may have some specific puzzles about some lines or phrases in the poem. For example, why is the worm invisible? Is it literally invisible or perhaps barely noticeable? Why does it make its first "appearance" in a howling storm? Why is the vehicle of its destructiveness a "dark secret love?" We need and, for the moment lack, answers to these various questions, general and specific. Clearly these are interpretive issues. Whatever answers we give will result in meanings we find in or assign to the poem in giving an interpretation of it.

There are many views about what we *should* do and what we *may* do in answering these questions. Let us begin to examine these.

Actual Intentionalism

One plausible starting point is to focus on the poet, and to see if what we can learn about him helps to answer the interpretive questions raised above about "The Sick Rose." However, there are different ways of doing this. One can engage in what can be called biographical criticism in which one tries to learn as much as possible about the life of the poet and then tries to, as it were, read off the meaning of the poem from what was going on in the poet's life around the time of writing.

There are several decisive criticisms of this approach. There is no reason to suppose that a poem, or more generally, a work of art, is a direct expression of what is going on in the artist's life. It might be, but, then again, the artist is just as likely to distance her work from her life in the act of artistic creation. Further, this approach to answering interpretive questions tends to distance the critic from something important: the details of the work. It will be virtually impossible to find nonspeculative connections between a poet's biography and her writing those precise words. Finally, even if such connections were found between the poet's life and words, these are likely to be private connections and certainly ones inaccessible to most readers. This makes them poor candidates for meanings, which must be capable of receiving uptake from the poet's audience. Few artists would rely on such connections when creating works to be introduced into the public domain.

Analogous to biographical criticism is an approach that seeks to discover in events contemporary with the poet a key that unlocks the poem's meaning, or at least, gives to it "a new historical resonance" (Mee 1998: 113). An example is a political interpretation of "The Sick Rose" (Mee 1998). The interpretation is based on the rise and fall of George Rose, a corrupt secretary and chief of public opinion in the Pitt government from 1784 to 1792. (Blake's poem was composed in the period 1791–2.) Playing on the politician's name, English newspapers were full of the equation between the rose (Rose) and corruption, for example, in the following verse from "The London Rose"

> *THE ROSE is called the first of flow'rs*
> *In all the rural shades and bow'rs*
> *But O! in London 'tis decreed*
> *The Rose is but a dirty weed.*

Is Blake's poem also referring to George Rose and to political corruption in the figure of the rose infested by the worm's dark, secret love? Is it "a total and profound vision of the corruptness of contemporary society" (Mee 1998: 117)?

There is some evidence that Blake *may* have followed the proceedings concerning George Rose in the early 1790s. We also know positively that Blake saw a connection between social and political decay and the disease of sexual repression, which leads to relationships of a dark and secret kind rather than healthy ones that are open and free. We know this because Blake is capable of making the connection quite explicit as he does in the poem "London," which is also one of the *Songs of Experience*. However, it is clearly the sexual issue that is explicitly at the forefront of attention in "The Sick Rose." The fact that Blake saw the above-mentioned connection and was capable of expressing it does not show that this poem has a sociopolitical "resonance." Nor is it shown by the fact that there were events contemporary with the poem's creation capable of being exploited for this purpose. What is missing in this equation is reference to something – some words or lines – in the poem that has the resonance that cannot be fully explained by the more explicit sexual concerns. Such a case may be makeable, but the mere existence of an external context that could have been exploited does not make it.

A more plausible approach, and one that might help to sort out when biographical and contextual considerations are relevant to a work's interpretation, is to ask what a poet (artist) is intending to do or convey with a poem (artwork). What was Blake's point in writing about the sick rose, in describing the worm as invisible, in making it first appear in a howling storm, in describing its destructiveness in terms of a secret love?

This approach is plausible because it reflects an important aspect of our explanatory stance when we are trying to understand human behavior and the products of human behavior. We typically explain what people do and make by appealing to their beliefs, desires, and the intentions they form in virtue of these. Why are you writing on that piece of paper? I'm filling out a withdrawal slip and am intending to use it to get money for the weekend. Why are you stirring those ingredients together? I'm making a cake and intending to have it for dessert. Notice this explanatory approach's common use when we are concerned with people's semantic doings, that is, when we are trying to understand what they are saying or writing. If we do not understand some part of a conversation, we are apt to ask, "What do you mean?" or "What are you getting at?" Once we are clear on that, our interpretive goals are usually satisfied.

It is plausible to carry over the same strategy to answering the interpretive questions about "The Sick Rose" and other works of art. If we do this, however, we should take care to make sure we are clear about what an interpretation is asserting and the sources of evidence for it. On the view under consideration – actual intentionalism[1] – we are looking at artworks as expressions of intention. Let us initially define actual intentionalism as the view that the correct interpretation of an artwork identifies the intention of the artist expressed in the work. Interpretations assert that a work expresses this or that intention, and they are true if and only if the intention in question is expressed in the work. In conversation the main source of evidence for interpretive claims are the words uttered in context. Similarly, the main sources of evidence for interpretive claims about artworks are features of the artwork understood in context. However, they are not the only source evidence. Just as we can ask an interlocutor what he means by his words, or make inferences about what he means from background information we have about the person, we can look for expressions of intention outside the artwork or use background information to help generate more plausible hypotheses about the artist's intention.

Actual intentionalism is often misrepresented. It is sometimes confused with the biographical criticism we have rejected above. It is also sometimes identified as the view that the correct interpretation of the work is the artist's interpretation of it, where this is not clearly distinguished from expressions of intention. This understanding is doubly confused. First, expressions of intention are not in general to be identified with interpretations of one's own behavior. "I'm planning on getting to the bank before it closes" is an expression (or at least a report) of intention and not an interpretation. "I think I went the bank just to get out of the house" is an interpretation of behavior and not an expression (or report) of intention. This is not to deny that there could be certain situations where these two things are hard to distinguish. Second, neither the artist's interpretation of her work, nor her expressions or reports of her intention that are external to the work, automatically constitute the correct interpretation of the work. The artist's interpretation of her work may be no better, and is often worse, than those of others. Expressions of intention can be inaccurate, insincere, or if issued before the work is completed, discarded rather than realized.

Criticisms of Actual Intentionalism

Despite its plausibility, there are a number of serious criticisms of actual intentionalism. One frequently expressed worry is whether we can ever know what the artist intends. The thought is that intentions are hidden and inaccessible. However, if they were, we would be permanent mysteries to each other. In fact, we can often know another's intentions, semantic and otherwise. The same is true with regard to works of art. As with other cases, some intentions are transparent, some we can figure out even when not obvious, and about some we can only form hypotheses that will never be decisively confirmed or disconfirmed.

Let us briefly return to "The Sick Rose" to see how this works in practice. Just as it is obvious that the poem is ostensibly about a rose, it is obvious that Blake intended this, and expressed this intention in the poem. Further, we can be sure that Blake intends the rose, the worm, the storm to be treated symbolically, and to say something about the human condition. (Notice that obvious though this is, we have already broached, if barely, a matter of interpretation.) Finally, the symbolism intentionally concerns, at least in part, human love and sexuality and the destructiveness of certain sorts of relationships having to do with sex and love. We have very good reason to believe this both from the words of the poem (the reference to the rose's "bed of crimson joy" and the worm's "dark secret love") and the surrounding context (the other poems in the *Songs of Experience*, many of which betray similar concerns). What is more a matter of hypothesis is the specific destructive relationship that Blake intended to symbolize in the poem – the other poems suggest several possibilities – *if* he intended something specific at all.

A second criticism is that, even if we can sometimes know what an artist intends, it is a mistake to identify the meaning of a work with the intention of the artist. One of the best arguments for this point begins by noting that we sometimes fail to do what we intend to do. This includes our semantic intentions; we sometimes fail to say what we intend to say. In these cases it is plausible to suppose that we have said something, but something other than what we intended to say, and hence, it is plausible that there is a distinction between what we meant (what we intended to say) and the meaning of our utterance (what we said). Therefore, the two cannot be identified (Beardsley 1970, Levinson 1996, Tolhurst 1979).

If the last objection to intentionalism turned on its inadequacy to provide a satisfactory definition of the meaning of a work (utterance), a final objections turns on a view about the proper aim of interpretation. Recall that we began by saying that when we interpret, we aim at (better) understanding and appreciation of an artwork. The present objection claims that we aim at maximizing such appreciation by maximizing enjoyable aesthetic experience. It is claimed that our interest in promoting enjoyment is best served by permitting a range of interpretations compatible with the artwork. The objection to intentionalism is that it unduly restricts the range of acceptable interpretations so that the proper aim of interpretation cannot be realized. Notice that this objection does not deny that intentionalism might be the right view in other interpretive contexts, but rather it claims that art and literature create a special context where different rules apply (S. Davies 1982, 1991).

These last two objections raise large issues within the theory of interpretation. One issue concerns whether there is a single proper aim of interpretation in the case of artworks or whether there are many legitimate aims (the proper aim issue). A related issue is whether this aim (or these aims) promotes an ideal of a plurality of acceptable interpretations of the same work, or an ideal of a single correct interpretation (the monism/pluralism issue). A final issue concerns whether there is such a thing as *the* meaning of a work (the work meaning issue)? We need to address these issues before we can fully evaluate the force of the objections to intentionalism.[2]

What Do we Aim At When We Interpret a Work?

The last objection claimed that intentionalism is false because it blocks the pursuit of the proper aim of interpretation. How does one decide what we *should* be doing when we interpret a work of art or literature? If there were a set of norms available a priori that we could appeal to, that would settle the matter, but anyone who appealed to such norms would likely be perceived as begging the question. What is available in a nonquestion begging way is actual (and possible!) interpretive practice. However, a straightforward appeal to this is not decisive because what people actually do (much less might do) is not necessarily what they should be doing. Nevertheless, if people engage in certain interpretive practices that make no straightforwardly false assumptions and that aim at valuable goals, then it is not clear how we can object to such practices. The aims of such practices would then at least be among the permissible aims of art interpretation. If there were just one actual or possible aim that passed this test, it would be the one we should be pursuing when we interpret the relevant works; but if not, a number of different aims would be options.

Both common sense and actual practice tell us that there are a number of different interpretive aims that meet the above conditions. There is plenty of critical practice that pursues the goal of identifying the intentions that artists express in works. Furthermore, there is no reason to think that this goal is less valuable here then it is in other interpretive contexts, where it is widely admitted to be the goal of interpretation. Even if the meaning of a work is not invariably identified with the intention expressed in the work, as the second criticism of intentionalism claims, identifying expressed intention may still be a perfectly reasonable aim of interpretation. However, there is plenty of critical practice that does not pursue this goal, and aims at other things such as value maximization. It is hard to deny that maximizing value is a valuable goal! These two aims are not the only ones we find when we examine what critics do. Some interpretations aim to find *an* understanding of a difficult work without claiming that it is either the intended way of taking the work or the only way. Some seek out a meaning that the work could have (or have had) for a certain sort of audience. Others attempt to identify how the work would be understood against the backdrop of certain large ideas or theories such as those of Freud, Marx, or those of some feminists. There may even be some interpretations that do not literally say anything about a work but that seek to get us to imaginatively contemplate certain actual or possible states of affairs.

We have now suggested a resolution to the first issue raised above: art interpretation does not have a single proper aim. Hence the value maximizers cannot criticize actual intentionalism for blocking the pursuit of this aim. We can, however, level a revised criticism at this view, although it is one that can be raised against value maximization as well. We defined actual intentionalism as a thesis about *the* correct interpretation of an artwork. We now have reason to think that this thesis is false. If art interpretation has a plurality of aims, it is quite possible that there are correct or acceptable interpretations of works arrived at in pursuit of some of these other aims that do not make statements about the artist's intention. On the other hand, there can also be perfectly acceptable interpretations that do not aim at or even contribute to maximizing our appreciation of the work by maximizing enjoyable aesthetic experience.

The Aims of Interpretation and the Value of Art

Before turning to the remaining issues, it is worth pointing out that there is a link between one's conception of the aims of art interpretation and one's view of the value of art. It is plausible that art interpretation should be in the service of appreciating what is of value in works of art. If one thinks that there is a single supreme artistic value – such as the provision of aesthetically valuable experiences – then it becomes more plausible to think that art interpretation too has a single dominant or primary aim, which in the case at hand would be to satisfy aesthetic interest in artworks. Even if one accepts this, it is still an open question which interpretive projects best serve an aesthetic interest in art. However, most of those who take this line argue that identifying the artist's actual intention is secondary to finding interpretations that enhance appreciation (Goldman 1995), that put a work in the best light (Dworkin 1986, Raz 1996), or that provide several different ways of taking the work (S. Davies 1991).

I would question both the principle just enunciated for determining interpretive aims – that the point of interpretation is enhanced appreciation – and the conception of artistic value featured in the previous paragraph. As I argue at greater length in chapter 4, if we have to settle for just one way of characterizing what we are trying to accomplish when we interpret works of art, then we should speak of the appreciative *understanding* of works, and not simply of the appreciation of their artistic value. We should recognize that one of main reasons we interpret artworks along with many other objects is that we find we do not understand them or that they have aspects (like the symbolic aspects of "The Sick Rose") that we do not understand. The point of an interpretation is to remedy this. Of course, we hope that this greater understanding will lead to greater appreciation. However, as we will show in chapter 4, understanding is not the same as appreciation, and the former can fail to lead to the latter without impugning the interpretive goal of improved understanding.

I would also argue for a more multivalenced conception of the value of art. There is not a single art practice, institution, or world, and there is not just one value that art is in the service of bringing into being. We do value art for the aesthetic experience it provides, but it also has cognitive, expressive, and many sorts of instrumental value. Among other things, we value works as the products and achievements of their creators, as explorations of possibilities, as ideal, novel, or perspicuous representations of objects, as exactly the right expression of a thought or feeling. If this conception of artistic value is accurate, to the extent that interpretation is in the service of appreciating what is of value in art, we would expect there to be a multiplicity of interpretive aims corresponding to the multiplicity of values. Arguing for this conception of artistic value is beyond the scope of this book, but I, and others, have offered such arguments elsewhere (Carroll 1986, Dickie 1988, Levinson 1996, Stecker 1997a: 247–304, 1997c, forthcoming).

Critical Monism and Critical Pluralism

The second issue is whether the aims of art interpretation promote an ideal of a plurality of acceptable interpretations or of a single correct interpretation. Those who believe that what is promoted is a single correct (true), comprehensive interpretation of a work are critical monists (Beardsley 1970, Hirsch 1967, Nehamas 1981). Those who believe that what is promoted is a noncombinable multiplicity of acceptable interpretations are critical pluralists (Barnes 1988, Fish 1980, Goldman 1990). It may seem as if what we have said so far supports the pluralist rather than the monist. After all if there is the variety of interpretive aims stated above, it won't make sense to combine them all together even if we could do so without outright inconsistency. The result would be a hotchpotch rather than a more comprehensive interpretation.

However, closer scrutiny suggests that we may not have to choose between these two ideals. Monism might be acceptable if its pursuit is properly contextualized within the domain of interpretive aims. Certain aims are properly pursued under the monist ideal while others are not. Intentionalist interpretation, for example, aims at finding the uniquely correct account of what the artist intended in the work, even though available evidence may be insufficient for realization of this aim. It would make no difference that the artist's intentions were ambivalent between different conceptions of the work or if he intended the work to be ambiguous in various respects, for a good intentionalist would seek to capture these things in a single interpretation. On the other hand, interpretations that aim at discovering what a work *could* mean, or at finding aesthetically valuable ways of taking a work, are best seen as pursuing the pluralist ideal. This is so regardless of the fact that such interpretations could be combined without inconsistency, since it is not inconsistent to assert that a work *could* mean that p and that it *could* mean that not-p. Though the interpretations can be consistently bundled together, it typically does not serve the aim of these interpretations to do so.

Theories of Work Meaning

This leaves us with the last of the three issues raised above, which we can rephrase as whether among the numerous aims of interpretation there is a special one of discovering the meaning of a work? *The meaning* of a work is to be distinguished from the various things that the work *could mean* or are merely taken to mean in the service of some interpretive aim. It is what the work actually *does* mean either in virtue of the artist's intention or, as the second objection to intentionalism suggests, on some other basis. Call this *work meaning*, for short. Is there is such a thing as work meaning?

There is currently no consensus how to answer this question. Some people suppose that, since interpretation is concerned with the ascription of meaning to works, there must be something – the meaning of the work – that is being ascribed. However, we have seen that meanings can be ascribed on many grounds in virtue of the many different aims with which we undertake interpretation. So, while we cannot deny that works can bear *meanings*, it does not follow that there is such a thing as *the meaning* of a work. Other people suppose that precisely because there is this multiplicity of aims, and that important among these is the aim of enhancing appreciation of the work, there could not be such a thing as the meaning of work. However, it does not follow from the fact that people interpret with many legitimate aims that there is no such thing as work meaning or that it is not an important aim to discover it.

The challenge that neither of the above arguments meets is to identify, or show why we cannot identify, a special kind of meaning-ascription appropriately thought of as the work's meaning. *Utterances* provide a good model for seeing how we can make this identification. An utterance is the use of language on a particular occasion (in speech or writing) to say or do something. "There are ten sheep in the field" standardly states that there are ten sheep in the field, but with certain sorts of common knowledge and with an appropriate context, I may be uttering this sentence primarily to say or do something else. It may be my conventional way of telling you that two sheep, in our twelve-sheep herd, have wandered off (in which case I am primarily using these words to say or imply something beyond what the words literally say), or I may even be telling you to go look for the two missing sheep (in which case I am primarily using these words to do something: get you to look for the sheep). Notice we can distinguish between what my utterance could mean (what I could say or do in making it) and what it does mean (what I actually say or do). It is the latter that we would identify as *the meaning* of the utterance.

We can extend this model to works of art by thinking of them as utterances of the artists who create them. The model applies most straightforwardly to literary works, which are, after all, literally complex linguistic utterances. However, whatever determines utterance (work) meaning may be applicable to other artworks as well.

It is common ground between intentionalists and, at least, some of their opponents to think of works as utterances. Some intentionalists claim that the meaning of an utterance or work is to be identified with the intention expressed in it. (Please notice, however, that this claim is not implied by the definition of intentionalism stated earlier.) As we have seen, opponents of intentionalism have shown that we can make utterances (or create works) in which we say or do something other than what we intended, and so the identification between intention and utterance/work meaning does not always hold.

Given that work meaning cannot be *identified* with intended meaning, what might it consist in? There are *three main alternatives* to consider. The first claims that work meaning is determined by conventions. For example, the meaning of a literary work is determined by linguistic conventions, literary conventions, and perhaps other cultural conventions (Beardsley 1970, 1982, S. Davies 1991). In general, artistic, linguistic, and other cultural conventions will be relevant in determining work meaning. (Linguistic conventions are almost always relevant to nonliterary artworks for many reasons. For one, most works have titles expressed in language. For another, many of the categories by which we approach these works, such as portrait or sonata, are enshrined in language.) Let us call this view conventionalism. Proponents of this view can, and do, differ about which conventions are operative in fixing work meaning. In the case of literary works, linguistic conventions will always be among these. However, one can disagree about which ones are appropriate since linguistic conventions change over time. Are they the conventions in place when the work is written, when the interpretation is offered, or at some other time? Among literary conventions, are conventions of interpretation relevant (if so, again which ones) or only conventions of writing or genre? Though a conventionalist would need to answer these questions, they may be moot for us because there seems to be a decisive objection to conventionalism as a stand-alone account of work meaning. The meaning of an utterance is normally not fixed by conventions alone. Context (and, possibly, utterer's intention) is always relevant. The content of utterances of "Richard is poor" will vary depending on who is being referred to, the relevant sense of "poor" (which might indicate the wealth, health, or another condition of Richard), and the speech act performed on the occasion in question. This is equally true of work meaning if it is to be understood on the model of utterance meaning. "The Sick Rose" does not need context to fix the reference of its singular terms, but it cannot be fully understood outside the context of the poems that accompany it in the *Songs of Innocence* and the *Songs of Experience*, of its historical period, and so on. An example of this is the choice of the rose as the sick flower. The rose had a conventional significance in Blake's poetic tradition as, for example, a symbol of fragile, transient beauty, but this hardly exhausts its significance in Blake's poetry, which can only be determined contextually. (Another poem in the *Songs* tells us, "The modest Rose puts forth a thorn . . . While the Lilly white shall in Love delight . . .")

While this is a decisive objection to a conventionalist account of work meaning, when such meaning is understood as a species of utterance meaning, the conventionalist might attempt to defend her view by denying that work meaning should be understood in those terms. A conventionalist could claim that a literary work is identical to a *text* or alternatively, and more plausibly, what I will call a "constrained text." Texts themselves can be understood in different ways: as a sequence of marks or shapes, as purely syntactic sequence, as a syntactic/semantic sequence, the semantic aspect of which changes as the language of the text changes, or as a syntactic/ semantic sequence, the semantics of which is fixed by the state of the language at a given time. Let us stipulate that the last of these conceptions identifies the texts that are purportedly identical to works. Such texts have the most determinate linguistic meaning among the alternatives just mentioned, but they have no literary meanings whatsoever, and their linguistic meaning is no guide to a literary appreciation of the work. The linguistic meaning of a sentence can be conceptualized as its potential to (be used to) say or do something when its referents and other variable features are fixed (typically by context or intention). Thus a text that contains several occurrences of the name "Richard Nixon" cannot even be assumed to be referring to the same individual in different occurrences of the name. It would all depend on what utterances the text is being used to make, and this is left wide open by the text itself. It would also be indeterminate whether we have a work of fiction or nonfiction. Thus a text gives us no characters, no plot, no theme, no elements, in short, that we take literary works to possess. While there are some who are willing to accept this consequence of the view that works are texts (see Goodman and Elgin 1988: 49–65), most theorists find this unpalatable.

The constrained text is the result of adding to the text *simpliciter* literary, genre, and other relevant conventions. This view is closer in spirit to conventionalism as we originally described it, and it might be adequate to determine such features of works as their fictionality, that they are stories with coherent characters, plot, and theme. Further, it might limit the reasonable choices regarding the exact determination of characters, plot, theme, and other interpretive issues rather than leave this wide open. The aim of interpretation, on this conventionalist view, might be to identify *a set of meanings* that can reasonably be assigned to the constrained text, rather than *the meaning* of the text.[3] Such a set of meanings is the closest we can come to identifying work meaning.

The objection to this version of conventionalism is that its constraints are still insufficient to provide a useful model of art interpretation. The reason for this is that, until we see the text as making or at least representing a complex utterance,[4] we cannot implement the relevant literary conventions. Perhaps literary conventions tell us that a novel is a story. But what story? We have to regard storytelling as an intentional act, that is, as someone's utterance, to figure out what story is being told. This criticism does not lead straight back to actual intentionalism, because it is arguable that the utterer in question is not the actual artist or that the intentions behind the utterance are not the artist's actual intentions. One way or another, however, we are led to considerations beyond those of mere convention. The only way that a conventionalist can save her view at this point is to argue that it is a convention that we should treat the work as an utterance and take an interest in intentions or contexts that might fix its meaning. However, this is unconvincing because, if it is indeed inevitable that we have to treat the text as an utterance, there is no need for a convention telling us to do this. In any case, conventionalism becomes indistinguishable from the nonconventionalist views discussed below if it simply tells us that it is a convention to treat texts as those views prescribe.

The idea of a second account of work meaning is that such meaning is properly identified not as what the actual artist actually intended but with what an audience should or would understand to be intended, given certain background assumptions. Call this a *hypothetical* intention and the view hypothetical intentionalism (Currie 1993, Levinson 1996, 1999, Nehamas 1981, 1987, Tolhurst 1979). It recognizes that audiences acknowledge the fact that artworks are the deliberate creations of artists by taking the features of works as intended. The innovative aspect of this view is that work meaning is to be identified with the hypothetical intention the audience is most justified in finding in the work. This puts hypothetical intentionalism in a position to take into account the considerations of context with which conventionalism was unable to deal. However, it allows for meanings that are not actually intended. Indeed, we are to identify work meaning with a hypothesized intention, even if we somehow come to know that something different was actually intended.

The view still needs filling out. It has to tell us more about the audience in question and about the considerations it may use in identifying hypothetical intentions. Is it the audience contemporary with the artist, the audience that the artist intends to address, or an ideal audience? Are the considerations that the audience takes into account only items that are *evidence* of the artist's intention? Or are other sorts of consideration also to be taken into account, such as whether the postulation of an intention makes the work artistically better? Are there restrictions on the kinds of evidence to be brought forward? That all these questions have to be answered is not a criticism of hypothetical intentionalism, but does indicate a challenge it must meet. There are different versions that answer these questions in different ways, and hypothetical intentionalists need to show us that there is a nonarbitrary way of picking the best version.

The last account of work meaning attempts to combine two views we considered earlier and found to be inadequate in their own right as accounts of such meaning. These are actual intentionalism and conventionalism, and the present view, call it the unified view, says, roughly, that work meaning is a function of both the actual intentions of artists and the conventions in place when the work is created.[5] When the artist succeeds in expressing her intention in the work (which, of course, will commonly involve the exploiting of conventions and context), that is what we should identify with the meaning of the work; but when actual intentions fail to be expressed, conventions in place when the work is created determine meaning.

Hypothetical Intentionalism Versus the Unified View

If one thinks that there is such a thing as work meaning, and that utterances provide the model for this meaning, the two views that are most plausible at this point are hypothetical intentionalism and the unified view. Is one of these views superior to the other? To answer this question, I briefly suspend the presentation of an overview of issues, to examine in some detail arguments for and against these positions.

Let us begin with hypothetical intentionalism (HI). I have already mentioned two things that motivate this view. One is that it is able to accommodate the fact that we think of works as deriving from intentions, and that our interpretations often explain works in those terms, while recognizing that work meaning can diverge from actually intended meaning. Second, it is able to take into account features of context, including some facts about the work's creator, as relevant determinants of significant artistic properties, and hence of work meaning. However, these aspects of HI give it no advantage over the unified view because the latter also accommodates precisely the same facts. Both of these views are trying to give an account of work meaning on the analogy with utterance meaning as distinct from an utterer's intended meaning.

Some, though not all, versions of HI have an additional motivating feature,[6] which, if based on fact, might provide an argument in its favor over the unified view. This is the thought that the artistic "utterance" differs from the conversational or the discursive one by the fact that evidence legitimately available for hypothesizing the artist's intention is restricted in the former instance, in a way that it is not in the latter instances. Since the unified view recognizes no such restriction, it would be defective *if* there were one. The purported restrictions tend to be set out along two parameters. First, the less publicly available a piece of evidence is, the more it is ruled out. Second, direct pronouncements of intentions by artists external to the work are excluded. It may be thought that the two parameters rule out the same pieces of evidence, but this is not so. A published interview with the artist, which contains a direct pronouncement of intention, is in the public domain in a way that private letters or diaries are not (until they are published). A rationale for the first parameter is that artworks are public in nature, and so admissible evidence of intention should also be public. However, if the "so" in the previous sentence indicates an inference from the first conjunct to the second, it is not a valid inference. The fact that works themselves are public do not tell us what evidence may be used to answer questions about those works. It is hard to imagine that works would undergo a change in meaning just because letters that were in private hands become publicly available. It looks, then, like the restriction required by the first parameter needs to be dropped in favor of the second one forbidding the consultation of any direct pronouncements external to the work.

We still need a rationale for that restriction. There are two on offer, but neither is satisfactory. One is that the consultation of direct pronouncements would distract our attention from the text. However, it would do so no more than the consultation of any other contextual feature, especially if we bear in mind, first, that we are consulting evidence to determine work (utterance) meaning, not utterer's meaning, and second that direct pronouncements of intention are not even authoritative for the latter, much less the former. They are merely one bit of evidence among others. The other rationale is that "the game" of artistic interpretation just *is* played with this restriction, or the aims of interpretation are best realized by obeying it. The point about how the game is played is surely an empirical claim for which proponents of HI *never* offer evidence. However, it appears to be patently false, as critics do routinely consult letters, diaries, interviews, memoirs, and so on in developing interpretations.[7] The point about best realizing the aims of art interpretation is normative rather than empirical. It indicates what critics should do. But why should they depart from their actual behavior? Not to avoid becoming distracted from the text (since that would reduce the second rationale to the first, and the distraction need not happen in any case). It is unclear what could underpin the normative claim, and our earlier negative conclusion regarding the question whether art interpretation has a single privileged aim should lead us to doubt it.

If hypothetical intentionalism is to be in a position to assert its superiority, it must be shown to be a superior account of utterance meaning in general, of which work meaning would be an instance. However, as an account of utterance meaning (work meaning), it faces counterexamples and a larger problem.

One counterexample consists in cases where a work W means P (perhaps for conventional reasons), but P is not intended, and the relevant audience of W is justified in believing that P is not intended. Then HI wrongly implies that W does not mean P. The other side of the same coin is the case where an artist intends W to mean P, it is known that the artist has this intention, but W does not mean P, but rather Q. Here HI wrongly implies that W does mean P. If works can have unintended meanings, they should be able to have those meanings whether or not we can detect that the meaning is not intended. We easily recognize such cases outside of the arts; for example, in slips of the tongue or the misuse of words. If I utter, "There's a fly in your suit," when all the evidence points to the fact that I am attempting to talk about an insect visibly floating in your soup (rather than a vent in trousers), the most justified hypothesis is that I meant to say that the fly is in your soup, but I actually said something (in virtue of the conventions of language) that located the fly elsewhere. And yet, if the meaning of my utterance is the intention an audience is most justified in attributing to me, given not just conventions of language but context, it looks, contrary to fact, that I said that there is a fly in your soup. Similarly if I utter, "You're a very perspicuous fellow," meaning you are very perspicacious, I actually say one thing, but the best hypothesis about what I intend to say will be something else.[8]

Suppose George Eliot wrote at one point in *Middlemarch* that Casuabon's house is 45 miles from Manchester, and at another point in the novel wrote that it is 54 miles from that city. Taken together, we have it fictionally in the novel that Manchester is both 45 and 54 miles from Casuabon's house, an unlikely state of affairs and one unlikely to be intended by Eliot. Perhaps we are most justified in believing that she intended the distance to be either 45 or 54 miles, and that it does not matter which distance is chosen. But again, that is not what is said in the novel.

Imagine a short story by Tolstoy, written in the latter part of his career, which is set up to contrast the virtues of peasants and the decadence of the landowning class. Suppose, as we read, we can detect subtle defects in peasant behavior, and some sparks of praiseworthy aspiration within the general malaise of the nobility. Suppose Tolstoy's *conscious* intention (the one he would sincerely offer if asked) was to present a stark contrast between peasants and aristocrats, without subtle gradations in order to communicate clear, strong emotions. This might also be the best hypothesis about his intention, given the overall structure of the story and his well-known, publicly available views about what constitutes good art. Yet it may not be the most accurate representation of the content of the work. Admittedly, that this is really a counterexample to HI is far less certain than in the other cases, because it is far less certain what would be the best hypothesis as to Tolstoy's intention. I suggest, however, this is because it is equally unclear what Tolstoy's actual intention might have been, which may be more complex than he would acknowledge.

These counterexamples illustrate what I referred to above as the larger problem for HI. HI justified itself by pointing out that utterance meaning can diverge from utterer's meaning, and that work meaning is better captured with the former notion than with the latter. However, it is then incumbent on HI to show that it provides a satisfactory account of utterance meaning, that is, of what someone *says* on an occasion of utterance. It now looks pretty clear that it does not do this.

The objections stated above are directed against the best-known versions of HI (Levinson 1996, Tolhurst 1979). There is a version of HI, which might escape the above objections, that claims that the meaning of a work is fixed by the intention of a hypothetical author who is fully aware of relevant context and conventions and flawlessly utilizes them to say what she intends to say (Nathan 1992).

This view escapes the "There's a fly in your suit" example, since it would attribute to the hypothetical utterer the intention to say that there is fly in your suit. Although it gets the meaning of the utterance right, what such an utterer is getting at remains mysterious. The unified view, which can identify both a failed intention and a meaning fixed by convention, provides a better take on the utterance. The proponent of this version of HI can also point to a failed actual intention, but then has to appeal to something purportedly completely extraneous to utterance meaning to explain what is going on in this situation.

Appeal to a flawless hypothetical author or utterer fares even worse in cases where there is something intrinsically wrong with the utterance. "You're a perspicuous fellow" does not have a literal meaning that makes sense, and so such a meaning cannot be attributed to the super-capable hypothetical author. The same goes for the *Middlemarch* example mentioned above.

Finally, there is another class of cases that can be directed against all versions of HI, characterized by the fact that the best hypothesis as to speaker's (artist's) intention may diverge from what the intention actually is. A number of writers have argued that, *where both candidates are compatible with relevant conventions*, it is actual intention that determines meaning rather than hypothetical intention (Carroll 2000: 84, Iseminger 1996: 323–5). One argument for this is that actual intentions tell us what is true regarding meaning, while hypothetical ones just tell us what we are warranted in asserting. This argument is less than decisive. It could be replied that *truth conditions* of meaning claims refer to hypothetical rather than actual intentions (Levinson 1999: 24). A crucial test case would be what proponents of HI say about the meaning of ordinary utterances outside of art in such cases. If they agree that actual intentions determine meaning in these cases, they have given up the game for work meaning as well.

Suppose I am speaking at a rally in front of a bank, on the roof of which several large sharks have been placed by antiglobalist demonstrators, to symbolize the sharkish nature of global capitalism. Unaware of the presence of these fish, I say, "As I speak, there are fish lying on the bank," intending to refer to a fish kill in a nearby river. It seems to me that it is unclear in these cases whether the ambiguity should be resolved in favor of intention or context, or perhaps left unresolved due to the differential pull of each of these factors. What is implausible is that the meaning of the utterance is *obviously* the one that the audience is most justified in believing to be intended rather than the one actually intended. If this is correct, it would be another counterexample to HI. (I borrow the gist of this example from Carroll 2000, who uses it to reach a more starkly actual intentionalist conclusion than I would endorse.)

Turning now to the unified view, it too faces serious objections. First, it is claimed that it relies on a notion of successful intention (an intention expressed in a work) which is circular because there is no way of explaining what success amounts to without an independent notion of work meaning (Levinson 1996: 180). Second, it can be charged that it lacks a clear account of the way intention and convention jointly determine work meaning. Third, it is not clear that the unified view can stop with recognizing only two determinants of work meaning (intention and convention). If it has to recognize others, it is at best incomplete. Fourth, the more nonintentional determinants of work meaning that we recognize, the less clear it is that we need intentions at all (Nathan 1992).

The first objection can be handled in one of two ways. First, one can find a way to identify relevant from inoperative or defective intentions that make no reference to success. (This tack is pursued by Livingston 1996: 628–30.) Alternatively, one can attempt to show one can use the notion of successful intention without falling into vicious circularity. I prefer this second strategy without denying that the first might be equally effective. An analysis of pictorial representation provides a model of how one can use the notion of successful intention without falling into circularity. A simplified version devoid of needed qualification, says O represents a just in case the creator of O intends viewers to see a in the work and properly prepared viewers would be able to do this. (A proponent of the unified view might add a further disjunct, viz., that conventions in place when O is created, not canceled in the work, permit, or require, seeing a in it.)[9] Here we have one condition that says an intention must be present, and a second uptake condition. The latter basically says that the work is such that the intention is capable of implementation, which indicates when we have a successful intention without, however, requiring an independent notion of work meaning. This basic analysis can be extended beyond the case of pictorial representation to work meaning in general. An intention is expressed in a work (the artist intentionally does something in a work) just in case she makes the work with the relevant intention, and the work is such that the intention is capable of uptake.

The second objection asserts that it is unclear how intention and convention work together to determine meaning. If it is unclear, it is because there is not a single way in which this happens. In the normal case, conventions (and context) enable me to implement my intention. However, when my intentions are inconsistent with conventions, this will sometimes make it impossible to do what I intend. For example, because "suit" refers to suits, but not to soup, I cannot say that there is a fly in your soup with the words "There's a fly in your suit."[10] However, other kinds of conventions (perhaps because they are less stringent) can be intentionally overridden or canceled. For example, in Blake's poetic tradition, a white lily might conventionally symbolize virginity, but Blake is able to cancel the conventional association with the words "The Lily white shall in Love delight," in the context of the *Songs of Experience* where the theme sexual love is front and center. (Blake may nevertheless be alluding to the convention to suggest that various kinds of conventional association are being turned on their heads.) So if there is obscurity, it is because there is a great deal of complexity in the interaction of intention and convention. Perhaps one can formulate some rules for some conventions (like those determining linguistic meaning), but one probably cannot formulate rules covering all interactions. However, it is not clear that this constitutes a serious objection to the unified view. That a view implies a certain complexity in the way its terms interact does not mean its is false.

The third objection is that the unified view is incomplete because intention and convention are not the only determinants of work (utterance) meaning. This objection is correct, and we should modify the unified view accordingly. Here are some illustrations of why we need to do so. Suppose I show you a snapshot in which you see a tiny goose in the upper right hand corner. I did not intend this goose to be in the picture. Nor is it convention that makes it true that we have a picture of a goose. A goose is there because it interacted with the photographic process in the right way when the picture was taken. That is a feature of the context in which the picture was taken. Hence, context also is a determinant of meaning. Again, recall my unfortunate uttering of "There's a fly in your suit." It is convention that determines that I am referring to suits and not soup. But what determines that I am referring to *your* suit (assuming you have a suit and are wearing it)? In part, it is linguistic convention again (I do say "your suit"), but in different contexts "your suit" refers to different people's suits, not always *your* suit. Hence, once again context plays a role in determining meaning (reference). Intention plays no role in this case, by the way, because I did not intend to refer to suits at all. So we do need to modify the unified view, but that does not mean we have to completely abandon it.

Unless the fourth objection is correct. This says that the more determinants of meaning we have, the less reason we have to suppose that intention determines meaning. Let us rephrase the objection in the light of the preceding paragraph. If we recognize that conventions and context determine work or utterance meaning, we do not need to refer to intentions at all. Reference to context and conventions always suffices, the objection claims, to explain why an utterance or a work has the meaning it has. For example, to return one last time to the suit–fly example, when I misspeak and say the now well-known unfortunate words, it is convention and context that determine what I say. Now suppose I utter the same words intending to say that there is a fly in your suit. Does this make any difference as to what determines what utterance I make? If context and convention sufficed before, shouldn't they suffice now? It would appear to.

I think this claim is fine when confined to a special case: when all that is needed to understand what is said is to take the words, *already disambiguated*, at the most literal level.[11] (For example, "suit" refers to articles of clothing and not to playing cards or legal actions in the case we have been discussing.) Since context and convention are what we utilize to convey our intention to say this or that, it is useful that context and convention do convey a clear meaning in their own right in the most literal and straightforward cases. Normally this just makes it easier to say what we intend, though occasionally, something goes wrong, and something is said, which is not intended. (For all this to work there must be a general shared intention to take words in certain ways.) However, once we leave this most literal level, we generally won't be able to fix what is being said without thinking about the intention or point of saying it. To return to an example used earlier, my ability to use "there are ten sheep in the field" to say that two sheep are missing and need to be found, relies on a shared understanding between you and me about my point in using those words. That may lead to the establishment of a miniconvention to enable me to express a certain intention in a certain context. (Of course something can go wrong, and I may end up saying something other than I intend.) Very often, there is not even a miniconvention: we have to figure out the point as we go. It is the point that makes certain uses of words ironic, that will constrain how we understand some metaphors, that will make something an allusion, and so on. It is only by getting a hold on Blake's expressed intention that will enable us to decide whether "The Sick Rose" has a political as well as a sexual dimension. Context and convention won't do it all in the business of determining meaning at all levels. That will be *at least* equally true when we turn to work meaning. So the fourth objection is not correct.

I certainly do not claim that this discussion of hypothetical intentionalism and the unified view is the final word on the debate between them. What I do claim is that HI needs to show that it provides a satisfactory account of utterance meaning, and that it faces serious obstacles to being able to do this. The unified view faced what looked like equally serious problems. However, I have tried to show that it has resources to provide promising solutions. One strategy that HI could contemplate is to restrict in some way the cases it covers. It might try restricting itself to cases where context and convention do not do all of the work. Alternatively, (though less promisingly in my view) it might try restricting itself to the meaning of artworks. However, *if* this turned out to make it harder to give counterexamples to HI, it also would make HI a less general theory with less explanatory power than the unified view.

I have spent some time examining the relative merits of two theories of utterance and work meaning. It is worth mentioning that the two views aren't all that far apart. They have a tendency to reach the same conclusions about the meanings works have, because the intention an audience is most justified in finding in a work will very often be the intention the artist expressed in it. We have seen that some hypothetical intentionalists want to restrict the evidence audiences may use to reach conclusions and to allow them to employ other considerations such as the aesthetic merit an interpretation bestows on a work. This seems to imply that the meanings they find in works will differ from those discovered by the unified view. This difference may be narrowed if proponents of the unified view want to introduce the idea that successful intentions are those that can receive audience uptake which could place some restrictions on evidence, and they may defend a principle of charity in choosing among rival hypotheses, which could introduce considerations of aesthetic merit. While the views do not collapse into each other, they are close relatives.[12]

In this chapter, we have set out three central issues that a theory of art interpretation must tackle. We have discussed various positions that have been taken on these issues, and have tried to give pointers toward what I take to be the correct or most plausible positions. In the next chapter these positions will be worked out in more detail and supported by further arguments in order to present a theory of art interpretation encompassing all of these issues.

NOTES

1　I speak of *actual* intentionalism (AI) here because this view will be contrasted below with another: *hypothetical* intentionalism. As introduced here, AI is ambiguous between a theory of what we are aiming for in interpretation and a theory of the meaning of artworks, one version of which would claim the meaning of a work is the intention the artist expresses in it. One should distinguish between these two versions of AI because one can think that interpretations aim at understanding intention (or expressed intention) without claiming that expressed intention constitutes the meaning of a work. Alternatively, one can believe that the meaning of a work is captured by the actual intentions of the artist, without believing that the only aim of interpretation is to identify work meaning. Of course, most actual intentionalists would accept both versions. Both claims – that interpretations aim at finding the intention expressed in the work, and that this constitutes the meaning of a work – will be evaluated below. In initially defining AI below as a theory about the correctness of interpretations, I deliberately exploit an ambiguity between pursuing the correct aim and identifying the correct meaning.

　　Some proponents of actual intentionalism are Carroll (1992, 2000), Harris (1988), Hirsch (1967, 1984), Juhl (1980), Iseminger (1992, 1996), Knapp and Michaels (1985), and Livingston (1996, 1998).

2　While I indicate my views about how these issues should be resolved below, these views will be set out more fully in chapter 3.

3 This conception of the meaning a conventionalist aims to identify corresponds closely with the views of S. Davies (1982, 1988, 1991). On the other hand, it departs from Beardsley's position (1958, 1970), which endorses the idea that interpretation aims to identify a single correct meaning. If the arguments in the text are correct, conventionalism does not supply the means to achieve this end.

4 Beardsley eventually came to suggest that a literary work contains representations of utterances, rather than actual utterances (Beardsley 1982).

5 Proponents of this view are Carroll (2000), Iseminger (1992: 96), Livingston (1996, 1998), and Stecker (1997a). The view is sometimes called modest actual intentionalism, which is why many of the proponents of actual intentionalism cited in note 1, are also cited here.

6 Levinson (1996) is notable for the emphasis he places on the claim that evidence of semantic intentions should be restricted, at least when interpreting literary works (his discussion being addressed to them). Nehamas (1981) places no such limitation on relevant evidence.

7 Carroll (2000) is particularly good at showing this. See also Livingston (1996) for support. More broadly, a number of critics of HI have argued that it is arbitrary or self-defeating to place limits on evidence of intention. (In addition to those just cited see Savile 1996, Stecker 1997a.) Iseminger (1996: 322–6) argues that such limitations are not required by considerations of the autonomy of art.

8 Dickie and Wilson (1995) make a somewhat similar point using a similar illustration.

9 See Stecker (1997a: 181–2) for another discussion of the circularity objection.

10 This is not to say that linguistic conventions can never be canceled or that they lack flexibility. For example, by inflecting one's voice appropriately, one can convey that one's words are intended, and should be taken, ironically rather than literally. Good writers manage to get us to "hear" such inflection as we read, thereby canceling the convention that we should take the words at face value.

11 However, it is very common that we need to do things like disambiguate to determine utterance meaning, and it is far from obvious that we can manage this without appealing to actual intentions.

12 This is so, in part because the version of HI on which we have focused is a species of traditional historicism. However, the distinction between hypothetical and actual intentionalism (or the unified view) is orthogonal to the distinction between traditional historicism and constructivism. It is only fair to point out that there are versions of HI, which are constructivist (Currie 1993). These versions permit a variety of widely divergent background assumptions about the artist and her context that differ from the actual historical context in which the work is created as the basis for perfectly acceptable interpretations of the work. Further, it is claimed that traditional historicist background assumptions are not privileged in the sense that they determine work meaning. Meaning is relative to background assumptions, and there are many equally legitimate sets of assumptions. (See Stecker 1995a for a critique of this position.) This is a relativistic as well as a constructivist version of HI. It is relativistic precisely because the correctness or acceptability of an interpretation is relative to a point of view and no point of view is acknowledged to be privileged over other legitimate points of view.

A Theory of Art Interpretation: Substantive Claims

I now turn to a theory of art interpretation.[1] In this chapter, I further explain and defend the set of theses proposed in chapter 2 as answers to the three central issues debated with regard to critical interpretation in the arts. In the next chapter, I resolve various conceptual and ontological issues raised by these theses.

I begin with a summary of the proposal on offer. Regarding the proper aim issue, I claim that (a) people interpret artworks with different aims; (b) such interpretations need to be evaluated relative to aims; (c) the aim of some interpretations permit, indeed require, them to be evaluated for truth or falsity, while the aim of others do not.

Regarding the monism/pluralism issue, I claim that (d) among the interpretations requiring evaluation for truth or falsity are those that aim to identify what an artist "does" in a work in a robust sense of "does" to be spelled out; (e) there is a single, correct, comprehensive interpretation with this aim for any given work; (f) also one can conjoin true interpretations of a work (whatever their aims) to form ever more comprehensive, true interpretations of it, though ones that may be too diffuse and unwieldy to be very useful; (g) everything that has been asserted so far is compatible with there being a plurality of good or acceptable interpretations of given a work.

Regarding the work meaning issue, I endorse a further claim (h) that the meaning of a work is set out in the interpretation mentioned in (d) and (e) above. However, I consider this claim as more optional, and as harder to defend, than claims (a)–(g).

Arguing for the Theory

In the following sections, I will argue for each thesis in points (a)–(h) in turn.

Aims of interpretation

To get at point (a), let us begin with what looks like a fairly clear contrast between two situations where we are engaged in interpretation. The first situation is one in which we are interpreting someone's behavior. Suppose your friend Jim has begun waking up in the middle of the night, going out of the house and poking around his backyard, then going back to sleep. That is all you know about his behavior based on a somewhat hasty telephone conversation. From this sparse information, you can think of many interpretations of your friend's behavior, which include:

1. He has insomnia, wants to get back to sleep and believes that the best way to do this is to get a bit of fresh air.
2. He is collecting night crawlers for an upcoming fishing trip.
3. He has become psychotic, and believing traps are being laid, is attempting to find them and expose the perpetrators.

An interpretation, in this context, would be a hypothesis about the explanation of the behavior. It is safe to say that, while you can think of many interpretations, that is, many possible explanations of the behavior, there are correct ones, though they may be complex in, for example, including both 1 and 2. Although your initial aim is to consider possible explanations, this is in the service of finding the actual causes of Jim's behavior, and you would throw out those you can determine to be incorrect. You certainly would not say something like "I accept 1 and 2 because they correctly explain Jim's behavior, but I also accept 3, because it makes Jim's behavior a lot more interesting than 1 and 2 do."

Turn now to the interpretation in the arts, such as the interpretation of poetry. Here we do get the assertion of interpretations as different as 1 and 3, and we also seem to get two different attitudes to the assertions of these. On one hand, just as in the case of the hypotheses put forward to explain Jim's behavior, different interpretations of a poem are regarded as rivals among which we need to choose, although, just as with 1 and 2 above, it remains a possibility that some seemingly rival interpretations are part of a more comprehensive correct interpretation, and hence not really rivals at all. The thought that interpretations are rivals is what permits interpretive controversies about particular works, of which there are many, including some famous ones such as the controversies over James's *Turn of the Screw* and Wordsworth's "A Slumber. . . . " On the other hand, there seems to be a considerable tolerance of a plurality of interpretations of the same work, a critical culture that encourages such diversity, and one that often expresses skepticism about the idea of an objectively correct interpretation. There does not seem to be a concerted and cohesive effort to look at interpretations as hypotheses to be confirmed or disconfirmed, or for one critic's work to build on the work of another in order to discover a more comprehensive set of interpretive truths about a work.

The key to understanding here is the realization that the situation with literary interpretation (and of interpretation within other art forms) is more complex than that regarding the interpretation of Jim's behavior, in that, in the former case but not the latter, there is not one question that dominates others (What *is* the explanation of the behavior?), not one aim that all interpreters are pursuing. Some seek to identify the artist's intention in creating the work. Some look for what the artist *could have* intended, where this allows for a number of different possibilities.[2] Others aim to discover what the artist does; for example, what attitudes get expressed, quite apart from, often in spite of, the artist's intention. (E.g., Brenda Webster claims that "Blake's rhetoric often serves as a cloak or defense that distracts the reader, and Blake himself, from seeing the aggressive or selfish nature of the sexual fantasies he is portraying" Webster 1996: 189.[3]) Some may seek merely *a way* of making sense of a work, a way it can be taken, where this may or may not be something the artist could have intended. While this is quite rare among academic critics if only because more is professionally expected of them, it is, I suspect, much more common among lay interpreters, nonprofessional appreciators of the arts, and understandable given the constraints of time and a limited knowledge of many works encountered. What is not rare among professional critics is attempting to find *a way* of understanding a work against the background of a set of large, culturally significant ideas, myths, or theories. (According to David Simpson, "Of all the major poets I know Blake is, along with Smart . . . and Joyce . . . the most open to analysis in terms set out by Derrida" [Simpson, 1996: 151].) Some aims are instrumental, such as the aim of making a work relevant or significant to a certain sort of audience, of identifying what is cognitively valuable in a work, or of enhancing the reader's aesthetic experience of a work. (In pursuing at least the first two of these instrumental aims, Laura Haigwood offers an interpretation of "Visions of the Daughters of Albion," and a criticism of earlier interpretations, in part to show that "feminist criticism which read feminine characters primarily as victims may intentionally . . . reinforce assumptions which support the very oppression it opposes. My more general political motive for making such a point is to find new ways of empowering women readers by contributing to the refinement and clarification of our 'visions' of ourselves and of the internal and external sources of oppression" [Haigwood 1996: 105].)

(b) Interpretations should be evaluated according to their aim. It would be foolish to criticize Brenda Webster's interpretation of the attitudes expressed in Blake's poetry either because the attitudes she identifies are not ones that Blake intended to convey or because her interpretation does not maximize the aesthetic experience of the poetry. Her interpretation should be evaluated for its truth and for the light it sheds on Blake's work. Her claims *might* receive positive evaluation on both counts independently of Blake's intentions and the maximization of aesthetic experience, though not without having a bearing on the artistic appreciation of the poems.[4]

(c) It follows from what has already been said that some interpretations require evaluation for their truth, consisting as they do of truth claims.[5] Already cited is Webster's interpretation claiming that Blake expresses certain attitudes in his poems. Similarly, interpretations claiming that Blake intended to do or say certain things in his poems, such as allude to political corruption in "The Sick Rose" (Mee 1998), or (more interestingly, perhaps) that he intentionally did or said those things, require this kind of evaluation. On the other hand, the situation is less clear with interpretations concerned with instrumental aims. They seem to claim at least that a work can be taken in a certain way (relative to some interpretive constraints including perhaps a limited set of agreed-upon facts about the work) and that doing so will have certain benefits. But they also can be construed as nonassertively offering such a way of taking a work for our contemplation without asserting it to hold and then commending the benefits of so doing. The only issue that would then be evaluable truth is whether entertaining the interpretive proposal has the touted benefits. I'm inclined to think that most interpretations make at least weak claims (e.g., that a work *could* mean p, our *can be taken as* meaning p), but I want to leave open that some interpretations are neither asserted nor true or false.

Monism and pluralism

(d) Among the interpretations that are truth evaluable is a subset that aims at a historically accurate statement of those things that the artist does in the work that are artistically significant. When I speak of what the author does, I have in mind an open ended list of acts which centrally include such things as saying, representing, expressing, presenting, alluding to, allegorizing, and so on. When I speak of a historically accurate statement of these things, I mean an identification of those doings that occur in virtue of the intention of the artist, conventions, or traditions in place at the time of creation that bear on the work, and any other relevant, meaning-creating, historical conditions. Much of what I have in mind here will be covered by what the artist *intentionally* does in the work, but some of what the artist does, such as the expression of certain attitudes, may be done unintentionally. What is not included here are things the artist does in virtue of circumstances that arise after the work is completed, even after the artist is dead. Among these would be acts that make possible anachronistic interpretations, such as Blake's enabling later readers to understand him as making a reference to the textile factories of the Industrial Revolution by using the phrase "dark satanic mills" in the poetic preface to the poem "Milton."

We should not confuse what an artist does *in* a work with everything an artist does *by* creating a work. Similarly we should not confuse what an artist intentionally does in the work with everything the artist intends by creating the work. An author may write a bestseller. That is something that the author does by creating the work, but not something he does in the work. An author may intend to write a bestseller. That is something the author intends to do by creating the work but not something intended in the work.

(e) Since the historically accurate statement mentioned above has many aspects, interpreters, whose aims fall within the broad boundaries of this project, may not see themselves as working toward a common goal. Nevertheless, just as there is one, possibly complex, truth about what explains Jim's behavior, there is one, certainly complex, truth about what the artist does in a work in virtue of his intentions, conventions in place at the time of creation, and historical context. There may be disagreement about what this is, and this may or may not be able to be settled relative to available evidence, but these are epistemic matters that do not bear on the main contention. Hence, ideally there should be a single, correct, comprehensive statement of what the artist does in the work (in the relevant sense).[6]

(f) It is also true that we can conjoin (or disjoin) any truths, including any true interpretations no matter how distinct their aims are. This would create some sort of fabric of interpretive truth, but one that does not represent a coherent project, and hence the point of attempting this is dubious.[7] Further, there is no particular reason to suppose there are a finite number of true interpretations (though, of course, at any time, there is a finite number that have been produced). Hence there is no reason to think that we would thereby produce a single correct, comprehensive interpretation of a work, if comprehensiveness consists in containing all the interpretive truths about the work.

(g) Ignoring the dubious project just mentioned in (f), even if all interpretations are truth evaluable, there is no reason to think they all sensibly combine into a single correct comprehensive interpretation. The many ways of *taking* works for the sake of the many different interpretive aims that critics (amateur and professional) bring to the task of understanding and appreciation guarantee a plurality of acceptable interpretations for just about any work. Given these different aims, the interpretations in question include those that speak to what a given work could mean, as well as what it does mean. It includes those with instrumental aims that attempt to find a significance in the work for the audience the interpreter addresses. Despite this diversity, it does not follow that these interpretations are strictly logically incompatible, as is sometimes claimed (Barnes 1988, Goldman 1990), but only that the aims of interpretation do not include one of combining all these disparate interpretations into a single, many headed, monster.

It is worth pointing out that there are different ways of defending the critical pluralism endorsed in the last paragraph. One is to emphasize, as was just done above, the diversity of aims in art interpretation and the pointlessness of combining even true interpretations that fulfill quite different purposes. Another is to point out that there are individual interpretive aims that allow for, indeed promote, plurality. This is certainly true, for example, of the instrumental, significance seeking aims discussed above. Simply because works can be significant in different ways and for different groups appealing to different interests, interpretations along these lines will be essentially noncombinable. Finally, if there are interpretations that are not truth evaluable at all, because instead of asserting something about a work, they are, among other possibilities, recommending or suggesting a way of taking it, these obviously could not combine into a single true interpretation.[8]

It is similarly worth making explicit what room is left to endorse critical monism, given what has just been said about critical pluralism. Critical monism is the view that there is a single, comprehensive, true interpretation for each work of art. This view cannot be true *tout court*, if what has just been asserted about pluralism in the preceding paragraphs of this section is true. We have already rejected the idea that we can take all the interpretive truths about a work, string them together, and claim that we have a single comprehensive, true interpretation.

What remains true is that monism holds within certain interpretive aims or projects such as the one outlined in point d above (as was pointed out in point e). Within those projects, it makes sense to look for the single, comprehensive, true interpretation of the work fulfilling the relevant aim. Further, if there is such a thing as the meaning of a work, then monism would have a special point because we could say that there is a single comprehensive true interpretation that identifies that meaning.

Work meaning

(h) Given the multiplicity of aims in art interpretation, hence the multiplicity of ways interpretations of a work can be acceptable, and, following from this, the truth of critical pluralism, does it make sense to speak of *the* meaning of an artwork or of what a work *does* mean?

The answer to this question is that it does make sense. Critical pluralism is, or should be, founded on the idea that there are various, legitimate interpretive projects that concern what works could (can be taken to) mean or the work's significance for various audiences. This leaves logical space for the question "Is there something the work does mean?" In order to answer this question, we should go back to the could-mean/does-mean distinction, set out in chapter 1. For some items, it does not make sense to ask what they mean. For example, there is a class of things I will call objects of fancy. We might see clouds or the cracks in an old wall according to an interpretation of our own invention. When we look at them in this way, they become objects of fancy. We might see clouds as engaged in a battle; we might see rivers and mountains in an old wall. We might get others to see the clouds or the wall according to these interpretations, but it would be ridiculous to ask whether the cloud or the wall really do mean these things. Rorschach inkblots are intentionally created items, meant to be treated like old walls in the previous example. They do have a point – to elicit experiences of seeing-in or seeing-according-to-an-interpretation, but they are not meant to express a particular pictorial content. So, unlike walls and clouds when subject to similar reactions, there is a correct understanding of Rorschach inkblots (viz., they are meant to elicit experiences of the type just mentioned), but nothing that they mean. There is no one experience they are meant to elicit.

Contrast Rorschach blots with paintings. There may be some paintings that are meant to function something like the blots in the sense of not being meant to present a content, but instead invite a variety of interpretive reactions. Even so, it is probable that they would have a more complex point – to exhibit the malleability of perception, to stand in contrast with other paintings, to allow spectators to "create" their own aesthetic experiences, to raise questions about the nature of the painting, and so on. When there is this complexity about their point, we are more inclined to think of their point as a meaning, and it makes sense to ask what they mean, even while recognizing that they invite a diversity of reactions as to ways they can be taken. This is even more obviously true with paintings that have a pictorial content.

Intentionally created things have a point, and grasping that point is necessary to come to a correct understanding of them. Artworks are paradigm examples of intentionally created things, and we understand them as products of the intentional activity that they result from. We can distinguish between point and meaning, as we did with Rorschach inkblots, but in the case of art, especially art with representational or expressive content, these concepts tend to get meshed together.[9] (There are natural phenomena that we tend to look at not as objects of fancy, but with a certain point in mind, and when we do this, we also tend to look at the information an item gives us with regard to this point as what the item means. We look at animal tracks this way, as giving us information about the animal that made them, which we regard as the meaning of the tracks.) The argument so far shows that accepting critical pluralism does not make it nonsensical to ask for *the* meaning of an artwork; and furthermore, artworks, at least those with representational or expressive content, are the sorts of objects for which this question is appropriate.

In the case of literary works, the meaning of a work (henceforth "work meaning") is identical to its utterance meaning.[10] Utterance meaning specifies what someone has said or done by using language on a particular occasion. The occasion for literary works is the presentation of the work normally by means of publication. Preparation for this occasion may be very lengthy and frequently interrupted. Further, in the case of even a short poem, much less a long novel, the writer does a great many things, but as long as we consider the work as the product of a project that the writer deliberately pursued, we should expect these many doings to mostly, if not perfectly, hang together as parts of a whole.[11]

Nonliterary artworks are not linguistic utterances (as I take literary ones to be), and possibly they are not literally utterances at all. If so, they do not literally have utterance meaning. Those that have meaning at all, do, however, have work meaning that is modeled on utterance meaning, namely, on what the artist does in the work that is artistically significant.

In the last chapter, I put forward two models as the most plausible accounts of utterance/work meaning: hypothetical intentionalism and the unified view and argued that the latter is the better of the two views. (Also see Carroll 2000, Iseminger 1996, Livingston 1996, Stecker 1997a: 173–85, 196–212.) The important point here is that there are views available that identify work meaning.

If we accept the unified view of work meaning, then we should regard the project, set out in point (d) above, of identifying a historically accurate statement of what the artist does in the work that is artistically significant, as identifying the meaning of an artwork. This is to be distinguished from meanings it could have, can be taken as having, and various significances that might be found in it by certain audiences.[12]

Results so far

One advantage of the theory of art interpretation just laid out is that it provides answers to the whole web of issues that has made the debate over the nature and point of interpretation so difficult to resolve. Another advantage is that it recognizes merit in most of the main positions people take on these issues. There is no single aim proper to interpretation, but the aims that have been candidates for this status are all aims of interpretation. There is truth both in critical pluralism and critical monism. There is such a thing as the meaning of a work, but that is not the only thing we are looking for in interpreting works. The notion of intention plays a role in understanding work meaning, but work meaning is not identical with the artist's intention in making the work.

We can see why it is inevitable that there are such a variety of interpretations put forward in the case of artworks, and why there is the dual attitude to these mentioned earlier. As long as we are individually and institutionally inclined to embody in our interpretive aims the many different interests we have toward artworks, plurality is inevitable and acceptable. However, this does not prevent individual interpretations from being truth evaluable, which gives the existence of critical controversies perfect sense. Nor does it imply incoherence in the notion of the meaning of a work. The theory proposed here still leaves unexplained some attitudes toward the interpretation of artworks mentioned earlier. For example, it does not explain the widespread skepticism about the possibility of objectively correct interpretations. Some reasons for this skepticism will be discussed in later chapters.

Objections

Some might regard a view that accommodates so many rival positions, not as an ideal compromise, but as compromised. But such a claim would have to be made good by showing real problems in the theory. I turn now to examine purported problems advanced by critics of the theory.

Second-class citizens

One objection to the theory is that it makes some interpretations "second best."[13] Which interpretations would deserve this title? It might be thought that it is the ones that are not part of the meaning of a work. Or perhaps it is the ones that lack truth value? The answer I would give to either suggestion is that if we take seriously the aims with which the supposedly "second best" interpretations are put forward, there is no reason to regard them in this way. So regarding them must be informed by the suspicion that the aims are not really legitimate. However, that is not my view.

A summary slogan for the view presented here is that we have monism with respect to some aims, pluralism with respect to other aims, and pluralism overall. We should recognize several, not always disjoint, classes of acceptable interpretations. There are those that belong to the class of interpretations lacking in truth value. Then there are those that belong to the class of interpretations given in pursuit of the different aims of interpretation. Some in this latter class will also belong to the former, but others will not. Among the truth evaluable interpretations are those that are not only acceptable relative to their aim but true. Among these true, acceptable interpretations, some ideally would combine with others to form the correct, comprehensive interpretation relative to a certain aim. Others do not, because there is no such comprehensive interpretation relative to *their* aim. But if the aim is a legitimate one, there is nothing second class about such interpretations.

An objection to work meaning and the utterance model

Some claim it is a mistake to think that identifying work meaning is an aim of interpretation, at least for certain cases and, hence, it is a mistake to think that the utterance model is helpful in these cases (Olsen 1982, Lamarque 2002). Literature, which is as central an instance of an object of interpretation as there is, has been put forward as one of these cases. If the claim is correct, we have a problem.

The claim is advanced by both an attack on the plausibility of seeking the meaning of a work, and by offering an alternative model. The attack is launched by asking what sense there is in requesting the meaning of a long work such as *Middlemarch* (Lamarque 2002: 264). To the reply that it is a request for the novel's utterance meaning, it is denied that the notion of utterance meaning transfers from conversational contexts to literary ones.[14] The production and criticism of literature, it is claimed, is a unique practice that aims at an appreciative experience. We only confuse the issue if we import interpretive concepts that have their home in other practices, such as conversation for the purpose of practical communication.

That is the criticism of work meaning. Here is the reply. The rhetorical question "What is the meaning of *Middlemarch*?" is answered by spelling out what work meaning consists in. On the view endorsed here, it is what the author does in the work in virtue of her intentions and historical contexts, including conventions in place when the work is put forward. The hypothetical intentionalist will have a slightly different, but equally coherent, account of work meaning. It is obviously something very complex, and not to be summarized in a few sentences. Hence, "What is the meaning of *Middlemarch*?" is not an appropriate exam question or even an appropriate question for a journal-length essay. This is why the question has an absurd sound if raised in such contexts.

Is the proponent of work meaning illicitly transferring a model that is operative in understanding conversations? Is the identification of an appreciative experience a better model for understanding literary interpretation? To answer these questions, first consider an example put forward to support the rejection of the utterance model, a bit of critical commentary by J. Hillis Miller on Dickens's novel *Our Mutual Friend*.

> A society in which personal relations reduce themselves to a struggle for dominance develops that drama of *looks* and *faces* which is so important in *Our Mutual Friend*. Scenes in the novel are frequently presented as a conflict of masks. Each person tries to hide his own secret and to probe behind a misleading surface and find the secrets of others. The prize of successful uncovering is the power that goes with knowing and not being known. (Quoted from Lamarque 2002: 249.)

If his commentary is on the mark, what Miller is identifying here is an aspect of the meaning of this novel, namely, that it represents a society in which personal relations have the character indicated in the passage. Further, the utterance model is most apt in characterizing this. It says that this is part of the meaning of the novel because Dickens has represented society in this way in the novel. To understand the novel, if Miller is correct, one has to understand this feature of it. Is this understanding likely to produce an appreciative experience? This is quite likely, but not guaranteed. No doubt Miller hopes that his interpretation will produce an appreciative understanding of this aspect of the novel, but this does not mean that it is better to think of interpretation as aiming at an appreciative experience.

That claim leaves out the way appreciation is achieved: by achieving an understanding of a perhaps unnoticed aspect of a work. Finally, it leaves out the possibility, discussed further in chapter 4, that achieving understanding will not lead to appreciative experience.

When we look for work meaning, we are not illicitly importing a model from the domain of conversation. We are using a model that applies across many domains, including the literary one. It is true that literary communication uses many techniques not typically found in everyday conversation. So, when attempting to understand a literary work, we look for themes, recurring images or symbols, emblematic passages, parallels or contrasts between characters and the like. You probably will not look for these things in a conversation with your neighbor about her holiday in South Carolina. That does not mean we are not seeking to understand the literary work. It just means that we need to understand different things.

An objection to monism

Here is an argument against monism about work meaning.[15]

1. Our interpretations of art depend on our (i.e., the interpreter's) background theories, interests, and values.
2. Several such divergent interpretations of a given work are equally legitimate.
3. Divergent interpretations of the natural world based on different background theories, interests, and values are not equally legitimate.
4. Therefore, art and nature differ in the following respect: there is a single complex determinate truth about the former, but there is no such determinate truth about the latter.

This is a defective argument. First the conclusion does not strictly follow. The conclusion is about determinate truth in the realm of art and nature. The premises are about legitimacy of divergent interpretations in these realms. The argument leaves us in the dark about how we should move from the latter concern to the former.

Second, while I grant premise 2, which is simply an affirmation of pluralism, the other premises are suspect. Consider premise 3. I take it that there are many "divergent" interpretations of nature that are driven precisely by different background theories, interests, and values. Consider the difference between a physicist's understanding of the movement of human bodies, a biologist's, and a psychologist's. All three are different due to different background theories and interests. Various engineering applications of theories are driven by the value of finding practical uses for the results of scientific research. This value may not inform "pure" theoretical research. Most important, the various truths discovered from these perspectives, while consistent with each other (I assume) do not all belong to a single grand theory of nature. At least, it is far from obvious that they do.

Regarding the first premise, if it is merely saying something similar about art interpretation, namely, that it can be done from a variety of perspectives or aims, it is unobjectionable. However, if, as is more likely, it is meant to imply that objectivity is ruled out because we cannot approach art without coloring it with our own *personal* interests or values, or those of a group *we* belong to, it is far from obvious (not to say question begging).[16] Does 1 permit us to try to find a historically accurate account of what an artist is doing in a work? If not, I do not see why we should accept it. If so, it is consistent with monism about work meaning, as the diversity of scientific perspectives is consistent with monism about scientific truth.

Underlying this argument is an assumption that will be discussed at great length in chapters 5 and 6, that the meaning of a work, unlike the truth about nature, is essentially indeterminate, until we bring something of our own perspective to it and construct one of an open ended number of complete meanings. All interpretations are such constructions, which are essentially disjoint and plural. I postpone until the later chapters a detailed examination of this view and the arguments that can be given in its behalf. However, when the view is simply assumed, as it is in the present argument, it is question begging rather than persuasive.

An objection to compatibility of monism and pluralism: Is the object of interpretation a work or a text?

An individuating feature of artworks is that they are objects (in a broad sense) that are produced in a particular historical context. (See chapter 4 for a defense of this claim.) For at least some types of artworks, such as literary and musical works, this means that a defining feature of such works is a relation that holds between artist and historical context on the one hand and a structural type on the other. In the case of literary works, this type is the text. In the case of musical works, it is a "sound structure" as would be indicated by a score (in cases where the work is scored).

When we combine this claim with others made in this chapter, we get the following three propositions: 1. Origin (historical context) is essential to a work's identity. 2. There is a single correct, comprehensive interpretation of the work that identifies what the artist does in the work, though this is usually set out in a number of less comprehensive interpretations (interpretation set A). 3. There are other acceptable interpretations *of the work* (interpretation set B) that are not combinable with interpretations in set A or with each other.

Here is an argument for the logical inconsistency of 1–3.

4. To the extent that contextual variables enter into the individuation of works, only interpretations that respect all of these variables are acceptable interpretations of works.
5. Only interpretations in set A respect all of these variables.
6. No interpretation in set B is in set A.
7. Therefore, interpretations in set B are not acceptable interpretations of works.

It follows that interpretations in set B either are not acceptable interpretations at all, or they are acceptable interpretations of something other than the work, such as the text, in the case of literary works, or the sound structure, in the case of musical works.[17]

In evaluating this argument, since the conclusion follows, we have to consider whether the premises are true. Premise 6 is true in virtue of the way we have defined the interpretation sets, but I doubt that both 4 and 5 are true. A lot depends on how we are to understand the vague idea of respecting "contextual variables," that is, essential facts about the origin of a work. Our evaluation of the premises also depends on whether interpretations have to be true to be acceptable. If an interpretation can be acceptable but untrue, it is very unclear why it has to be consistent with some particular set of facts, even facts essential to identifying the works. Such inconsistency can only serve to make interpretations untrue, but by hypothesis this is not necessary for acceptability. The argument can be dismissed immediately if there can be untrue, but acceptable interpretations. To put the argument in the best light, let us assume truth and acceptability go hand in hand.

One thing that respecting contextual variables can mean is that one's interpretation is consistent with them. This is not a difficult condition to meet as long as care is taken about what one's interpretation asserts. If what it asserts is that a work *can be taken* in a certain way, or that it *could* mean so and so, then it can be consistent with contextual variables that imply the work *does* mean something quite different. So Blake's "Preface" to the poem "Milton" *can be taken as* containing a reference to textile mills, even if facts about the origin of the poem imply that it *does not* contain one.

It may be objected that, if, as we have been assuming, the contextual variables determine the very identity of the work, then a work not only does not, but could not mean something incompatible with these variables, since any work that did mean these other things would not be the work in question. The legitimate point here is that there is *a sense* of "could" (which philosophers sometimes call the metaphysical sense), in which a work not only does not but could not mean things incompatible with the relevant facts about the work's origins. Specifically, there is no possible world in which the work *does* mean those things. However, there are other senses of "could" which do not have this implication, and are more relevant to the interpretive context. It is quite possible, in fact more likely, that what critics are asserting when making interpretive statements relies on one of these other senses. For example, it would make perfect sense to say, when one first hears of Jim's insomniac behavior, that it could be a symptom of psychosis. One thing we could mean is simply that, relative to our evidence or what we currently know, this is a possibility. This is the epistemic sense of "could." This is certainly a sense that it would be reasonable for critics (both amateur and professional) to utilize, since critics are quite commonly working with evidence that is incomplete. There is also what can be called the pragmatic sense of "could," where we assert that a work could mean something relative to a point of view or set of constraints. We ignore or bracket off something we do know about the work for the purpose of pursuing a particular interpretive aim. Here, we intentionally bracket off certain facts about the work, even if we know they are essential to identifying the work, for certain interpretive purposes. For example, we may know a work has an essentially polemical aspect, but may want to bracket it off to see if we can find a more general significance in it.

So, if all we mean by respecting contextual variables is that our interpretation is consistent with them, then premise 5 is false. Interpretations in set B also respect contextual variables if formulated with sufficient care, or, alternatively, if taken in the right spirit.

Of course, something stronger can be intended by the requirement that we respect all the contextual variables. One possibility would be to require that only interpretations that make reference to *all* of them, or use all of them in their formulation, respects the variables. This requirement would certainly rule out interpretations in set B as being among those that respect the contextual variables. But it would also rule out many, if not all, of the individual members of set A, since it is unlikely that any would make reference to all contextual variables. So 4 would now be false, not only for wrongly excluding from acceptability interpretations in set B, but also individual members of set A from acceptability. This point could be circumvented by claiming that there is "really" only one interpretation in set A, that consists in the single, true, comprehensive statement of what the artist does in creating the work, and this interpretation does respect all the contextual variables in the current sense of "respect." Seemingly less comprehensive interpretations should be seen as really being part of the comprehensive interpretation.

However, there is another problem with the argument understood as requiring that an acceptable interpretation make reference to all the contextual variables essential to the work's identity. This is simply that this is not a reasonable requirement of *acceptable* interpretations. Nothing like such a requirement is recognized in any community of critics (amateur or professional). Nor is such a requirement reasonable, since it would imply that individual critics virtually never offer acceptable interpretations of a work. Hence, if we understand "respect" according to the current suggestion, premise 4 is almost certainly false.

It would not quite be legitimate to conclude that the argument under consideration is unsound, since there might be a sense of "respect" that is both reasonable and, according to which, the premises are true. We can conclude, though, that it looks unlikely that there is such a sense, because we can see emerging from the stated objections to the premises a general dilemma that the argument faces. The dilemma is that, when the understanding of "respect" is reasonable (so that premise 4 is true), it fails to exclude interpretations in set B (so that premise 5 is false). When it excludes those interpretations, it does so at the cost of requiring an unreasonable understanding of "respect" (rendering premise 4 false). Hence, though we haven't demonstrated it, we have good reason to think the argument is unsound. Hence also, we lack a good reason to think 1–3 is inconsistent.

Before leaving this issue, perhaps we should try to reformulate it without reference to the semantics of "respect for contextual variables," since it might be thought that the main point of the argument has been evaded via technical problems raised by particular words used to formulate the argument. The main point, it may be said, is that interpretive claims about a work, even claims about what it *could* mean, should satisfy the following condition: We are either saying something false about the work or speaking of *something else* if the meanings ascribed to it do not accord with meanings it has in virtue of constitutive or *essential* features of the work, be they structural or contextual. Call this the accordance condition.

There are two problems. First, "being in accord with" is no clearer than "respect," and so it brings us no closer to a resolution. Let us stipulate that what it is saying is that no meaning may be correctly ascribed to a work that is inconsistent with what it could mean in the *metaphysical* sense. The second problem with this condition is that it gets the desired result by legislating when an interpretation is of the work and possibly true. It simply rules out by definition the possibility of interpretations employing the pragmatic sense of "could" and "can be taken" mentioned above. Of course, I do not accept this stipulation. Suppose I say, "Richard III could be any totalitarian ruler. He shares their motives; he shares their methods." Now, this might be false because (the fictional) Richard's motives or methods are not those of most dictators. But is it false, because, strictly speaking, this is not in accord with the contextually fixed meaning of *Richard III*? It is, after all, a constitutive property of the play that it fictionally represents a former king of England, a member of the House of York, who fought in the War of the Roses, that brought his family to power. So the play does not represent a totalitarian everyman. Yet I might, and people have, interpreted the play that way without being ignorant of its contextually fixed meaning. The point, of course, is to bracket off something true, in fact essentially true, of the work to bring out a more general significance.

One at least needs an argument for the accordance condition. One argument that might be given is that it clearly defines when an interpretation is of a work, whereas, on the alternative view, it is vague when we have bracketed off too much to be still talking about the work. However, the clarity is illusory, but, even if it obtained, it is not necessarily desirable. The accordance condition merely shifts the area of vagueness to another location. First it tells us that certain interpretations are not about the work *or* they are, but they are false. Which disjunct should we go with? Suppose we go with the first. Then what is the interpretation about? It could be the text or it could be a possible work similar to the actual one. If the latter, which one? Or is it not one but a set?

Suppose, though it is unlikely, that there are definitive answers to these questions. Is it better to exclude certain interpretations as having the work as object or, instead, making it a default assumption that interpretations are about works unless we are forced to say otherwise? Comparing interpretations to performances is, in this instance, illuminating. A performance of a play or opera may leave out or alter the order of scenes, thereby failing to possess essential structural properties of the work. It may also fail to possess certain contextually fixed properties of works in, for example, some modern dress versions of Shakespeare. We may like or dislike these productions. We can also agree that such productions sacrifice accuracy in presentation for a purported gain in other artistic values. It is usually allowed, however, that they are productions of the work. So it is with interpretations that employ the pragmatic "could."

It should be added that I am not arguing that a structural type such as a text is never an object of interpretation. Abstract structural types do exist, even if they should not be identified with works, and it might come about that one such turns out to be what a critic is interpreting. This could happen in more than one way. A sophisticated critic might prefer to consider how a structural type could be taken to what a work means. This might be so because such a critic might enjoy a sense of greater freedom in discerning what meanings could attach to a given structure. Alternatively, a critic might be operating under the false belief that the work is the text, in which case the most charitable way of understanding what such a critic is doing is that she is interpreting the text. Furthermore, it might be difficult to distinguish some interpretations of works that belong in interpretation set B, and some interpretations of texts or other structural types, unless one can become clear about what the critic is aiming at.

NOTES

1   This is a revised version of some earlier attempts to set out such a theory (Stecker 1993, 1994, 1997a).

2   Among the aims that fall under a search for what the artist could mean or intend are those of various versions of hypothetical intentionalism and conventionalism. On the former approach, we try to determine an intention that some audience (intended, original, ideal) would hypothesize as the artist's, based on some weighting of epistemic and aesthetic considerations. Defenders of this view are Currie (1993), Levinson (1996), Nehamas (1981), and Tolhurst (1979). On a conventionalist approach, we try to determine what intentions are compatible with the artwork against a background of conventions in place when the work is created. A defender of this view is S. Davies (1991). These two approaches do not exhaust the possible ways of approaching what an artist *could* have meant.

3   The reference here and below to recent Blake criticism are motivated by an interest in finding out what aims are actually being pursued with respect to a poet and a body of earlier criticism with which I have some familiarity.

4   Webster's interpretation of Blake is an instance of what Noël Carroll calls the "hermeneutics of suspicion," which consists of the interrogation of works for (largely unintended) expressions of racism, sexism, imperialism, and other unsavory attitudes. Not only does Carroll correctly recognize this as a legitimate aim of interpretation, but he also provides an excellent account of the consistency of this aim with modest actual intentionalism and, a fortiori, the unified view defended in chapter 2 and below under point (h). (See Carroll 1993.)

5   This ignores the view that denies that interpretive statements have bivalent truth values, and, in particular, lack the value *true*. This view is discussed in chapter 6.

6   Unless such an interpretation cannot be expressed in a finite set of statements,

in which case there would only be more and more comprehensive interpretations of what the artist does in the relevant sense.

7   This is a departure from views I have previously expressed. I was, in the past, more sympathetic to the monster just condemned (Stecker 1997a: 149).

8   These points should suffice to answer doubts raised by Michael Krausz whether one can defend pluralism (in his terminology, multiplism) by appealing to the multiple aims of interpretation. His doubts are based on the claim that interpretations made on the basis of different aims are "congruent" with each other (Krausz 2000: 120). Krausz does not explain what he means by "congruent." If "congruent" means that such interpretations are logically consistent, the claim is true, but irrelevant. We still could have a plurality of acceptable interpretations that emerge from the pursuit of different aims. This is so, because the mere fact that a pair of interpretations is consistent does not show that they can be combined into a single acceptable interpretation. In fact there is reason to think that many interpretations that pursue different aims could not be so combined. If "congruent" means, not logically consistent, but rather combinable into a single acceptable interpretation, Krausz has not shown that the interpretations in question are congruent after all, for reasons just mentioned. Finally, recall that there is an additional defense of pluralism derived from multiple aims of interpretation, namely, that some aims themselves promote multiple, noncombinable interpretations. These interpretations, which derive from the same interpretive aim, completely evade Krausz's problem.

9   There are art forms, such as architecture and ceramics, where talk of the meaning of the work does not come naturally, while it is more natural to ask about their point or the point of a part or aspect.

10   See chapter 1 above, Levinson (1996), and Stecker (1997a) for further exposition of and arguments for this claim.

11   This would be my answer to Lamarque (2002: 265), when he asks, "what could *on a particular occasion* mean for a novel that took several years to write . . . ?"

12   In Stecker (1997a: 156–85). Jerrold Levinson (1999), though he defends a somewhat different conception of work meaning, comes to a similar conclusion about the possibility of combining interpretations identifying parts or aspects of the meaning of a work into a single comprehensive interpretation.

13   Lamarque (2002: 276–7). Lamarque is responding to an earlier version of my view, which emphasizes more than I do now that some acceptable interpretations lack truth value. I point out (in Stecker 1997a) regarding the work Lamarque discusses that if we confine critical monism to a claim about work meaning, then we can recognize *true*, acceptable interpretations that are not part of the comprehensive interpretation of the work's meaning. My earlier view (stated in Stecker 1997a) has evolved further here to that stated below and in the previous section.

14   Part of the problem with Lamarque's critique of the utterance model is that he takes utterance meaning to be something like sentence meaning, a view that would be rejected by all the proponents of the utterance model. Consider: "These features [of *Moll Flanders*], the pattern of theft, the 'contradictions,' the 'double vision' of the heroine, are not properties of the linguistic *text* inherent in the language" (Lamarque 2002: 270. See also 272 and note 20 on 283 for similar claims). It is precisely the point of those who endorse the

utterance model that these properties of the novel are not properties of the linguistic text, but properties that result from Defoe's *use* of the text to make the particular literary utterance that he does. The hypothetical intentionalist variation on this is that the best hypothesis about Defoe's intention is that he is using the text in this way.

15 This argument is based on Kieran (1996). Also see Thom (2000a: 11–14). Both writers have, to my puzzlement, defended pluralism against my enthusiastic support for that view. Thom's criticisms appear to be based on a misunderstanding. He takes me to claim that all acceptable interpretations of a work can be seen as part of its single comprehensive interpretation. This, however, is not my view.

Kieran, at times, does something similar. He recognizes that I claim that monism is compatible with pluralism. However, he too at times understands this claim in such a way that it essentially does away with interpretive plurality. He attributes to me the following model. A work has a core meaning with which any acceptable interpretation has to be consistent. This meaning leaves some further questions about the work unanswered. Different answers are acceptable if they are permitted by the core meaning, and will form part of a single comprehensive interpretation of the work. Kieran goes on to argue, as does Thom, that these sundry acceptable interpretations are not part of a single comprehensive interpretation. I, however, do not claim they are, and it is not part of my defense of monism that they all are part of such a single interpretation. In earlier work (especially Stecker 1994) I claimed that all the *true* ones could be seen as part of a single interpretation, while emphasizing that many acceptable ones needn't be true. I now argue that monism should be seen as holding within specific interpretive aims.

16 Kieran suggests that there is such a limitation on objectivity in art interpretation in a number of passages. The following gives the gist of his view: "In order to imaginatively engage with the artwork, the viewer must bring to bear his own understanding, assumptions and associations" (Kieran 1996: 243).

17 Points 4–7 are an attempt to reconstruct an argument proposed in D. Davies (1996).

A Theory of Art Interpretation: Conceptual and Ontological Claims

The theory of art interpretation presented in chapters 2 and 3 raises a number of conceptual and ontological issues. This chapter will set these out and try to resolve them.

Conceptual Issues of Art Interpretation

In chapter 2, art interpretation was characterized this way: it is thought or discourse about a work that attempts to understand or appreciate it, or better understand or better appreciate it by discovering, or at least ascribing on some basis, a meaning in or to the item in question or determining what significance the item has for us.

Implicit in this formula are several distinctions, and it is a matter of controversy just how they should be made out and what their implications are for a theory of interpretation. These are the distinctions between discovering meaning and ascribing meaning, between understanding and appreciation, and between meaning and significance. A final issue concerns whether the proper scope of a theory of art interpretation should include performance interpretation as well as the critical variety.

Kinds of meaning ascription

When we try to understand a work, there are at least four different things we can be doing: identifying (1) what it could mean, (2) what it does mean, (3) what it was intended to mean, and (4) what its significance is to someone. In this section I am concerned with the first two of these, and whether one or the other is the primary focus of art interpretation. However, first a word about the distinction itself.

A number of writers on interpretation have recognized the distinction. The recognition has found a variety of forms of expression. Levinson distinguishes between looking for what something could mean, and looking for what it does mean.[1] This distinction figured in a large way in chapter 3. Thom distinguishes between adequational and constructive interpretation (Thom 2000a: 40–7). Gracia also makes a similar distinction between meaning interpretations and relational interpretations (Gracia 2000: 47–50). I have distinguished between looking for the meaning of a work (the correct understanding) and looking for a way of taking it (an understanding) (Stecker 1997a: 120–1). While all of these distinctions may not precisely map onto each other, they are all pointing in the same direction.

A *sentence could* mean many things. That is, it can be used to make many different utterances. "Hilary is a man," might refer to many different people and might say of one of them many different things: he is no longer a boy; he is male; he or she has done something "manly"; he has completed his long desired change of sex, and so on. We can also wonder what a particular *utterance* of a sentence could mean, perhaps as a preliminary to deciding what it does mean (as Levinson 1999: 19 points out). Normally, however, there is something that an utterance does mean, among the various things it could mean. This is so even if it has, say, a double meaning. The meaning of the utterance combines, in an appropriate way, both meanings.

When a sentence is used to make an utterance, there is something the utterance does mean. If we at first do not know what this is, and then find out, we have made a discovery. We have discovered the meaning the utterance does have. Contrast this with simply thinking of possible meanings an utterance could have. When we think of one such possibility, and then, for some reason, take the utterance as having that meaning, we are ascribing a meaning to the utterance without discovering (or, necessarily, claiming to discover) the meaning it does have.

As noted in chapter 3, there are things of which it would not make sense to ask what they do mean, but only what they could mean. It would not make sense to ask of a Rorschach inkblot what it does mean. (It would not make sense to ask what the meaning, the correct understanding of it, is.) One could only ask what it could mean, or better, what is a way of taking it.

"Could" has different senses, and it is reasonable to ask which sense or senses are at stake in this discussion. At the end of the last chapter we considered three senses, which I called the epistemic, pragmatic, and metaphysical meanings of "could." As just mentioned, if I am trying to figure out what something does mean, I might consider what it could mean given my current evidence or beliefs about it. An assertion, in this context, that it could mean so-and-so, uses "could" in its epistemic sense. When attempting an interpretation, I may well consider epistemically possible meanings before venturing a conjecture about what the object in question does mean. So the epistemic sense of "could" is one of the senses relevant to the interpretive context. However, it is not the only one. It is clearly not the sense in use in the Rorschach case. Since there is nothing an inkblot does mean, there is likewise no evidence that it means this rather than that. Nor is the metaphysical sense in question here, since we are not considering the meaning an inkblot does have in various possible worlds. Rather, the relevant sense is what I am calling a pragmatic one: meanings an item pragmatically could have are possible meanings (ways of taking) relative to a point of view or set of constraints. In the case of the inkblots, the relevant point of view is my subjectivity – whatever I see in it. However, the point of view that contextually defines the pragmatic "could" on a given occasion is often much more constrained. We might be interested in what something could mean in its historical context, but abstracting from the specific intentions of the object's creator. Or, what something could mean, if we look at it from the Freudian point of view. Notice that these may be things that are metaphysically impossible that the item actually means. In the case of the inkblot, for example, it is plausible that it is metaphysically impossible that there is *anything* it does actually mean.[2] The metaphysical "could" also has a role to play in the interpretive context. It is particularly important when we are trying to figure out what something does mean. It is here that it may be helpful to first ask what it (metaphysically) could mean.

There are different views about what the appropriate question is when we are interpreting works of art. Some people think it is "What could it mean?" or "How can it be taken?" Some think this because they believe that, like Rorschach inkblots, there is nothing that works do mean (Lamarque 2000, Olsen 1982, Stout 1982). Some think this because, though they need not deny that there is something that works do mean, they believe that the aim of art interpretation is best served by looking for the several things a work could mean. They might think, for example, that the aim of interpretation is enhanced appreciation, and that this is best served by making available the various things a work could mean (S. Davies, 1991). Others think the appropriate question is "What does it mean?" or "What is the correct understanding of it?" (Beardsley 1958, 1970, Hirsch 1967). My view, already defended in chapter 3, is that both sorts of questions are appropriate in art interpretation and not just in the sense that the former are a reasonable preliminary to the latter. Rather, they are both appropriate independently of the other. Which is appropriate depends on the interpretive aim. We will look at some alternatives to this view when we examine constructivist conceptions of interpretation in succeeding chapters.

Understanding and appreciation

We interpret artworks (and a number of other things) to understand or appreciate them. Are understanding and appreciation different things, and if so, when we interpret, are we sometimes aiming at one, sometimes aiming at the other? There is a distinction to be drawn between understanding and appreciation, but it is not hard and fast, or, more precisely, not every use of the words "understanding" and "appreciation" preserves the distinction. Sometimes, perhaps, "appreciation" can be used to mean understanding. If I appreciate the destructive force of an approaching storm, this may (but need not) come to little more than understanding what its destructive force really is. "Understand" can be used to mean appreciate, as when we say, "Do you understand how powerful (poignant, unifying) that image is?"

The distinction is this: The appreciation of something normally implies finding value (positive or negative) in it, whereas understanding does not imply this. Understanding involves making sense of something, which can involve a number of different things, two of which were discussed in the previous section. The point is that making sense does not always lead to valuing. One can say with perfect intelligibility, "Now I understand what you are saying (doing), but I do not know yet what I think (how I feel) about it." That is a case of understanding without appreciation.

The typical aim of art interpretation might be best described as appreciative understanding or an understanding that leads to appreciation. In chapter 2, we discussed various interpretive questions that it is natural to raise about Blake's poem "The Sick Rose." Answering those questions (or, alternatively, deciding that some either are inappropriate or have no answer) is essential to *understanding* the poem. However, we also assume that we will only be able to *appreciate* the poem when we come to understand it. We expect understanding will have an appreciative payoff, and we know there will be no such payoff without it.

Sometimes however, we can understand but not enjoy or find a positive payoff. Two different things could then happen. We might negatively appreciate the work, that is, find negative value in the work based on our understanding of it, or we might understand it but not appreciate it. This is the situation with James Joyce's *Ulysses* and me. When I first read it many years ago in a modern literature class, I was passionately interested in such works, and worked hard to understand the novel. I think I succeeded as well as anyone in the class – better than most. But I was left cold. Time and rereading, which has led to the revaluation of many other works, has not changed my reaction to *Ulysses*. That, however, has not led me to a negative valuation of the work. I put it down to incompatible sensibilities. Lack of appreciation may also be due to oneself rather than the work. Overfamiliarity, for example, can produce a lack of appreciation of a work on a given encounter without a corresponding reduction in understanding.

Normally, we do not sharply distinguish between seeking understanding and seeking appreciation. We typically are aiming for both realizing that the latter usually accompanies the former, which is a necessary condition for appreciation. We are aiming for appreciative understanding. But sometimes we do not get it. We just get cold, hard understanding.

Significance

Significance is always significance *for* someone or some group. One finds significance[3] when one relates the meaning or one's understanding of a work to something outside the work that one already feels is important. Significance is essentially a relation between a work, a particular audience of a work, which may be a single individual, or a subgroup of the work's total audience across time, and something outside the work that the audience finds important. It is by definition not something that everyone must take into account to understand or appreciate a work, or it would be part of the meaning of the work rather than a significance the work has for someone. In contrast with the relation between a work and its meaning, the significance relation between a work and a member of its audience is always contingent, and sometimes transient. Some cases of significance are straightforward, for example, the phenomenon called "identification." When one identifies with a character or situation in a novel, one finds, or at least believes that one finds, a connection between the character or situation and something in one's own life. A literary work might have greater significance to someone just because the thematic material coincides with that individual's current concerns or with some salient experiences. Here is D. H. Lawrence, writing about Hester and Dimsdale in *The Scarlet Letter*:

She dished him and his spirituality, so he hated her. As Angel Clare was dished and hated Tess. As Jude in the end hated Sue: or should have done. The women make fools of them, the spiritual men. And when, as men, they've gone flop in their spirituality, they can't pick themselves up whole anymore. So they just crawl and die detesting the female . . . who made them fall. (Lawrence 1962: 49)

Lawrence is finding significance in Hawthorne and Hardy in relation to his own ideas about men and women. If one doubts this, the giveaway is the remark about Jude (the obscure): he "hated Sue, or *should have done.*" Lawrence is a master at finding significance of this type in the work of other writers.

Unlike these instances, the basis of significance may not be easy to identify. The following lines from Robert Pinsky's poem, "Song of Reasons," gives expression to such a case as well as some of these features of significance:

> . . . *A child has learned to read, and each morning before leaving*
> *For school she likes to be helped through The Question Man*
> *In the daily paper: Your Most Romantic Moment? Your Family Hero?*
> *Your Worst Vacation? Your Favorite Ethnic Group? – and pictures*
> *Of the five or six people, next to their answers. She likes it;*
> *The exact forms of the ordinary each morning . . .*
> (Pinsky 1984: 35–6)

It is sometimes said that to find significance in a work, one first has to identify the meaning of a work (Hirsch 1967: 133, Harris 1988: 63–5). However, this is not quite right. What is needed is some conception of what is going on in a work. One has to form *an* understanding, identify something the work could mean. On the basis of any of these things as well as a (typically partial) identification of what a work does mean, one may legitimately find significance in a work. This does not imply that one cannot be mistaken in believing that a work bears on one's life or concerns, but it does imply that there are a number of different routes to the work having this bearing.

While there is a sharp distinction between what a work does mean and its significance for a person or group, there is no such sharp distinction between what a work could mean and significance. When a critic relates a work to the ideas of Marx, Derrida, or Lacan, to issues concerning race or gender, or to current political concerns, it *may* be equally natural to say the critic is ascribing to a work a meaning it could have and that she is making it relevant to (identifying significance it has for) a certain audience. However, such a significance creating understanding would have to be based on some prior understanding.

If one seeks understanding *and* appreciation, one of the most effective, though not essential, bridging devices is finding significance. Its holding, I suspect, makes an enormous difference in the appreciative experience of a work. Yet the contingency of the significance relation might raise doubts about the legitimacy of one's appreciative experience due to significance. Both points are noted by W. H. Auden:

> There are a few writers . . . who are artists and apostles . . . Readers who find something of value in their message will attach unique importance to their writings . . . But this importance may be shortlived . . . Should I later come to think the message false or misleading, I shall remember him with resentment and distaste. (Auden 1968: 278)

Other contingent relations in which one can stand to a work that tend to make it personally important, are usually discounted from one's artistic appreciation of the work. For example, if a piece is your song because it was being played when you became engaged to be married, or a novel can never be enjoyed because it was inflicted on you long before you were ready for it by a sadistic seventh grade teacher, it is true that you enjoy the song more and the novel not at all as a result of these experiences. However, it is not true that one's artistic appreciation of the song is enhanced simply because it is your song. Your artistic appreciation of the novel is blocked, but this has nothing to do with your coming to see that the novel has little artistic value.

The difference between these two cases and what we have (technically) defined as finding significance in something is that the latter is based on an understanding of the work, while in the former, one's attitude to the work is independent of *any* understanding of it. If a work has significance to oneself, one is in the best position possible to appreciate features that one understands the work to have. We can say that one's appreciation is actually enhanced if the significance one finds in the work is based on an acceptable understanding (interpretation) of the work.

While significance can exist without its being laid out in an interpretation, there remains the question of what interpretations have to say about significance. Some want to distinguish the sort of commentary that brings out significance from interpretation (Harris 1988: 65). This is a terminological matter. I prefer to include all of the above under the "interpretation" label, because it is more in keeping with current practice, and it is better to avoid revisions in such practice unless there is something really wrong with it. Some identify bringing out significance with any commentary that picks out something a work could mean (independently of what it does mean). This conflation is too sweeping. Some attempts to say what a work could mean do not aim at establishing a significance relation. They could aim simply at finding a coherent reading of a puzzling work.

The contingency and even transience of the significance relation is no bar to attempting to identify it in personal encounters with artworks and in the interpretations of ordinary members of a work's audience. (I do not think such nonprofessional interpretations should be ignored in a theory of interpretation.) However, these features obviously do pose a problem in professional criticism, which addresses a general audience. This does not mean that the significance of a work need be ignored. There are two strategies to interpret a work for its significance that deal with this problem. One is to present the significance a work has to oneself in such a way that others are likely to find that they share the reaction. This is what Lawrence hopes to do in the passage quoted above. Alternatively, one can show how the work bears on something that one knows in advance is of importance to a sizeable group. This is what I called above making the work relevant to that audience.

Critical interpretation and performance interpretation

The characterization of critical interpretation given above does not fit one kind of interpretation common in the arts, namely, performance. Is this a problem? It is, only if we cannot understand the former kind of interpretation without seeing that it has an essential similarity with the latter. Is there something crucial we are missing by ignoring the sorts of interpretations of works provided by performances? Not everyone even wishes to call performances interpretations, preferring to think of the latter as underpinning the former. The thought is that for some performances (there could be others that do not involve interpretation at all or involve it in some other way), there is at least one critical interpretation that motivates or guides it, though without the performer(s) necessarily being able to articulate the interpretation. However, let us not take this tack. Following ordinary usage, let us say that some performances are interpretations.

The question is whether it is important to find a conception of art interpretation, or of interpretation per se, that covers both the critical and performance varieties without which we lose something crucial for understanding the critical species. I will argue that we lose little by keeping these notions separate, and that we are in fact better off by doing so.

One proposal for bringing critical and performance interpretation under a single definition is as follows: An interpretation is a representation of an object under a governing concept that makes sense of the object or endows it with significance.[4]

To marry performance and critical interpretation, this definition calls them both representations of a work (object) that make sense of it. But are performances really representations? Are they representations in the same sense that an interpretive statement is? For that matter, is an interpretive statement a representation of a work?

A performance *presents* a work. If the work is uncut, the performance presents the whole work. Any work of the right sort can have different performances, each of these (after the first) re-presents the work (presents it again and differently). A given interpretive performance may have a single guiding conception, or may blend several different conceptions, including conceptions that stand in tension with each other. A critical interpretation never presents a work or is even a representation of a complete work, cut or uncut. It *says, hypothesizes, suggests, and so on, something* about the work by focusing on some aspects of it. (I will henceforth abbreviate these sundry propositional attitudes or speech acts simply by speaking of what an interpretation *says*.)

Every performance of a work involves, consciously or unconsciously, filling in details that the work leaves undetermined. Many of these fillings in would not be regarded as interpretations from the critical point of view, but can radically affect how we understand the work through a performance. Examples of this include details about the appearance and dress of characters in a play.

The "making sense" that the critical and performance interpretations do is also quite different. This is indicated by the fact that an audience might be reasonably led to different critical interpretations of work after watching the same performance, even if the performance is guided by a single coherent conception of the work.

If performances and critical interpretations are both representations of works, they are so in quite different senses. If we ignore these differences, we can easily be misled to make invalid inferences. Performances are necessarily constructive; that is, they necessarily add features that the work leaves vague or undetermined. We cannot infer from this that critical interpretations are ever constructive either in the sense of adding something to the meaning of a work or creating a new work on the basis of the original. Some may do this, but it cannot be inferred from the constructive character of performances.

There is one lesson that might be learned from thinking of these two types of art interpretation together. *One* aim of critical interpretation can be to provide a basis for an aesthetically viable (interesting, vibrant) performance, and a performance may suggest one or more critical interpretations of a work. On the whole, however, it is better not to yoke these two kinds of interpretation under one overly vague and potentially misleading concept.

Ontology of Interpretation

I turn now to the discussion of two ontological questions that have important implications for a theory of interpretation. One concerns the relation between interpretations and objects of interpretation, and what entities are the terms of this relation. The other concerns the nature of one of these entities: the object of interpretation.

One of the advantages of the view presented in this chapter, though I take it to be a minor advantage, is that it requires only the simplest possible ontology. Some of the alternative theories we will consider entail not only a more complex ontology, but ones involving entities, the natures of which are more obscure, or the postulation of which is ad hoc.

The interpretation relation and its terms

Suppose Peter gives a critical interpretation of *Macbeth*. On the surface, we seem to have *mentioned* three entities: Peter, Peter's interpretation, and *Macbeth*. Basically, the claim maintained here is that this surface view is the correct one. There is one further thing we implicitly referred to in the first sentence of this paragraph, namely, something Peter did in virtue of which he *gave* an interpretation of a work. Typically this will be an act of producing an interpretation (though it could be one of borrowing an interpretation. Peter may give Stein's interpretation of *Macbeth*). While recognizing its existence, I won't worry about the act in what follows. Nor will I worry about Peter, which would be more appropriate in a different branch of philosophy. When Peter gives an interpretation of *Macbeth*, there is an interpretation such that *it* is an interpretation of (an aspect of) *Macbeth*. What we have to worry about is the sort of thing an interpretation is, the sort of thing that the *being an interpretation of* relation is, and the sort of thing "*Macbeth*" refers to in this context.

Interpretations can exist in thought or in a public medium such as writing or speech. When presented in a public medium, an interpretation says something about a work. Like literary works, it is a kind of utterance, and we would find out the content of an interpretation, what it says, by finding out what propositions it asserts, hypothesizes, and so on. When I repeat an interpretation offered on a previous occasion, or if someone else interprets a work exactly as I do, either because he borrows my interpretation or comes up with the same interpretation on his own, on each occasion an utterance of the same type is being made. On each occasion the same propositions are asserted, hypothesized, or whatever. An interpretation, repeated on different occasions, is an utterance type.

Being an interpretation of is a relation between a thought or an utterance on the one hand and an object of interpretation on the other. In the case of art, as noted in the first part of this chapter, an utterance about a work is *an interpretation of* the work, only if it says something about the meaning of a work, about a meaning it could have or was intended by its creator to have, or about the work's significance. This does not mean that every proposition that an interpretation contains will be directly about one of these things, but something won't be an interpretation unless it contains propositions that are about at least one of them.

"*Macbeth*" refers to *Macbeth*, that is, the drama that Shakespeare wrote. Whatever sort of thing the artwork (of this type) is, that is what *Macbeth* is. This may seem to be the most trivial of truisms. I would agree, except that the supposition that objects of interpretations come in more exotic varieties is quite widespread. It is sometimes claimed that the object of interpretation is an intentional object. This can mean different things (the possibilities will be set out in chapter 6), but one thing it is sometimes taken to mean is that the object of interpretation in the case of *Macbeth* is the play *as it is conceived in the thought of an interpreter.* "The intentional object of interpretation is that toward which the act of interpretation is directed. It is identified via a set of features believed by the interpreter to apply to it . . ." (Thom 2000a: 20. See also Krausz 1993, Margolis 1995a). This view, call it the intentional view, seems to me to confuse the object being interpreted with the interpretation. It is the latter that tells us how an interpreter conceives of an object, but then it is always open to us to ask, "Is the conception true or false, plausible or implausible, adequate or inadequate, useful or not useful, and so on?" If the object of interpretation is simply an object as conceived in an interpretation, it is not clear how we could sensibly ask these questions. The conception is automatically true of and adequate to the intentional object, since it is defined as having just those properties it is conceived to have. Given this, it makes little sense to go on to ask whether it is either useful or plausible to conceive the intentional object as it is defined to be.

To this it might be replied that there are some conceptions of objects that are prior to particular interpretations of the objects. This is certainly a possibility and, where one identifies a prior conception with the object of interpretation, one could not say that this object is being confused with the interpretation. It would remain a mistake, however, to make this identification. For we can still ask, of the preinterpretive conception, the set of questions mentioned in the previous paragraph. With respect to the work, is this conception true or false, adequate or inadequate, useful or useless? If we can sensibly answer these questions, the work is the real object of thought, the conception being some beliefs about this object prior to and quite possibly facilitating an interpretation of it. It is only if we cannot sensibly answer these questions that it would be plausible to say the conception itself is the object of thought and interpretation, but the idea that the questions make no sense is one few would want to accept.

The intentional view also seems to confuse the role of conception in thought. When we form a conception of something, that is, when we come to think of an object as having certain properties, this conception is not the object of thought, but the vehicle or content of thought. What we think about an object shouldn't be confused with the object being thought about. We will explore these points in more detail in chapters 5 and 6.

Proponents of the intentional view, as well as others, sometimes claim that the interpretation relation is not a two-place relation as I have just claimed, but is one that has three terms. The idea is that interpretation always involves two objects (in addition to the interpretation itself). There is an initial object that prompts us to interpret, and a subsequent object that is the product of our interpretation.[5] The subsequent object is constructed from the initial object by the interpretation. This conception of interpretation is sometimes used to attempt to fend off objections like those just raised to the intentional view. How this is to be done depends on the way that we think of the initial object. (The subsequent object is always understood as intentional.)

One line is that the subsequent object is constructed by selecting "material" found in the initial object (Krausz 1993). This suggests that the initial object is a nonintentional object such as a work or text. We can now sensibly ask of the subsequent object whether the properties it purportedly selects from the initial object are really possessed by it, whether it is plausible that initial object has those properties, whether it is a useful selection, and so on. The problem with this approach is that it is completely unnecessary to hypothesize the subsequent object to understand what is going on when we engage in interpretation. Suppose that the initial object is the work, which is the most plausible assumption. The interpretation itself already selects features from the work in order to make various claims about it. It is the work, after all, that is the object we are interested in understanding and appreciating. It is the feature-selecting interpretation that accomplishes this understanding. There is not only no need to postulate another subsequent object, but doing so does not help us to see how interpretations illuminate *artworks*. Supposing that interpretations construct subsequent objects is a prime example of confusing or conflating the interpretation and the object of interpretation.

A second line of thought supposes that both the initial object and the subsequent object are intentional objects. The initial object is the intentional object defined by the sort of preinterpretive conception mentioned above. The subsequent object constructs a richer, more significant intentional object (Thom 1997: 184). So, for example, suppose we have two interpretations of Macbeth's "life's but a walking shadow" speech. One claims that it represents only Macbeth's frame of mind at this point in the drama. Another claims that it represents not merely how Macbeth sees human existence, but the play's vision of life. On the present view, the initial object is our conception of this speech prior to either interpretation. There are two subsequent objects, each supplementing the initial object with one of the two interpretations. There are two main problems with this line. First, we seem to have completely lost the play *Macbeth* as an object of interpretation, since the play is identical with neither the initial nor the subsequent object. The play exists independently of any individual interpreter's conception, while the initial and subsequent objects just mentioned do not. This result is unfortunate because we want interpretations to illuminate artworks, not merely supplement our conceptions of artworks. Second, it is very obscure how we are to evaluate competing interpretations on the present view. We cannot turn to the prior objects since they are completely silent on interpretive matters. They simply lack the properties predicated to the subsequent objects. My initial conception of Macbeth's speech is silent on whether it just reflects Macbeth's state of mind or presents a vision of life endorsed by the play. To evaluate these interpretations, one has to consult what is so far missing – the play. However, if we have to do this anyway, there is a much simpler conception of interpretation at hand, namely, that the object of interpretation is neither an intentional initial object nor an intentional subsequent object, but rather the artwork (or other nonintentional object) about which the interpretation makes claims as to its meaning and significance.

The object of interpretation

The objects of art interpretation are artworks or aspects of artworks, and artworks are not intentional objects in the sense discussed above. (Recall that there are other senses.) Can we say something more positive about what these objects are?

My own view aligns, at least roughly, with views expressed by Richard Wollheim, Jerrold Levinson, and Stephen Davies among others (Wollheim 1980, Levinson 1990, 1996, S. Davies 2001). Each of these philosophers holds different views but they share in common the following ideas: 1. Artworks are ontologically diverse. There is no single sort of thing that all artworks are. 2. All share at least one thing in common: that the identity of a given work in part depends on the historical context in which it is created. 3. Musical and literary works are "context-sensitive" structural types.[6] 4. Some artworks, such as paintings and some sculptures, are physical objects. Note that it is not being claimed that context-sensitive structures and physical objects are the only types of thing that artworks can be. Call this position "heteronymous contextualism" or "contextualism" for short.

There are alternative ontologies that have the apparent advantage of giving a single, uniform account of works of art. Three among these are that artworks are mental entities (which is close to the intentional view as characterized above if it went so far as to identify artworks and objects of interpretation);[7] that artworks are either type (Currie 1989) or token (D. Davies 1999) events, actions, or processes of some sort; that artworks are culturally emergent entities – neither pure abstract structures, actions, or physical objects, but tokens-of-a-type embodied in physical things (Margolis 1980, 1999a, 1999b).

It is not my purpose here to provide a detailed examination of these alternatives. Rather, I mention these alternatives to heteronymous contextualism primarily to exhibit both the main advantages of and the most serious challenges to the latter view. However, let us first offer a quick, thumbnail assessment of the alternatives.

The suggestion that artworks are mental entities runs counter to their public character. It also runs counter to the fact that many kinds of artworks are made or constituted from materials appropriate to a medium. A closely related problem is that many properties of artworks are incompatible with having a mental status. Buildings can be occupied, used, possess rooms with specific dimensions, and so on. Sculptures have measurable dimensions; they can be walked around and touched. Similar things can be said about paintings, photographs, and other art forms. None of these things is true of mental entities like thoughts, conceptions, emotions, or sensations.

It is no more plausible to think of certain types of artworks as events, actions, or processes. It is unclear how we can say of an event, action, or process (type or token), that it has a material composition, that it hangs on a wall, that it is read at a single sitting. Buildings, sculptures, paintings, and novels simply are not eventlike, even if performance art, dance, and music are. (It might make sense to think of a musical work as a context-sensitive sound event type, rather than a context-sensitive sound structure, if there is a significant difference between these alternatives.)

What initially appeared to be an advantage of these two views – that they offer a uniform ontology of art – turns out to be one of their greatest liabilities, since it seems particularly easy to find some artworks that neither view easily covers. Both the views of artworks as mental entities and as actions appear to be recommending that we reconceive the object of art interpretation and appreciation. They are revisionary theories of the art object, and they are plausible only if revision is needed. The view that artworks are action types or tokens is fairly explicit about this. The motivation typically provided for this view consists precisely in attempting to show that more widely accepted alternatives are unworkable (Currie 1989: 63–4, D. Davies, 1999).

The third alternative is the view that artworks are emergent, materially embodied entities. Margolis, the main proponent of this view, combines this claim with another: that artworks, like other cultural entities, are to-kens-of-types. What this latter claim comes to is to me both obscure, since Margolis denies that types exist (though they are in some sense "real")[8] (1999b: 388–90), and does not seem a good fit with literary and musical works which seem more like types than tokens, however, construed. Though I am sure Margolis would object, I will detach the first claim from the second, focus on the former's plausibility and usefulness in connection with a difficulty for the contextualist position to be mentioned below.

The main advantages of the contextualist position are two. First, it captures a strong intuition that there is a significant difference between paintings and uncast sculptures on the one hand and literary and musical works on the other. (This is not meant to imply either that there are no ontologically significant differences within these categories or that there are not other significant categories of artworks.) Second, the way the position attempts to capture the difference seems to be roughly right, namely, that the former category contains concrete things, while the latter contains things that are abstract, and therefore not physical. This is so because a given work in this category has many instances, and in virtue of this, there is no physical or concrete thing one can point to and say without qualification, "That is the work."

However, despite this rough rightness, there are important problems for both the idea that some works are context-sensitive structures and that others are physical objects.

An abstract structure is an object that is capable of many instances. The square is a two-dimensional geometrical structure – an arrangement of lines and angles. Musical works have sound structures, and literary works have linguistic structures (texts). Some claim that musical and literary works just are the context-independent, abstract structures specific to them (Kivy 1993: 35–94, Goodman and Elgin 1988). There are three objections to this view. One is that such structures cannot be created but only discovered.[9] But works of music and literature are created, so they cannot be mere context-independent structures. Second, different works can share the same abstract structure, so these structures alone cannot individuate works.[10] Third, a work has crucial artistic properties that derive, not from their structure but from their context. This supplies a reason to suppose that their individuation in part depends on the context of creation. So abstract, context-independent structures cannot give the whole story about the identity of works.

If one accepts all or some of these objections, but plausibly believes that a structure is essential to a work's identity, then it would be natural to suppose that a work is something like a structure-given-in-a-context. This is because this view promises to capture the three intuitions behind the objections to the claim that some musical and literary works are abstract or context-independent structures: namely, that these works are created, that different works can share the same structure, and that some of their essential properties derive from context. The best known version of this view is that a work is an indicated structure, that is, a structure indicated by an artist at a time in an art-historical context (Levinson 1996: 146) where the time is the time the work is created (discovered), and the context is the artist's cultural world at this time.

This view has problems of its own. First, one might doubt that indicating a structure really is creating anything (Predelli 2001); second, one might find the idea of an indicated structure obscure or doubt that there really are such entities; and third, one might find that the view individuates artworks incorrectly (Currie 1989).

To elaborate: the first problem is made vivid when we think of indicating in completely literal terms. Indicating is normally a matter of pointing or some other kind of demonstrating, and demonstrating is not creating. Imagine that a person is "standing next to" an abstract structure (perhaps embodied in a text or score) and pointing at it. He creates nothing new simply by pointing to a structure, and so, to say there is an entity that results from the structure and my pointing to it, is wrong. No doubt, Levinson does not mean us to take indicating so literally, but that raises the question of what is meant. This immediately brings us to the second problem, the claim that the idea of an indicated structure is obscure. The third problem is most commonly supported by the claim that if the same structure is put forward by different artists in the same context at roughly the same time, the result will be that each artist produced one and the same artwork, not two different ones. Hence the identity of the artist is not essential to the identity of the work.

One response to these objections is to retreat to a more modest version of contextualism. One proposal is to say that a work is a structure made normative in an art-historical setting (where "made normative" indicates that the structure is put forward in such a way as to determine correct and incorrect instances of it) (S. Davies 2001).[11] The first two objections are handled by substituting "made normative" for "indicated", while the third is handled by allowing that two artists might produce the same work in the same setting.

I find this response unsatisfactory. The main reason is that the same structure and the same art-historical setting are insufficient to guarantee identity of work. Identical scores might be produced in the same musico-historical setting, but if one is made with the intention that it be played to parody the other, it is plausibly a different work. More generally, the same art-historical context leaves room for artists to do quite different things with the same structure. That is sufficient for the making of different works.

I endorse a different response, which claims that literary and musical works are structures-in-use. What do poets actually do when they "indicate" structures? They put words together to make lines, and lines together to make a poem. They use words and lines to do something. Writers working in other literary forms, and composers, do similar things. We can think of an indicated structure – a work – as a *structure-in-use*. It is very common for humans to use abstract structures. For example, that is what we constantly do when we use language. We take abstract structures – sentences – and use them to say something. When we do this, we produce something new. We say things that the sentences by themselves did not say. What we say is a proposition, which is also an abstract entity, and is not literally created by us. To identify the proposition correctly, however, it is not sufficient to refer to the sentence, but we also must make reference to the context of utterance.

We should think of literary and musical works on this model. Writers and composers use abstract structures to do something, thereby producing something new: the work, the product of what writers and composers do. Works come to us when a writer or composer uses a structure at a given time in a historical context. This should be regarded as no more obscure than using language to say something. Talk of using structures, by the way, shouldn't mislead us into thinking that structures are found whole and ready for use like a preassembled trampoline. Writers and composers have to assemble the structures they use. That is also true of most of the sentences we use to make utterances. Like utterances, works have properties that abstract structures considered apart from the context of creation do not and could not have. However, musical and literary works are still abstract entities.[12]

In order to flesh out this view further, let us consider how it answers the following questions: If works are structures-in-use, does it follow that they are, or are not, norm-kinds? Are they tied to a single agent (artist or ensemble of artists)? Are they created?

The view that some artworks are structures-in-use is compatible with the idea that one of the things that the artist does in using the structure is to make certain properties normative, and further, in doing this, the normativity of the property is made an essential feature of the work. If this makes a work a norm-kind, then it is consistent with the structure-in-use view that works are norm-kinds. It does not, however, strike me as obvious that making some property normative is something artists do across the board in using a structure. It is an apt idea in the performing arts where, in making works, artists at the same time create instructions (e.g., scores) for performing those works. For nonperforming literary works, what is made normative are conditions for creating a good text of a work, which depends on having the *correct* sequence of symbols.

Is a work essentially tied to a single artist (or ensemble)? Or can different artists be responsible for the same work? Different people can make the same utterance, that is, say the same thing. So there is some plausibility in saying that it is logically possible, if most unlikely, that two artists, in the same art-historical context, working at roughly the same time might do the same thing with the same structure, thereby "indicating" the same work. On the other hand, the set of properties essential to understanding and appreciating artworks is far richer than the semantic and pragmatic properties essential to understanding conversational utterances. The former set may include, for example, relational properties connecting this work to other works in an artist's *oeuvre*. Suppose Haydn wrote a symphony – his lost last symphony – that is note for note identical with Beethoven's first symphony. It is plausible that these symphonies would have, and have essentially, some very different musical and historical properties. So, while I do not claim that the matter is entirely settled, on the structure-in-use view, given the sort of essential, contextual properties works possess, the more plausible view is that a work is essentially tied to a single artist.

Are works literally created by these artists? I do not find it obvious that abstract entities, abstract structures included, cannot be created. Consider the design for the 1995 Buick Skylark. Since artifacts are certainly things that are created, it is not obvious to me why their designs or structures are not created too, rather than discovered. This view is endorsed by Amy Thomasson (1999), who recognizes a class of created abstract entities that she calls abstract artifacts. Among these are some that are brought into existence by the acts of their creators in a particular historical context, the origin of which is essential to them. Dodd (2000), on the other hand, argues that even context-sensitive structural types are not created, since they are still types, and that all types are eternal. His test for the existence of a type is the existence of an associated property that supplies conditions that must be satisfied for something to be a token of the type. Consider a type partially defined by the property "being created in 1995." This property is eternal even though only things created in 1995 have the property. Similarly, for Dodd, the type is eternal. However, one needn't accept this. First, it is not clear that all properties are eternal (Howell 2002b). Consider the property of being a remake of the Spencer Tracy–Katherine Hepburn film *Father of the Bride*. Could that property exist before the existence of actors and film? Second, one can require, for a type to exist, not only that there be the associated property, but, among other possibilities, either, that there be tokens of the type in existence (Margolis 1980) or at least instructions or designs for creating such tokens. There is some plausibility in saying that the whale does not exist until there are whales (tokens of the type) and that Mozart's Clarinet Quintet does not exist until he wrote the score – the instructions for creating tokens. (Further arguments for such a view are given in Howell 2002b.) My sympathies lie with Thomasson and Howell rather than Dodd. It is counterintuitive to suppose that the 1995 Buick Skylark existed in the age of the dinosaurs. So I conclude that types can be created, and structures-in-use would be apt candidates for being created types.[13]

I now turn to the claim that some artworks, such as drawings, paintings, and uncast sculptures, are physical objects. An initial objection to the claim that paintings and the like are physical objects hinges on the idea that they too are really structures or at least structures-in-use. Every drawing or painting has structural features, though, as with literature and music, there are different ways of defining structure. The structure of a drawing might be an arrangement of lines and shadings, or it might also include the way three-dimensional space and objects conceived as volumes are represented. The objection is simply that we should opt for a more uniform ontology of art by conceiving of all works, including paintings and drawings, as structures-in-use potentially with multiple instances, if not always so in practice.

The answer to this "objection" is that it is really a suggestion for revising our conception of the artworks under discussion for the sake of conceptual tidiness, and conceptual tidiness is not a good enough reason to do this. I believe conceptual change along these lines might be justified, but only if there were insuperable problems for our current conception, or at least advantages for the new conception more substantial than tidiness. I will concentrate on defending the coherence of the physical object conception of paintings and the like.

An objection of more substance to the view that paintings are physical objects is that such works have properties, "intentional properties," that physical objects cannot have (Margolis 1980, 1995a, 1999a, 1999b). "Intentional" here is being used in a different way than its use above in connection with intentional objects. At least a partial characterization of *intentional property* is this: Human beings have intentional properties in virtue of having intentional psychological states, that is, contentful states like thoughts, beliefs, desires, intentions. Objects have intentional properties in virtue of expressing some of those psychological states. So intentional properties of a painting might include its representing a lion, its symbolizing injustice, its expressing indignation. However, it is not clear why physical objects cannot have both sorts of intentional property. The possibility that they do is a very live option, so this objection is less than decisive.[14]

A third objection concerns the modal properties of artworks and physical objects. A painting is created when a quantity of paint is applied to a canvas and arranged in a certain way. Similarly a sculpture of a man is created when a piece of clay is molded into a certain shape. Obviously the piece of clay existed before it was so molded and will survive another change in shape. So the sculpture is not the same physical object as the piece of clay. It is not even the same physical object as the man-shaped piece of clay, because being man shaped is a contingent property of the piece of clay but an essential property of the sculpture. While there is no reason to suppose that the man-shaped piece of clay would not survive a change in shape, there is every reason to suppose that the sculpture would not survive a change in shape. So either the sculpture is not a physical object, or, if it is, there are (at least) two physical objects occupying exactly the same place at the same time – the one that would not survive a change in shape and the one that would. Similarly for the painting: there is the object that could not survive a rearrangement of paint on canvas and the one that could. The problem is that there cannot be two objects of the same kind in the same place at the same time. If there are two physical objects where the painting or sculpture is, we appear to violate this principle. If paintings and sculptures are physical objects, we appear to have too many of them at a given time and place.

To solve this problem it may look appealing to replace the claim that paintings and sculptures are physical objects with the claim that they are culturally emergent, materially embodied objects. We now seem to get a different kind of object occupying the same space as the physical paint on canvas. Further, paintings can only exist and acquire identity conditions in a cultural context. So the suggestion not only seems to solve the problem but seems apt. However, this appearance is illusory. The reason is found when we inquire further into what these culturally emergent entities are. One condition they must meet is that they possess some properties of the material object that embodies them (Margolis 1980: 21). Which properties? Presumably physical properties like weight and dimensions. However, it is a principle at least as plausible as the one cited in the previous paragraph that what possesses physical properties is a physical object. So it turns out that culturally emergent, materially embodied objects are physical objects after all. If so, we are back to square one.

Here is an alternative solution. The problem we are discussing applies to artifacts of all kinds, not just certain types of artworks. Consider an iron wheel. Where the iron wheel is, there is also a wheel-shaped lump of iron. A lump of iron is a physical object. If the wheel is a physical object, and there cannot be two physical objects in the same place at the same time, then the wheel is the lump of iron. But the wheel and the lump have different modal properties. If the piece of iron were put in a press and made into an iron cube, the lump would survive, but the wheel would not. So an iron wheel is not a physical object. This conclusion is absurd. So the principle that leads us to it is false. A plausible alternative principle says that we can have different physical objects in the same place at the same time as long as they are different kinds of physical objects (Wiggins 1980). There is no reason why the identity parameters of some physical objects, especially functional objects made by human beings, should not be interest-relative and culturally conditioned. So wheels and lumps of iron (even wheel-shaped lumps) are both physical objects, but different kinds of physical objects with different kinds of identity conditions. The same is true for painting and sculptures on the one hand, and paint on canvas and lumps of clay on the other.

In the next two chapters I will consider alternative conceptions of interpretation according to which an interpretation is a construction of some kind: it is either the construction of a new object or, alternatively, of the meaning of the original object, the work. This will give us the opportunity to consider in more detail conceptions of the object of interpretation and of the interpretation-relation that are alternatives to those endorsed here.

NOTES

1   Levinson (1999) contains one of the best discussions of this distinction.

2   In asserting this, I am assuming that certain facts about the origin of the ink-blot are essential to its identity. In particular, that it was made for the purpose of eliciting reactions rather than being a representation of a bat or an abstract artwork is an essential property of that inkblot.

3   The distinction between meaning and significance is put forward in Hirsch (1967, 1984) and by Harris (1988: 63–81). The distinction proposed here, though in general agreement with Hirsch and Harris, is not identical to theirs as is indicated below.

4   This definition is a composite of several characterizations in Thom (2000a). It does not perfectly correspond to any single characterization of his. For the best argument for the conceptual distinctness of performance and critical in-terpretation, see Levinson (1996: 60–89). For a reply, see Thom (2000a: 56–62).

5   For the purpose of clearly setting out this view, I have invented the terminol-ogy of initial and subsequent objects. There is other terminology in use, but it seems to me less clear than that adopted here. The subsequent object is some-times referred to as an object-of-interpretation (Krausz 1993), which, unless made very clear which is meant, could refer to either the initial or subsequent object. Thom (1997) refers to the initial object as a "further" object and the subsequent object as the object-as-represented. "Further" misleadingly sug-gests coming, or being attended to, later; while on a view, like Thom's, where both initial and subsequent objects are intentional, they are, strictly speaking, both objects-as-represented.

6   For Levinson, these are *indicated* structures, that is, structures that an artist puts together or identifies in some way in a context at a time. The identity of the artist, time, and context are all essential to the identity of the work (Levinson 1996: 146). For Davies, only context and time are essential (Davies 2001). Robert Howell (2002a) has convincingly challenged the claim that all literary works are structures partially defined by a specific word sequence, and would issue a similar challenge regarding musical works. In the light of this, the thesis should be restricted to some types of literary and musical works.

7   R. G. Collingwood is a philosopher who comes closer to explicitly accepting the mental entity view (Collingwood 1938). I doubt that proponents of in-tentional objects would accept this ontology despite the fact their concep-tion of objects of interpretation encourages, if not implies, it.

8   Margolis (1999b) says, in the cited passage, that types are "predicables." This does not clarify matters. "Predicable" might refer to a type of predicate, that is, a word or a property. But types are neither. They are certainly not in all cases words. They are also not properties. Types, such as The American Flag, the letter L, the word THE, occupy subject positions in sentences, and have objects rather than property particulars as instances.

9   I will argue below that some abstract structures are created. The structures referred to in this objection, however, are eternal, hence uncreated, patterns, to use Robert Howell's terminology (Howell 2002b).

10   The idea that one can have different artworks with the same abstract structure derives from arguments offered by Danto (1981) that one can have indiscern-

ible artworks and thought experiments like that provided by Borges in "Pierre Menard, Author of the *Quixote*." This objection and the next are linked. If different works can share the same structure, then other factors must be responsible for crucial artistic properties, and broadly contextual factors are obvious candidates.

11   The idea of a "norm-kind" was first advanced in Woltersorff (1980). Levinson himself appeals to the concept of a norm-kind to help flesh out the notion of an indicated structure (1990), but this cannot be his whole story if indicated structures are essentially tied to specific artists. Norm-kinds need not be so tied.

12   It might be objected that the idea that musical and literary works are abstract structural types, and, in particular, structures-in-use is just as revisionary as the view that such works are mental entities or that they are action types or tokens. The truth in this claim is that the concept is a theoretical one not in ordinary use. However, what makes this theoretical concept nonrevisionary is that it captures a maximal set of shared intuitions about such works – that they have many instances, that they are nevertheless created, that historical context plays a role in their individuation. One might think it a stretch to think of very large structures – such as the text of *Middlemarch* – as used to do something such as make an utterance. However, one would only have that thought if one's paradigm utterance were conversational speech. It is *precisely* true that George Eliot uses the text of *Middlemarch*, sentence by sentence, to create a novel, just as it is true, as we noted in chapter 3, that there is such a thing as the meaning of *Middlemarch*, though it would not make sense to ask for it in an exam question.

13   Howell perspicuously writes, "When, through the coming into existence of a community practice, a pattern takes on the property of functioning to carry such semantic, formal, and expressive qualities – or when the pattern simply takes on the property by being singled out, through the existence of the practice, for production and recognition by the community – the pattern becomes the type. The property here is not the property that underlies the pure pattern itself . . . Rather, it is a property *of* the pattern, roughly the pattern's property of actually being used in the community to carry out those qualities" (Howell 2002b).

14   A cousin of the view under discussion is the idea associated with Danto (1981) that works are pairs consisting of a "real thing" such as a physical object and an interpretation. The intentional properties of the artwork are found in the interpretation. This view is discussed in chapter 5.

Radical Constructivism

There are works, like *Hamlet*, that receive an almost endless multiplicity of interpretations. (This is equally true of some philosophical works such as Hume's *Treatise of Human Nature* and some historical events such as the French Revolution.) There are other works where the available interpretations boil down to two main alternatives, though these in turn may be fine-tuned into almost endless variations on the theme of each alternative. *Turn of the Screw* is perhaps the most famous example of the latter phenomenon, but it is by no means the only one. Watteau's painting *Embarkation on the Isle of Cythere* and Orson Welles's film *Citizen Kane* are two other examples. Regarding the painting, the interpretive issue is whether the people depicted in the painting are departing for or from the Isle. Concerning the film, the issue is whether the portrayal of Kane "illustrates the point that the nature of a person is ultimately a mystery; a person is all things to all people, and, correspondingly, a multiplicity of selves . . . [or whether] Kane's personality is explicable by some such notions as 'lost childhood' or 'lost innocence'" (Carroll 1998: 153). Interestingly, when the interpretative controversy about a work boils down to a pair of fairly stark alternatives, inevitably a third interpretive option eventually surfaces, namely, that the work somehow embraces both of the original options. Did Henry James and Watteau intentionally create ambiguous works? Does *Citizen Kane* invite audiences to consider both the view of Kane as enigma and the view of Kane as victim in order to draw audiences to consider both views of human life (Carroll 1998: 161)? When there are such stark fault lines between works-as-conceived under alternative interpretations, one might wonder whether there is just one object of interpretation or whether the three different conceptions of these works create three different objects.

There are various ways of conceptualizing interpretive phenomena. One that will concern us for much of the rest of this book is the constructivist conception of interpretation – the idea that interpretations are not simply instruments for discovering properties already to be found in works, but contribute to the creation of such properties. The reader may recall that there are two main versions of constructivism. One claims that interpretations or other factors change the meaning of the objects we interpret (moderate or historical constructivism). This view will be discussed in chapters 6 and 7. The present chapter concerns the other main version: radical constructivism.

Radical constructivism (RC) is the view that interpretations create new works, new objects of interpretation. More precisely it claims that novel interpretations – ones never before attributed to an object – create new objects distinct from themselves (Percival 2002b). RC itself has two versions. The strong version says that all novel interpretations do this. The weak version says that some do this. Let's call the process by which an interpretation creates a new object distinct from an interpretation "a radical construction" or "a construction" for short. For RC, each new interpretation of *Turn of the Screw*, *Embarkation on the Isle of Cythere*, and *Citizen Kane* create a new object of interpretation, in a sense, a new work of art.

Ontology of Radical Construction

When a radical construction occurs, there must be three objects involved. One is the interpretation, and another is the new object distinct from and created by the interpretation. But there is a third object, the one that initially elicits the interpretation. I'll call this "the initial object," and call what is constructed the "subsequent" or "created object." The initial object must be distinct from the object created by the interpretation because it exists before the interpretation is offered. It is in some sense what is being interpreted, the object of interpretation. When a construction occurs, an interpretation is placed on the initial object to create a new object. However, while an initial object is in some sense what is interpreted in these cases, the newly created object can also be regarded as what is interpreted. It is the object that has the meaning assigned by the interpretation. The initial object does not have that meaning, or at least, not just that meaning, else an object with (just) that meaning would preexist the interpretation, and hence could not be created by the interpretation. So in cases where a construction occurs, "object of interpretation" is always ambiguous between initial object and created object. This is worth pointing out if only because there could easily be confusion over which referent of "object of interpretation" is in effect on a given occasion.[1] It is also worth pointing out in order to contrast constructions with other interpretations, if there are any, where the object that elicits an interpretation is the same as the object that possesses the meaning assigned by an interpretation.

To make this more concrete, consider the objects involved in radical construction in three domains: literature and other arts, law, and history.

Beginning with literature, can we cash out talk of initial objects and created objects into more familiar talk about works, texts, and their meanings? If so, what gets identified with what? In chapters 2 and 3 it was argued that the meaning of artworks is to be understood on the model of utterance meaning. In the case of literary works, their work meaning *is* their utterance meaning. An utterance is made by using sentences – the text of the work – to say or do something.

Let us explore the possibilities. One is to say that the initial object – what the artist brings into being – is a work in its own right, produced by using a text to make an utterance. A proponent of weak RC could admit that some interpretations simply are of this work. Some of these interpretations identify its utterance meaning, that is, its original work meaning. However, sometimes the interpretations that critics give construct new works that make new utterances. A proponent of strong RC, if he were to take this line, would have to say that, although artists create works, the interpretations of critics *invariably* transform these into something new, making a new utterance.

A second alternative is to say that the initial object – what the artist provides – is simply a text. A radical constructivist could think of the text in more than one way. A standard way of doing so is to think of a literary text as a string of sentences bearing syntax and conventional linguistic meanings, perhaps fixed by the state of the language when the text is produced by the artist.[2] Such syntax and linguistic meanings typically do not by themselves determine what a sentence is used to say on a particular occasion. For example, consider the first few sentences of "Notes from the Underground": "I am a sick man. I am a spiteful man. I am an unattractive man. I think my liver is diseased." The fictional status of the utterance and the (fictional) referent of the first person pronoun is not fixed by the syntax and linguistic meaning of the sentences, but by other factors such as author's intention, context, or literary convention. Or consider the very short text "I shall return." It could be an expression of intention, and if so, could be a more particular type of one such as a threat or a promise. It could be a prediction. It could express a hope or a fear, a premonition, a recurring anxiety. It could refer to a place or something else. The literal linguistic meaning of the sentence (text) tells us nothing about which specification is the right one for a particular utterance of the sentence.

If one thinks of the text in this way, a subsequent object – a work – is created by an interpretation, by supplying, as it were, additional meaning that transforms a syntactic/semantic string into an utterance. Utterances may assert something or make a statement, but there are utterances of many other kinds – that ask a question, issue a command, consider a possibility, or make something fictional.

Of course, constructions, like any interpretations, are likely to do more or go further than simply creating an utterance. They may also speak of symbols the work contains, its wider significance, abstract from its characters, actions, settings, plot structures, and provide an analysis of these items. This is perhaps a misleading way of putting the matter because there is less of a distinction, for radical constructivists, between creating an utterance, and further interpretive acts than has just been suggested. Rather, it might be said than an utterance is created precisely by those interpretive acts.

A proponent of RC that adopts this second alternative may acknowledge that the artist may have her own interpretation of the text she produces. But the proponent of RC could deny that this is part of the public object the writer gives us, claiming that the public object is confined to the text. A proponent of weak RC might claim that the pair consisting of the text and the artist's interpretation is just one among the many utterances the text can be used to make. Each new interpretation creates a new utterance, a new (subsequent) object. Each is as legitimate as any other if it is faithful to the text.

A third model, a variation on the second, identifies work and text. Not only is the public object that the artist gives us a text, but this is what we should identify as the work (of art). Interpreters do not create new works on this view, but works are things necessarily incomplete. Interpretations, by providing the means for a text to say (or do) something – to make an utterance – complete works, thereby creating a subsequent object.

There are other models that will not be given special attention now. All of these regard the subsequent object, and some the initial object, as intentional objects. Since we discussed and rejected some of these views, where intentional objects are understood as objects-as-conceived by someone, in chapter 4's discussion of the ontology of interpretation, we do not have to consider them again here. Other versions will be discussed in chapter 6 in connection with moderate constructivism.

To summarize, we have three models of initial and subsequent objects for the realm of literary interpretation. The first thinks of works and texts as distinct, acknowledges that the writer creates a work, but claims that some (all) interpretations create new works distinct from the writer's. The writer's work is the initial object, and the interpreter's is the subsequent object.

The second model also thinks of texts and works as distinct, but claims that the only public object that the writer gives us is a text. This is the initial object of interpretation. Works are made by pairing an interpretation with this object. This could be the writer's interpretation, but it could be the interpreter's own. Works, conceived of as text/interpretation pairs, are the subsequent objects. The last model identifies works and texts. Interpretations do not create works, since the work/text is the initial object, but they complete them by transforming a text into an utterance. The utterance purportedly created by giving an interpretation to a text is the subsequent object.

It might be objected that the appearance of three distinct models of initial and subsequent objects of literary interpretation is illusory. The objector claims that there is really just one workable model. Return to the first model. It claims that interpretations are of works made by writers, and works are distinct from texts. "How," the objector asks, "can one interpret a work, as the first model understands it, without the interpretation being about the artist's utterance?" One cannot, since that is what the work essentially is. However, if the interpretation is about the artist's utterance, it cannot create a new object distinct from that utterance. So if an interpretation does create a new object, it cannot be about the work as the first model understands it. It must be about the text, as the other two models claim. As for the distinction between them, the objector claims that it is merely semantic. They recognize the same entities: texts and text/interpretation pairs, but call them by different names. One calls the latter but not the former a work; the other does the reverse. But this semantic difference is not a real difference.

There are essentially two objections here. The first is against the suitability of the first model to the radical constructivist agenda. A radical constructivist attracted to the first model might reply that there is a sense in which our interpretations are about the artist's utterance – since, as noted above, "object of interpretation" is always ambiguous in the case of radical constructions – but this does not rule out such interpretations being creative of new objects. Interpretations can be creative misreadings, as Harold Bloom has claimed (Bloom 1975). When this happens, sometimes a new work can result from the interpretation of the old (See the Madagascar argument below for a fleshing out of how this can happen.) Again, an interpretation may be about the artist's utterance, but under strict constraints about admissible evidence. As an example, suppose that only facts about conventions in place when the original work was created count as admissible evidence constraining interpretations. Then, the reply claims, one can think of the interpretations of the work as graphing it onto a set of works consistent with those conventions, and in doing so creating a set of new works. Alternatively, even if the initial object is a work understood as the artist's utterance, it may be an utterance that is indeterminate in various ways. An interpretation may take this indeterminate thing and create something determinate or more determinate. Finally, someone might claim that the original work is just too rich in meaning for any single interpretation to capture it all. A new object is created by an interpretation, by isolating and making salient one coherent way of understanding the original. (See the section "Super-rich texts and indeterminate works" for a discussion of these last two replies.) These counterarguments show that the objection to the first model is too quick.

The second objection claims that there is a mere semantic difference between the second and third models, and this semantic difference is not a real difference. I am not sure whether the difference is not better described as conceptual rather than semantic, but whatever name we give it, how we are to think of the work of art is not an insignificant matter. (The object of interpretation has already been discussed in chapter 4.) The grain of truth in the second objection is that any argument that shows that a text is the initial object of interpretation could be used in support of either the second or third models (see the section "Artist/critic parity" for such an argument) with the proviso that some further argument would be needed to sort out the issue of work identity.

This is not to say that I think all three models of radical constructivist interpretation of literature are fine. In the end, without significant qualification or weakening, I think none is fine, because interpretations do not construct works, or subsequent objects, in the way that any of these models claim. For the time being, however, let us give the radical constructivist the benefit of the doubt, and ask whether the models have a similar prima facie applicability to other art form beyond literature, to the law, and to history.

The obvious problem with applying these models to art forms beyond the literary ones is that they lack literal texts. Scored music is most easily accommodated, since one can think of a score as a text bearing a musical syntax (though much more questionably a semantics), which elicits an interpretation that on the constructivist view *creates* a musical work.

However, if we generalize from syntactic/semantic structure to a structure of a sort appropriate to a given artistic medium, and think of an art interpretation as using a structure to do something of artistic significance that is not done by the structure alone, then something very like the text(structure)/utterance (artistically significant doing) distinction can be carried over to the other arts. One will always face choices in picking out the relevant structure that elicits an interpretation. For example, with regard to drawing, one can perhaps take the structure to consist of the two-dimensional array of lines, shadings, hatch work, and so on, or one can include in addition some three-dimensional representational elements. Again there can be choices about which of the representational elements should be included. However, one also faces choices in deciding what is included in a literary text. There are simply different ways of construing the text/utterance distinction across the board.

Just as no one disputes that art is created, no one disputes that positive law is created.[3] In the arts, the dispute between radical constructivists and others is over who are the creators and in what manner creation occurs. Something similar can be said about law. When the law is interpreted by judges and jurists, does that (at least sometimes) create new laws, does it (at least sometimes) modify an already existing law, or does it always simply (purport to) clarify what the law is. Some sort of constructivism, moderate or radical, has considerable plausibility for at least some bodies of law such as common law and American constitutional law. A main idea in common law is that it is shaped (which surely means at least modified) by legal decisions. Similarly, it is plausible that appellate and ultimately Supreme Court decisions at least sometimes modify constitutional law. (See chapter 7 for a defense of the moderate constructivist view of legal interpretation.)

The radical constructivist view is that novel interpretations create new objects, and the most plausible new objects in the case of legal interpretation are new laws. So RC would either claim that legal interpretation has legal texts as its initial object and laws, brought into existence by interpretations, as subsequent objects, or old law is the initial object and new law is the created object. If RC is coherent at all, there is no problem transferring it to the legal realm.

As we will see in the next section, there are historiographers who are also attracted to a radical constructivist position, but it is not so clear what are the initial and subsequent objects of historical interpretation. Historians engage in a number of activities that it is tempting to call descriptive. They try to determine what events occurred in the past, what social structures were in place, how groups interacted, the practices of a culture, and so on. They also offer explanations of the events and states of affairs they describe. Let historical interpretation cover both these descriptive and explanatory activities. Historians who embrace radical constructivism seem to think of their initial object as something that might be called the historical record, that is, the items that it is appropriate to count as evidence recognized as acceptable within the study of history. According to them, interpretations construct events, states of affairs, or explanations of these sorts of things from this "text."

Arguments for Radical Constructivism

So far we have looked at the types of claims radical constructivists make, and the entities that must exist for these claims to be true. It is time to ask, "Are there good reasons for believing that RC is true?"

Arguments from mediation

What might lead someone to accept strong RC? One argument is based on the idea that all thought is mediated, by concepts or conceptual schemes, by assumptions or methodological frameworks, by one's historical situation, and so on. The following quotation from historian Leon Goldstein illustrates the thought at its most basic:

> If in history there is no referent except as it is constituted or constructed by means of the techniques of historical investigation . . . then it is hard to see how reference in history is achieved by a reaching out from within that framework of knowing to facts and events of an unmediated real past. Put another way, if the reference of an assertion is determined by attending to what is looked for by those who are qualified to determine its truth, the realist view of the matter seems to have little in its favor. (Krausz 1993: 134)

Joseph Margolis makes a similar point: "We make or constitute nature . . . . because the only nature we address intelligibly is 'nature' already (somehow) formed (or preformed) in accord with whatever way human understanding functions . . ." (Margolis 1995a: 89).

Goldstein and Margolis point out that any historical or scientific investigation, any attempt to think about the past (or about anything else in nature), will employ concepts and methods of our own devising. From this they conclude that we can never find out about a concept-independent past (nature). Rather, we construct the past and the world around us. Presumably this is true of each attempt to do history. So every historical interpretation creates its own object. Something similar could be said about scientific explanation.

If this is true for historical interpretation, it could also be true for art interpretation: "Meanings are the property neither of fixed and stable texts nor free and independent readers but of interpretive communities that are responsible for the shape of a reader's activities and for the texts those activities produce" (Fish 1989: 322). In particular, an interpretive community supplies a set of tacit assumptions and beliefs, which mediate our interaction with a text that is always there, but is always an interpreted object.

Now the premise of this argument is obviously right. There is no think-ing without concepts (beliefs). It is equally obvious that the conclusion is either trivially true or a non sequitur depending on how we interpret "con-cept-independent past" (belief-independent text). If it means a past (text) that we *discover* without (applying) our concepts (methods, beliefs, and so on), of course, there is no such past (text). Trying to think (discover some-thing) without concepts or beliefs is like trying to eat without a means of ingesting food. It won't happen. However, if "concept-independent" means *existing* independently of our concepts, the conclusion plainly does not follow. The past we discover through applying our concepts, methods, and so on may very well exist independently of our concepts. I cannot think of a cat as a cat unless I apply to it the concept *cat*. What *follows* about the concept-independent existence of the cats I am thinking about? Nothing.

Since many people, including many good thinkers, are exercised by a thought along the lines indicated by Goldstein, Margolis, and Fish, there must be an appeal to additional premises that generate more plausible ar-guments.

Some people (including Goldstein) seem to have the following thought. What we form beliefs about is a concept-shaped past. (You may substitute your favorite instrument of mediation for "concept-shaped." The idea is that the object of belief is a mediated object.[4]) If someone were to claim that these beliefs are true of a concept-independent past, we could only test this by comparing the concept-shaped past with the concept-independent past and seeing if there is a match. But one can never make this comparison because to do so we would need to have unmediated access to the concept-independent past, and it is agreed by all that unmediated access is impossi-ble. So the idea that our beliefs are about a concept-independent past is meaningless, or at least pointless. An idea that is meaningless or pointless shouldn't be taken seriously. So our beliefs are not about a concept-inde-pendent past.[5] Call this the impossible-comparison argument.

Let's accept the verificationism implicit in this argument, not because it is ultimately right, but because quarreling with it would distract us from the argument's main flaw. This is a misunderstanding of what concepts are and do. Concepts are vehicles of thought, not (typically) objects of thought. (Of course, we can make them objects of thought if we decide to think about our vehicles of thought.) Suppose I am investigating Nazi terror. There is a sense in which my concept shapes what I study. I need to decide what I will count as Nazi terror, and in doing this I will define a conception of my subject. I might confine it to acts of violence or intimidation ordered by Nazi officials, or alternatively, to such acts carried out by Nazi organiza-tions or personnel whether or not on orders, or as yet another alternative, in addition, to acts carried out by civilians due to a climate that permitted violence toward members of certain groups. These are distinct conceptions of Nazi violence. It need not be arbitrary which conception is chosen, but for certain purposes one might be better, for other purposes another might be. What this means is that the *idea* (concept) of Nazi terror is constructed by historians. We use the idea to study actions, the agents and victims of those actions, their causes, effects, and so on. These are the objects studied, and it is precisely the non sequitur mentioned above to go from the claim that the ideas are constructed to the claim that the objects are.[6] These objects are sorted by concepts, but it does not follow that their *existence* depends on the historian's concepts. Because that is so, the idea that we are studying a concept-shaped historical reality, to which we then have the impossible task of comparing a concept-independent past that we do not and cannot study, is a red herring. So far, we have no reason to believe that the concept-*shaped* past (i.e., the one studied using ideas shaped by historians) is not the concept-independent past. The same goes for the concept(method, assumption)-shaped interpretation of literature.[7]

Of course, these are only the beginning moves in a very long chess game, or rather, a number of possible games that share this start. Since following all these moves would take another book, we will just examine one or two more.

One reply that a proponent of radical constructivism might make is to grant that, when we examine a single concept, no constructivist conclusions follow about the objects that fall under it. However, when we think of that concept as belonging to a conceptual scheme, or an interpretive community characterized by a shared sensibility or set of assumptions, we can see that concept-shaped reality is not identical to concept-independent reality.

How does putting a concept in the context of a whole conceptual scheme change things? The *counting argument* offered by Hilary Putnam (1990) can be used to illustrate how this might be thought to work. (Nelson Goodman offers similar arguments.[8]) Consider a "world" that consists of three circles. How many objects does this world contain? Some claim that it depends on conceptual scheme. A conceptual scheme (A) that, with respect to this world only counts explicitly bounded geometrical figures as objects, claims that the world contains three objects. (This scheme may recognize other types of objects, but these do not exist in our "world".) Another conceptual scheme (M) that not only counts the circles as objects, but also counts mereological sums of circles, tells us that there are seven objects. Now the concept-independent world cannot contain exactly both three objects in total and seven objects in total. Therefore, either the world shaped by scheme A or the world shaped by scheme M, or neither scheme-shaped world, is the concept-independent world. (Most who accept this conclusion will be inclined to opt for the last disjunct, even though it does not strictly follow.)

The argument is invalid. Its premises are compatible with asserting that both schemes *are* talking about concept-independent reality and are simply saying something false about it. It is true that there are three circles in the imaginary world, but not true that these are the only kinds of things that can be counted in the world. For example, if a world contains circles, it surely contains semicircles, diameters, radii, arcs, planes, and so on. If a given conceptual scheme cannot recognize this, it is just not adequate to the reality of that world, though it can recognize some truths about it. (If we ask how many semicircles the world contains, the answer is uncountably many.) Conceptual scheme M is more adequate than A since it recognizes some objects not recognized by scheme A, but is certainly not much closer to being adequate to identifying all the objects in the world than A is. In fact, we can generalize the point by saying that no conceptual scheme that limits a two(or more)-dimensional world to a finite number of objects is going to be adequate to that world. So the counting argument does not establish that, when we consider whole conceptual schemes, or even consider how the world looks from different conceptual schemes, the world that we think about is not the world that exists independently of our concepts.[9]

I will attempt to formulate one last way to fill in the mediation argument. It begins by pointing out that my reply to the counting argument presupposes a choice of conceptual framework that encompasses both of the frameworks that Putnam considers (and more). Relative to my framework, Putnam's are inadequate, and so can be said to make false claims about the objective world. However, I haven't shown that claims of objectivity are not relative to conceptual framework: there are always competing conceptual frameworks. 'The objective world' is always constructed relative to such a framework.

There is a sense in which it is true that there are always competing conceptual frameworks. Consider two. One requires that we think of circles as partless monads, which also cannot be parts of anything else. Another allows that circles can have parts, and that they can in turn be parts. Notice that I am able to cognize both frameworks and to compare them. Further, I can evaluate each for adequacy as cognitive tools. When I do this, the second framework wins hands down. This tells me that choice of framework is as much shaped by independent reality as that my beliefs about reality are shaped by the concepts I happen to use. So I reject the claim that the objective world is always shaped relative to a given conceptual scheme. That overlooks that competing schemes can be noticed at one and the same time and compared for adequacy. (The relativism implicit in this argument is discussed further in chapter 8.)

At this point one might simply insist the comparisons just alluded to only make sense within a given social practice or form of life which is now put forward as the favored instrument of mediation. But this just restarts the dialectic we have already been through. In the light of that dialectic, the insistence that objects of thought are constructed within one of several strictly partitioned practices is question begging.

Let me conclude the discussion of the argument from mediation with one comment on the very idea of a conceptual scheme. My purpose is not to argue, a la Davidson (1986), that there is something incoherent about supposing there are diverging conceptual schemes. My present point is simply that it is hard to tell when they would exist. Consider the possessors of schemes A and M above. We have assumed these are different because the possessors of M have something that the possessors of A lack: the concept of a mereological sum. But then my neighbor also lacks that concept. Do he and I have different conceptual schemes? Surely people do not have different schemes just because they do not have *all* the same concepts. Here people might refer to different forms of life, different culturally embedded thick concepts, and so on, but, as far as I can see, these raise exactly the same questions as the one just raised about conceptual schemes. I think we are owed some sort of method of individuation on this score.

Artist/critic parity

The next argument I will consider, is based on *artist/critic parity*.[10] This claims that, if an artist can create a work by intending something (successfully) regarding a text, namely, that it make a novel utterance, a critic can create a new work by giving novel interpretation to the same text. This view is best thought of as a way of defending weak, rather than strong, radical constructivism, because it admits that artists create works by intentionally doing something with texts. In making this admission, barring skepticism about the accessibility of the artist's intention, critics are given the option of attempting to uncover texts, thereby discovering meaning in already existing works. But the proponent of artist/critic parity claims that critics can also create new works by producing novel interpretations of the same text.

Artist/critic parity is suggested by a claim once made by Arthur Danto.

In chapter 5 of *The Transfiguration of the Commonplace*, he argues that a work is a product of an object and an interpretation, a view he expresses in several different ways in the space of a few pages. For example: Interpretations are functions that transform objects into works; each new interpretation of an object constitutes a new work; the esse of a work is interpretari (1981: 125). Despite the fact that the second of these ways of expressing his view is a perfect formulation of strong RC, I doubt that Danto himself is a radical constructivist. The reason he is not is indicated by another claim he makes about interpretations and works: "To interpret a work is to offer a theory as to what the work is about" (1981: 119). Danto's real view is that a work is an object that has a content, an object that is about something. (This is to state a necessary, not a sufficient, condition for being an artwork.) Any abstract or physical structure is capable of being about many different things. That is why, for Danto, there are indiscernible works. But in saying that an interpretation is a theory of what a work is about, there is the strong suggestion that there is something a work is about prior to interpretation, which aims to find out what this is. This also suggests that with regard to a given work, say Breugel's *Fall of Icarus*, an interpretation can get this right or wrong. An interpretation that proposes of *that* painting that it is about industry on land and sea, and claims that Icarus's legs are those of a pearl diver, gets it wrong.

How then can Danto say that an *interpretation* transforms an object into a work? Only by using "interpretation" equivocally. Just as every belief consists in an attitude of acceptance toward a proposition, for Danto, every interpretation theorizes about the content of a work. "Belief" can refer to the attitude toward the proposition in question or to the proposition itself, the belief's "content." Similarly, "interpretation" can refer to a theorizing about the content of a work or to the content itself. In the quotation from 1981: 119 Danto refers to the former. In the formulations from 1981: 125 he refers to the latter. It is having a content that is necessary for transforming an object into a work. What needs to be understood is that, for Danto, it is not the interpretive theorizing that fixes the content. It is something understood in traditional historicist, indeed, intentionalist, terms that does this.

However, it is at this point that a proponent of RC might appeal to artist/critic parity. The claim is that if an artist's (successful) intention can bring it about that an object is about something, so can a critic's novel interpretation bring this about, as long as he is interpreting the text (object) and not the *artist's* work. If a work consists of a text that has been given an utterance-meaning in virtue of an interpretation (intention), then, at least sometimes, novel interpretations of texts create new works.

This claim can be made more plausible if we can equate the artist's intention that her work will have a given content with the artist's interpretation of her work as having that content, or if we can say that in having the intention, the artist adopts an interpretive attitude toward her work. Alternatively, someone could claim that interpretations express readers' intentions about the meaning of a text.[11] Claims such as these suggest that artist and critic are doing the same thing with the text. Either an artist is interpreting a text just as a critic does, or a critic forms an intention just like the artist's and (sometimes) successfully carries it off. If the artist creates a work from a text, so can the critic. The main difference between them is that the artist is responsible also for fashioning a novel text, whereas the critic co-opts the artist's text.

There is a grain of truth in the idea that both artist and critic are interpreting a text. When an artist (speaker) uses a text to make an utterance, it is plausible that he presupposes, though not necessarily consciously, that the chosen text allows him to make the intended utterance in the situation at hand. Similarly, when a critic interprets a text as making a certain utterance, it is plausible that a similar presupposition is made. If we like, we can call this presupposition an "interpretive attitude" toward the text. This is the grain of truth in the idea that both artist and critic interpret a text.

However, normally "interpret" has a far richer meaning. When one interprets, one makes claims, statements, conjectures, recommendations, gives explanations, and offers reasons for these. One tries to uncover, or at least, attribute, meaning or significance to a text or work. In all these cases, one is saying something about a text or work. When one uses a text to make an utterance, or even when one intends to do this, one is not doing any of the things just mentioned. One is (intending to) constitute something meaningful rather than saying something about it or about the text from which it is constituted.

Of course, a critic does intend to constitute something meaningful, when offering an interpretation as well as doing some of the various things mentioned in the previous paragraph. However, as pointed out in the chapter 4, this is an intention regarding the interpretation itself, not an object being interpreted. Only by confusing the object of interpretation and the interpretation of the object, could one suppose that a critic has this intention with regard to the former.

There is also a grain of truth in the idea that artists and critics have, or rather could have, similar intentions. Here I do not merely mean that their intentions have something in common, for example, that they both concern the meaning or significance of work or text (though typically in different ways). Rather, a critic or "reader" can form an intention to co-opt a text, and use it to make a novel utterance, to constitute something with a new meaning rather than say something about it. This is perhaps what Roland Barthes had in mind when he spoke of writerly reading (Barthes 1974). When one engages in this type of reading, one becomes a producer, rather than a consumer, of a "text" (meaning that one finds in the text novel utterances of one's own devising).

However, it is instructive that Barthes goes to great pains to distinguish writerly reading from interpretation.[12] If one engages in writerly reading, one is adopting a role more like an artist's than a critic's. The clearest examples of such co-opting are those made by bona fide artists in order to produce bona fide artworks. There are numerous examples in recent art history, such as Roy Lichtenstein's borrowing of the "text" of an Erle Loran diagram to make a new "artwork that consists of what looks like a diagram" (Danto 1981: 142), *Portrait of Madame Cézanne*. Ironically, in this case the "text" of a work of criticism is co-opted for use in creating a work of art.

When one moves away from examples like the one just cited, it typically becomes more obscure what is going on. A hearer or reader may understand or take someone's words in many ways, but would not intend them to have a certain meaning, would not intend to make an utterance with them. If you say to me, "We will meet at the bank," I might say, "I take that to be a riverside appointment," but it would be truly odd for me to say, "*I* intend a riverside appointment" when referring to *your* words. This is because it is not easy for anyone lacking the "transfiguring" mission of an artist (or a thief), to take a text put forward by another to make an utterance, and wholly ignore his or her intent. Even highly revisionary interpretations are typically of a work, not merely a text. For example, a Freudian interpretation of *Hamlet*, or *Merchant of Venice*, introduces various sorts of subconscious motivating forces into the world of the play, which it would be entirely unable to do with the syntactic/semantic string of these plays' texts. They need Shakespeare's character's, which can only be "found" in the plays, not the texts.[13]

We should conclude that intending to use a text to make an utterance is not to be identified with interpreting a text. Utterance(art)-making intentions just are different from interpretation-making intentions. Artist/critic parity is a misconception.

Yet *there is* an interpretation-making intention the carrying out of which comes *close to* radically constructing a work from someone else's text. Suppose a critic realizes a text could be used to make an utterance when placed in a context, and there is much to appreciate in such an utterance, although the critic is equally aware that this utterance bears little or no resemblance to the one made by the original artist. The context might consist in thinking of the text as making an utterance that comments on some contemporary social arrangements. The value of the utterance might lie in its being a hilarious parody of those arrangements. To make the text into a work that is such a parody is an artistic act. But to *assert* that the text can be taken to bear that meaning, can be understood as such a parody, and to offer reasons for thinking of it in those terms (pointing out the artistic value of the parody) is an interpretive act. It is not quite right to say a critic has created the work in question so much as identified a work that might be created from the text. Whether critics actually do this is one thing. That they might is the grain of truth in artist/critic parity.

Before moving on, the reader might find it helpful to have a summary of the argument from artist–critic parity and my evaluation of it. The basic argument goes like this:

1. An artist creates a work by making a text and intentionally using it to make a novel utterance.
2. If an artist can create a work by intentionally using a text she creates to make a novel utterance, a critic can create a work by giving a text a novel interpretation (artist/critic parity).
3. Therefore, novel interpretations sometimes create new works.

I suggested two claims that, if true, enhance the plausibility of premise 2. We can add these as premises to the main argument:

2A   When an artist intentionally uses her text to make a novel utterance, she does so by interpreting her text in a novel way (adopting a novel interpretive attitude toward her text).
2B   In offering a novel interpretation of a text, a critic is intentionally using a text to make a novel utterance.

However, both the additional premises are false. Hence, we do not have reason to accept 2 as it stands. But we can, however, accept:

2C   If an artist can create a work by intentionally using a text to make a novel utterance, a critic can identify a possible work by giving a text a novel interpretation.

From 1 and 2C, the consequent of the latter can be inferred.

The Madagascar argument

The argument from artist/critic parity shows that interpretations of texts can sometimes identify possible works, works that the text could be used to make. It also shows that texts can be co-opted to actually make new works, though this is an artistic rather than critical activity. It would be more interesting if it could be shown that interpretations of *works* sometimes create new objects of interpretation rather than "merely" illuminate an already existing work. In part this is because actual interpretations are typically of works rather than texts.[14] Further, this would be a more telling way to demonstrate the transformative power of interpretation. When a text is appropriated, the work is not in any way transformed because the critic is never talking about the work in the first place.

The Madagascar argument attempts to do just this. It attempts to show that interpretations that are intended to illuminate works might end up altering those works or actually creating new ones (Hence, either a proponent of moderate or of radical constructivism might employ the argument.) It is not claimed that an individual interpretation accomplishes this in one fell swoop. Rather, it is claimed that it is accomplished by a series of interpretations or by an interpretation that initiates a social process that ultimately produces a new (or modifies the original) work.

The strategy the Madagascar argument uses to reach its conclusion is to consider a series of purportedly analogous cases where a meaning assignment to an object (often an initially incorrect assignment), ends up achieving broad social acceptance. As a result, the original object has a new meaning or a new object with the new meaning comes into existence. As we will see, which of the two readings of the examples is preferable varies from case to case.

The argument derives its name from Gareth Evans's Madagascar example (Evans 1982). In this case, an object, namely, a word, acquires a new referent (meaning) through an unintended social process. (Alternatively, one might conceive of this as a case where a new word with one referent comes into existence by gradually supplanting in use a homonym with a different referent.) "Madagascar" originally referred to an area on the African mainland. Apparently through (what were originally) unintended misapplications of the word to a large island off the coast of Africa, and through the gradual general acceptance of this new application, "Madagascar" now refers to Madagascar (the island). I prefer to look at this as a case of meaning change of a single word rather than the creation of a new word. Words are objects that are subject to such changes through contingent historical causes. The meaning of words is historically constructed.

However, other, apparently similar examples at least suggest a different treatment. First consider Bob's sign, a piece of board on which is inscribed the words "Back in five minutes." In Bob's language, these words mean "No trespassing," and Bob uses the sign to warn trespassers to keep out of his garden. Now suppose 1,000 years later Sally digs up the sign in her garden. Sally's first thought is that this sign says, "Back in five minutes," and makes plans to use it in her shop window when she has to close to run a short errand. Everything works out fine. Sally puts the sign out and people realize that she will be back in five minutes. Has the meaning of the sign changed?

If a sign should be understood on the model of an utterance, the meaning of the original sign did not change after Sally discovered the board in her garden, or at any later time. Rather, Sally took the board and made it the case that it was a sign that she would be back in five minutes by intending that it would be so used and placing it in a context where this intention received uptake. Bob used the same board to make a different utterance. The fact that Sally's sign and Bob's sign made use of the same board with the same shapes inscribed on it should not mislead us into thinking that there is just one sign. There is one board, but two signs.

Notice that for Sally to transform the board into a sign that suits her purpose, she does not have to mistake it as a sign that always indicated that someone would be back in five minutes. She could be an amateur archeologist, and know that the board was originally a "No trespassing" sign. Perhaps hundreds of such signs have already been discovered in her area. So this sign has little archeological value, but it could save Sally the cost of making a new sign.

Do we have to take a sign on the model of an utterance? I suppose not. We could take it as a semantic tool. A tool is an artifact made to fulfill one or more specific functions, but which can acquire new functions in use. (There is more to a tool than this, but that won't affect what is said here.) I assume that the screwdriver was invented to turn screws, but people came to discover that it is also quite good for prying things open. It is fine to say that prying things open is a function of screwdrivers even if this was not intended when the tool was invented. Screwdrivers may cease to turn screws (because screws go out of use), but continue to exist to pry things open. If a sign is a semantic tool, it can acquire new semantic functions and still be the same sign. (Of course, a sign, like virtually anything that has a material embodiment, can acquire nonsemantic functions as well.)

Next consider an idol, a piece of carved wood intended to stand in for the god Nur. It fulfills this function for several hundred years. Eventually though, it becomes lost in a region where the god Artifa is worshiped.

Rediscovered, it comes to stand in for the god Artifa for several hundred years. Perhaps it is intentionally put forward as an idol of Artifa by a particular individual. Alternatively, perhaps it was generally misconstrued as having been made to serve this function, and its treatment as such eventually establishes a social convention to so use it. Finally, it might be known that it was intended to be an idol of Nur, but the pragmatic tribal members decide it would be a handy stand-in for Artifa. It is a fact that there is one carved figure that stands in for the god Nur for several hundred years and later stands in for the god Artifa for several hundred years. There is one carved figure. Is there one idol or two? I would be inclined to say two, just as I was inclined to say there were two signs. But I'm fully cognizant that there is no obvious right answer, and perhaps no fact of the matter.

Assuming that there are two signs and two idols, but one word ("Madagascar"), what explains this difference? A word is a very short text.[15] It is ripe for different employments even when its linguistic meaning is fixed; but just as tools can acquire new functions, words can acquire new meanings while remaining the same word. If the view we entertained above that signs are semantic tools were correct, then they too would be best thought of as texts, linguistic items ripe for different employments. (I suggested above that [language] texts might be best thought of as having a linguistic meaning fixed by the linguistic conventions in place when the utterer [artist] first put it forward. If we stick with that, then what I am talking about here are not strictly texts, because these are syntactic strings capable of semantic change. We could call them ur-texts.) However, the view I prefer is that signs are utterances, and utterances are not ripe for different employments. They are employments and hence, given the different employments of the inscribed board, we get two signs.

In addition to these differences between texts (and ur-texts) on the one hand and utterances on the other, there is the question whether the intentions and activities of sign makers are best thought of as analogous to art-making intentions and activities or to interpretation-making intentions and activities. The answer is clearly the former. In making a sign, whether that is done from scratch or by appropriation, one is not putting forward claims or hypotheses about it. One is constituting something meaningful rather than saying something about it. In the case of Sally's sign this is obscured by the fact that in one scenario, Sally is interpreting (indeed misinterpreting) something, namely, Bob's sign. Notice, however, that this has no effect on Bob's sign. Further, if Sally were simply offering an identifying interpretation of Bob's sign in preparation for display in a museum, then she simply would be mistaken, and would remain mistaken even if her interpretation were widely accepted. What brings about a new sign is Sally's appropriation, the intention with which she appropriates, and the fact that her intention receives uptake from her audience. We can see this is so from the fact that there are other scenarios where Sally accomplishes the same result without misinterpreting Bob's sign.

The example of the idols also seems to be basically a case of appropriation. But it raises the issue anew of what is appropriated. In the case of the signs it was an (ur-)text given two different employments. In the case of the idols, is it a structure (the as yet uninterpreted shape of the wood) analogous to a text, the piece of wood that constitutes the idols, or is it simply that one idol is commandeered to serve as the other? One might also use this example to try to blur the distinction, which I have tried to maintain, between appropriation and interpretation. Suppose what happens is this. Joe finds the piece of wood near his house and takes it to be an idol of Artifa, that is, something made with the intention to be used for that purpose. He puts it on the idol shelf in his house and so uses it. When friends and neighbors visit, they also take the piece of wood in the same way and treat it appropriately. In this scenario, unlike some of the other scenarios discussed above, an informal interpretation (taking the piece of wood to represent Artifa) is the agent of appropriation. However, it is because there is an appropriation that there is an idol of Artifa in the first place. If Joe were simply offering an identifying interpretation of the idol in preparation for display in a museum, he would be mistaken and would remain mistaken even if his interpretation was widely accepted.

Now consider an (imaginary) painting, a pictorial work of art. The painting resembles the faces/vase ambiguous figure (from one perspective this shows the profiles of two faces facing each other; from another a vase), but in fact was painted in a land that forbids the representation of the human face and was intended simply as a representation of a vase. So it was understood when it was initially exhibited in the land. However, the painting is moved to a conquered region whose people relish the representation of the human body. They see faces as well as a vase, and a rumor begins that this is a subversive painting cleverly representing human faces under the guise of being a vase picture. This becomes established in the local art history, and generations in the conquered land take the painting this way, long after independence is regained.

The issues are clearer and starker in this case. Here we have a case where it is a *work* that is being *interpreted* which leads eventually to an understanding of the work that pervades a society. The work, so understood, even becomes an important cultural symbol in the society. The view I would like to maintain is first that the radical constructivist option is not workable here. Because the entrenched interpretation is about the original work, and it is that work that has become a cultural symbol, we do not have a case of appropriation. Hence, there is no second work that comes into existence from an appropriative act. Further, if the distinction between texts and utterances that I have employed throughout is correct, the interpretation originally misunderstood the work (utterance). But none of the examples we have considered so far has suggested that *utterances* acquire new meanings by a misinterpretation of them becoming widely accepted. Hence a moderate constructivist understanding of the example also seems wrong.

A work of art does not change its meaning either on the basis of "innocent" miscontrual or the fact that a new way of taking it is "handy." Sometimes the artist who created a painting is misidentified. For example, paintings were attributed to Rembrandt, when they were done by lesser members of his school. When these attributions are corrected, it is not uncommon for our understanding and evaluation of the painting to change, even if an earlier understanding is well established in art history. The discovery that the vase painting was neither intended nor received (by its original audience) as an ambiguous and subversive figure, and that the contrary view was based on a false rumor, would require a similar art historical and critical reevaluation.

It is plausible to conclude that, even if misconstrual is based on something other than mistaken authorship, once the misconstrual is uncovered, understandings of a work based on the misconstrual are given up no matter how well established, unless other grounds are found for them. Further, if misconstruals are not uncovered, they would not be genuine agents of meaning change. In a similar vein, we do not believe poems change their meaning when a word used in the poem has since acquired a new meaning, and it is handy to interpret the poem according to this new meaning. The relevant meaning(s) of the word are one or more that it had when the poem was written.

A different example is provided by A. E. Housman's poem "1887 written on the occasion of Queen Victoria's Golden Jubilee." Here the poet's *expressed* intention was that the poem was an expression of patriotism with no irony intended, but from the moment of publication it was often read as ironic. Such a case is intrinsically less clear, even from an intentionalist point of view. This is because there is a genuine question about the poet's literary intentions as well as what he did in the historical context in which the poem was first issued. Either he was not fully in touch with his intentions at least by the time he came to express them subsequent to writing the poem, or his expression of intention was not wholly sincere, or there is a question whether his intention were successfully implemented.

Super-rich texts and indeterminate works

The discussion so far has been cast in terms of what I have been calling the standard conception of texts, and in terms of works regarded as utterances. I will briefly consider the possibility that RC can be better defended if we look at either texts or works in a different light. An alternative to the standard notion of a text is the super-rich text, a text so full of aspects that, in order to give it sense, we have to make a selection from it. A subsequent object is created by such a selection. As far as I can see, it makes little difference whether we say it is a text that is super-rich, or whether we say this of the work and go on to claim that the interpretations make new works from old ones by selection.

Whichever terminology we use, one illustration of the idea is provided by ambiguous figures (Krausz 1993: 67–78). Consider a duck/rabbit picture. It has a pictorial structure such that we can interpret the figure it presents as a duck or we can interpret it as a rabbit, and it might be claimed that each interpretation creates a new object: a duck picture and a rabbit picture. Similarly, we might treat interpretation of what has sometimes been regarded as ambiguous artworks, such as *Turn of the Screw* and *Embarkation on the Isle of Cythere*, as creating several unambiguous works through the judicious selection of aspects.

However, such claims would be unwarranted. There is no reason why we cannot take the "interpretations" of the duck/rabbit as of the original picture, for there is nothing incoherent in pointing out that it has both aspects even if it is difficult or impossible to grasp both in a single perceptual act. In fact the claim that we have an unambiguous rabbit (duck) picture is false rather than object creating. If the artworks mentioned above are indeed ambiguous, then exactly the same thing should be said about them. All that the strategy recommended in the previous paragraph accomplishes is to leave us with several artificially individuated simpler works, rather than the far richer one the artist gives us capable of multiple interpretations.

Turning now to a different idea, it is noteworthy that works are in many respects indeterminate.[16] No musical work or drama will answer every question as to how it should be performed, and so will leave room for different performances. These, however, are not the only works that leave a variety of questions unanswered. Perhaps all works do, but not all these questions are interpretive questions. How long Hamlet's nose is typically is not. Some unanswered questions certainly can be interpretive. For example, "What motivates Hamlet to delay?" may not have a fully determinate answer, though the play is not silent on the matter either. Suppose *Hamlet* is indeterminate in this respect, and suppose an interpretation is on offer that gives a determinate answer to this question. Should we say that such an interpretation creates a new object of interpretation – one in which Hamlet's motivation is determinately fixed? For now, let us be content to point out that there is certainly no *need* to say this. We can instead construe it as an interpretation of the already existing play and say one of the following: 1. the interpretation is false; 2. it gives us an optional way of looking at Hamlet's motivation (which may be very useful or satisfying). Which of 1 or 2 we should say depends on what the interpretation asserts. If it asserts that the play determinately fixes Hamlet's motivation, it is false. If it proposes a way of taking Hamlet's motivation in the light of particular interpretive aims, then it may provide a welcome option.

Neither the thought that texts are super-rich nor the thought that works are indeterminate provides plausible lines of argument for RC. We will take the latter idea up in much more detail when we consider moderate constructivism in the next chapter.

Objects-as-represented

Interpretation necessarily involves re-presentation. Suppose you hear me say, "Let's send the pudding to the moon." If you ask me what I meant, it is obfuscation, not interpretation, to say, "I meant, 'Let's send the pudding to the moon.'" On the other hand, it is informative or illuminating to say that my utterance was part of a child's game in which putting the pudding in the refrigerator counts as sending it to the moon. So we start out with "Let's send the pudding to moon." We end up with "Let's put the pudding in the refrigerator," and an understanding of the connection (in make-believe) between them. Interpretation involves the re-presentation of the object of interpretation in other terms.

We can call the re-presentation just discussed "recovery." We recover from a proposed make-believe action, a real action that would count as the make-believe action in a game. We also recover an intention to create certain make-believe equivalencies. Another thing we can recover is an intended action that is not equivalent to the actual action performed. Suppose the second shelf from the bottom of the refrigerator is the part of the moon known as the Sea of Serenity, and the third shelf is the part known as the Sea of Tranquility. Suppose it is decided to put the pudding in the latter part, but by mistake I put it in the former part. Once you are in on the make-believe, you might be able to figure out that I intended one action but did another. Yet a further thing interpretations can recover is hidden or deeper meanings. Suppose, for example, the underlying point of the pudding game is this. The pudding in question is tapioca, and the child, with whom I am playing the game, hates tapioca. To mollify the child, we are sending the pudding to a faraway place – the moon. The deep meaning of our game is BANISHING THE PUDDING. That too could be recovered by an interpretation.

There are other re-presentations that interpretations bring about. No actual interpretation of an artwork will take into account every feature of an artwork. It will simplify and abstract – idealize – to identify features important for understanding and appreciating the work. It might propose an organization of the work not manifest in the work itself. It also might propose a reconception of a work. For example, an interpretation of a novel that had always been read as naturalistic might propose that it be reconceived as an allegory.

Now someone inclined to accept RC might claim that these obvious facts about the nature of interpretation shows that RC is true. Each time we have a new re-presentation of the work, such a person claims, what has happened is that we start out with an initial object and end up with an "object-as-represented" by applying a particular interpretative concept, scheme or principle.[17]

If this is all that the radical constructivist wishes to claim, that is, that whenever we have an interpretation, we start out with an object that we are trying to understand, and end up with a representation of that object which is our attempt to understand it, then there is really little to quarrel with. The claim is true, but terribly obvious.

However, true and obvious though the claim is, it is also misleading. It is misleading if this claim is thought to imply that the object that really ends up being interpreted, the real object of interpretation, is the object-as-represented. In fact, in most cases, speaking of an object-as-represented is simply a fancy way of talking about the interpretation, not an object of interpretation. As noted above, "interpretation" can refer to an act or a product of that act. The act is the attempt to understand or appreciate something. In order to carry out this act, we need to do some of the things we have just been talking about: recovering, idealizing or simplifying, reconceiving, and reorganizing. When we do these things, we end up with a product, our interpretation of some object. *It* represents the object in certain ways that help us to understand or appreciate the object. Your interpretation of my pudding game represents my putting the pudding in the refrigerator as sending it to the moon, putting it on the second shelf as putting it in the Sea of Serenity, while intending to put it in the Sea of

Tranquility, and represents the deeper meaning of all this as banishing the pudding. So the representing is to be found in the interpretation itself, the product of your act of interpreting. There is no need for a new object – the object-as-represented.

One reason that might motivate someone to posit an objects-as-represented (distinct from both the initial object and the interpretation per se) is that there is a plurality of good interpretations of some things such as artworks. If one has two good interpretations of an initial object that cannot be combined into a single larger interpretation, it might be thought that we have to say that each interpretation is about two different objects-as-represented derived from the initial object. But this is not so. There can be more than one good way to take the initial object, and that is all that is needed for pluralism to go through.[18] There is no need to construe such interpretations as of anything other than the initial object, telling us what it *could* (though not necessarily does) mean.

A not unrelated reason to posit a distinct object-as-represented goes back to the idea, discussed in the previous section, that works can be indeterminate with respect to certain interpretive questions. If the initial object is indeterminate with respect to a property, and an acceptable interpretation assigns that property to the object, do we not have to suppose that, after the interpretation is given there is some object that has the property?[19] One possibility, to be discussed in the next chapter, is that the initial object *now* has it, having been altered by the interpretation. The possibility that the proponent of RC favors is that a subsequent object-as-represented has it. But in the absence of further arguments, we are not forced to either of these views. We can say once again that the interpretation gives us an optional way of taking the initial object, optional precisely because of the above-mentioned indeterminacy, but acceptable for the nonce, relative to an interpretive aim. The representation of the initial object as having the property is already found in the interpretation, so there is no need for a further subsequent object that really has the property.

Can Radical Constructivism Be Refuted?

So far we have distinguished between strong and weak radical constructivism, and looked at some arguments for each. The arguments have suggested that there is something to weak RC. A text can be used to make different works, and an interpretation can identify a possible work that could be made from a text. In general, however, the transformations envisioned by even weak RC require an act of appropriation and, while such acts might be initiated by a (mis)interpretation, and facilitated by a series of similar interpretive acts, something more is always required. Appropriation is never merely interpretation. It requires an intention (individual or collective) to use something in a certain way, not merely claims or conjectures about what an item is saying or doing, about how it can be taken, or about its significance for an individual or a group. So, at least with respect to signs, idols, games of make-believe, and artworks, weak RC is not strictly true. What there is to weak RC is that it suggests insights about meaning-creating social processes. If weak RC is not strictly true of art interpretation, strong RC could not be true either. So RC is not true.

However, these are conclusions that should be regarded as provisional. They are based on our evaluation of some arguments for RC. There might be other arguments for RC, and these might suggest different conclusions. This will always be a possibility, unless we can put forward independent reasons to doubt RC.

There are good reasons to doubt strong RC, the idea that every novel interpretation creates its own object rather than discovers meaning in an already existing object. First note that this could at best be a restricted thesis – restricted to some objects but not others, or to some meaning assignments and not others. For suppose this thesis was true of everything to which we assign meaning, for example, not only of artworks but of ordinary utterances, and true of all such assignments. Then a meaning could never be conveyed. If it was, we would grasp a meaning something already has, rather than create a new object. RC would apply to interpretations as much as to anything else. To understand an interpretation, we would have to assign it a meaning. But any attempt to do this would just create a new object of interpretation. This is just as true of our attempts to understand our own interpretations, as attempts to understand those of others. So interpretations would create "objects" that no one, including the interpreter, could identify and assign them "meanings" that no one could grasp. That is a world without meaning rather than one in which meaning is radically constructed.

A defender of RC has a number of strategies to regain coherence. One strategy is to claim that we can sometimes understand without interpreting (a plausible claim), and so there are cases where meanings are conveyed. Perhaps interpretations (or some interpretations) do not themselves need to be interpreted, while the artworks, historical events, and laws require interpretation. Alternatively, strong RC might hold for some domains (such as art interpretation) but not others (such as interpretation interpretation). Finally, perhaps the most plausible position for proponents of RC is to combine both strategies.

So suppose that the claim is that every novel interpretation of an artwork creates a new object of interpretation, but these interpretations themselves can be understood without creating a new interpretation of the interpretation. Further, there are things we can understand about artworks that do not require interpretation such as (in the case of literary works) the literal meaning of many of its sentences and certain obvious "facts" concerning the fictional world of the work. For example, with respect to the play *King Lear* no interpretation is needed to know that it is fictional in the play that Lear is a man, he is still a king at the beginning of the play, he has three daughters, and divides his kingdom between two of them. However, strong RC claims that, as soon as we begin to interpret the play, we create a new object of interpretation.

There is still an insuperable problem for strong RC. If we can look at the lines of *King Lear* and gather the information just set out, then we have to admit that the author of *Lear*, Shakespeare, has not just given us a syntactic string with a linguistic meaning, but something with utterance meaning. That is why it can be fictional that the play refers to the man and his daughters, and so on. Once this is admitted, we can always go on to ask about other meaning characteristics of Shakespeare's utterance (the play). We cannot rule out such interpretive questions as being among those we ask. If these are questions about Shakespeare's utterance, answers will be about the same thing. It matters not whether the answers are true, false, or neither. In these cases, the object of interpretation, Shakespeare's utterance, is not an object created by the interpretation. Hence we can rule out strong RC.

Nothing similar can be done with weak RC. Here matters should be left exactly where they were in the first paragraph of this section. We have provisional reason to believe that weak RC is not strictly true, though it is a source of various insights. However, this is barring further argument, or further models of meaning construction that might make weak RC work.

However, if art interpretation is typically of already existing works (as I take to be the case), rather than something that creates works from texts, or new works from old ones, then the interesting version of constructivism is moderate constructivism or historical constructivism. It is to these that I turn in the next chapter.

NOTES

1   See Percival (2002b: 184) for an example where the ambiguity is exploited: "If an artist interprets a text he has fashioned and a critic interprets a text he has borrowed, interpretations by artist and critic alike focus . . . on the same

object . . ." Percival asserts this to dispute my claim (Stecker 1997b: 49) that for (strong) RC, every (novel) interpretation has its own unique object. However, since I was referring to the object to which meaning was assigned, my claim remains true even if the artist's and critic's interpretations are elicited by a common initial object.

One conception of the subsequent object discussed below is an ordered pair consisting of an initial object and an interpretation. On this conception, it is perhaps infelicitous to speak of the subsequent object as being an object *of* interpretation, rather than simply an object created by interpretation. On the other hand, it is also infelicitous to speak of the initial object as the only object of interpretation, because that would imply it has the meaning set out in the interpretation, in which case there is no need of a subsequent object at all. What these infelicities point to, I believe, is the incoherence of the underlying conception of interpretation.

2   There are other ways of conceiving a literary (linguistic) text. One can think of it as a sequence of shapes, or as a purely syntactic sequence in a single language, or as a string of sentences bearing a syntax and a conventional linguistic meaning, but one not fixed to a particular state of the language, and hence capable of change over time.

3   At least everyone wants to *accommodate*, if not literally endorse the idea that artworks are created. Some believe that artworks are structures conceived as abstract entities always in existence, and hence not literally created. This view was discussed in chapter 4.

4   This idea is a close cousin, or perhaps the identical twin, of the idea that the object of thought is an intentional object. Since different things can be meant by "intentional object," the exact relation between the two claims will vary depending on how we pin down the latter idea. I criticize the proposal that the object of interpretation is an intentional object, understood as a conception of an object, in chapter 4. The different senses of "intentional object" and the role they play in constructivist argument are discussed in chapter 6.

5   This is a widely used argument. It is explicit in Goldstein's denial that we can (metaphorically) "reach out" from the "context of knowing" to "realistic objects" (Krausz 1993: 132). Shusterman also appeals to it (1988a: 54).

6   See Hacking (1999: 10–11), from whom I borrow this point.

7   Confusing vehicle of thought with object of thought is by no means confined to the constructivist argument under consideration. Berkeley's master argument for idealism is another instance of such a confusion as Thomas Nagel has pointed out in describing the flaw in the argument in these terms in Nagel (1986: 93). Also see Williams (1966).

8   Goodman (1978) and Goodman and Elgin (1988) are rich sources for such arguments.

9   Searle (1995: 160–7) also criticizes the counting argument. Searle's criticism of Putnam is different from mine. His point is that the existence of a concept-independent reality is compatible with the idea that our grasping of that reality is conceptually relative and, hence, an incompatibility claim does not follow from the premises of Putnam's argument. People do make the claim Searle is criticizing, which he correctly identifies as an error. I am not sure if Putnam makes this claim, because I find his position elusive. Stanley Fish does repeatedly: "There is no document 'in and of itself,' no document waiting to be

configured by a grid of purposes. Documents come into view only in the light of purposes already in place . . ." (1993: 61). Notice how Fish is willing to deny the very existence of documents on the basis that they always come into view in a grid of purposes (concepts), and notice that the latter point in no way implies the former.

However, many who appeal to conceptual relativity do not quarrel with Searle's point. Perhaps there is such a reality, they admit, but it is not the one we *think about*. My point is to challenge this latter claim.

10 For an excellent discussion of this idea, see Percival (2002b). Much of my discussion is shaped by his exposition.

11 As does Shusterman (1988b: 400): "The necessary meaning-securing intentions can belong to readers of texts rather than to its original author."

12 Margolis (1995a: 36–45) argues that writerly reading is a form of interpretation.

13 A radical constructivist could say that, while the interpretation requires characters, *it* creates them, rather than finding a work already containing them.

14 For some possible exceptions, see chapter 3, p. 69. Percival (2000) puts forward Madagascar arguments as a way of defending constructivism. The sign and idol examples discussed below are due to him. The vase painting example was first used in Stecker (1997b).

15 Goodman and Elgin (1988: 58–60) also treat words this way. See their discussion of the words "cape" and "chat."

16 This claim is strongly qualified in the next chapter.

17 Paul Thom (1997, 2000a, and 2000b) takes this line, although I do not always find it clearly expressed. His words can sometimes be taken, unobjectionably, as identifying what he calls the object-as-represented with the interpretation, while at other times with a constructed object of interpretation. Ironically, when he does the latter, the interpretation sometimes disappears from view. See, for example, 2000a: 107. His considered view seems to be that interpretation has a "three tiered structure" consisting of an object, an interpretation, and an object-as-represented. As I argue below in the main text, there is no reason to suppose there is such a thing as the object-as-represented over and above the interpretation itself. Its postulation is an ad hoc measure to save constructivism. The categories of recovery, idealization, and reconception mentioned above are taken from Thom (2000b).

18 See chapter 3 for a more elaborate explanation of this point.

19 Sherri Irvin raised this point.

Moderate and Historical Constructivism

In this chapter we look at the idea that the meaning of things changes. In the case of art, this is the view that a work's meaning changes over time subsequent to its creation by an artist. Similar theses might be advanced about law or history: that the actual content of a law (e.g., a constitutional amendment) might change over time, or that the historical "meaning" of events might change.

It might just seem to be common sense that this is true. How could one deny that *Hamlet* means something different to us than it did to its original audience? There is a multitude of reasons in support of this intuition. We use very different concepts than did Elizabethans. So when we see the play, or think about it, we do so employing these different concepts. Won't this lead to the ascription of different meanings to the play and to different kinds of appreciation? Also, we are the beneficiaries of hundreds of inter-pretations of the play. This has unquestionably influenced the way the play is performed and both because of this influence and independently of it, affects our reception of the work. The most famous example of this is the idea that Hamlet's hesitation is to be explained by his being in the thrall of an Oedipus Complex. But this is only one of many interpretations that affect our thinking about the play. Further, when we see the play now, it is in the context of a rich history of later drama. It is natural to apply some categories from later drama to it just as, when we read philosophy from a different era, it is natural to reformulate some of its issues in terms of con-temporary debates. In short, the play *Hamlet* comes to us overlaid with so many contexts and concepts from later periods that one might think it inevitable that the play itself has a different meaning now then it did in 1603.

However, despite these reasons to accept moderate constructivism, if this thesis is not to reduce to trivial truth, it is important to keep in mind the distinction between the meaning an object of interpretation possesses and the significance it has for someone. Obviously the significance of an artwork, law, historical event to a given person or group of persons is capable of constant change. Dostoyevsky was once my favorite writer. This is no longer true. When I do go back to his works, the features that are important to me now are different from those important to me thirty years ago. The significance an item has to someone obviously can change without the item changing. It can change because the person (or group) changes. It can change because of an alteration in the person's relation to the item. It can change because the comparison class in which the item is placed changes. Hence, it is inevitable that *Hamlet* has a different significance for each of us today than for Shakespeare's contemporaries, but from this it does not follow that its meaning has changed.

We should also distinguish meaning change from another sort of change that an interpretation of an item can bring about. When we give a new interpretation of an object, we are thinking of it in a new way and, in virtue of this, the object acquires the property of being thought of in this new way. When this happens, what has primarily changed is us. The property of being thought of in a new way is a by-product of this change in us. It is not meaning change. (See Lamarque 2000: 114–15, a qualified dissent from this claim.) Hence, the fact that we think differently about *Hamlet* now than did Shakespeare's contemporaries does not show that the meaning of the play has changed.

With regard to artworks, to get a sense of work meaning not tied to the traditional historicism defended in chapter 3, let us provisionally stipulate that the meaning of a work is the important artistic properties of a work that are at its core, that is, the properties of the work that would have to be taken in to have a full appreciation of a work at a given time.[1]

Moderate constructivism claims that novel interpretations can change a work's meaning – change the important artistic properties of a work.[2] As with radical constructivism, one can distinguish between strong and weak versions of the doctrine. The former asserts that all interpretations alter a work's meaning, the latter that only some do. However, only weak moderate constructivism has plausibility, and only it will be under discussion here.

Moderate constructivism is a species of historical constructivism.[3] This is the view that events that occur, or contexts, conventions, or traditions that arise, or objects that come into existence after a work is created, either directly contribute to the meaning of a work or contribute to bringing it about that the work undergoes a change in meaning. Or, to put it more concisely, changes that occur in the course of a work's history and in the history of the culture in which the work is embedded, change its meaning.

Moderate constructivism claims that interpretations are the agents of such change.

In what follows I will first consider the merits of moderate constructivism, by first posing a dilemma for that view, and then seeing if it can escape it. The dilemma, however, does not apply to the broader view I have called historical constructivism. I will consider that view in the second half of this chapter.

A Dilemma for Moderate Constructivism

As mentioned above, many people would be inclined to accept the claim that interpretations change the meanings of their objects. However, there is a dilemma moderate constructivism faces, which provides a substantial reason to doubt this view. The dilemma goes like this: Either interpretations make statements that are truth valued (true or false), or they do not. If they do, then, when they are true, their objects already have the properties attributed to them; while, if they are false, their objects do not have those properties and will not acquire them in virtue of such false ascription. What if interpretations lack truth value? I can change you by uttering certain things that lack truth value: if I say "Walk," you might start walking, and that would be a fairly robust change in you. However, this does not carry over to artworks and other objects of interpretation. I cannot change an artwork by issuing a command, recommendation, or by imagining something with regard to it. The best I can do is bring about a change in myself or another human being, by doing these things. An artwork might acquire new properties by my doing these things, but only of the trivial sort mentioned above. So, it appears, that on either supposition, interpretations do not change their objects.[4]

Is the Dilemma Flawed?

One argument against the dilemma claims that the properties of various items including artworks can stem from people's intentions.[5] To take a simple example: Suppose that in representing how a battle unfolds, I use a banana to represent a regiment. I say, "This banana represents the fourth regiment" or "Let the banana represent the regiment." What brings it about that the banana represents the regiment is my intending this, my expressing the intention in the presence of the banana, my receiving uptake from the audience, and so on. But, it is claimed, interpretations are on a par with intentions. Therefore, the properties of various items, including artworks, can stem from interpretations. If the properties stem from true interpretations in virtue of their truth then the first horn of the dilemma is false. If they stem from interpretation, but not in virtue of their truth, the second horn is false.

The crucial premise here is the claim that interpretations are on a par with intentions. This claim closely resembles the thesis of artist/critic parity discussed in chapter 5. I will argue below that the present claim is similarly problematic.

Of course it is true that intentions and interpretations have things in common. Both can be formulated in indicative sentences that express mental states of their utterers. But these similarities do not show that intentions and interpretations are on a par. The intention to represent a regiment with a banana contributes to a regiment being represented by a banana because it is a necessary (or at least normal) condition of the act of representing a regiment by a banana. Interpretive acts (normally) accomplish quite different things. They make claims, conjectures, recommendations, suggestions, or offer explanations. (Note that some of these things would typically be evaluated for truth, some not.)

Suppose Phyllis actually does represent a regiment with a banana, and I am trying to interpret what she did. I do not represent a regiment with a banana afresh, by claiming or conjecturing that the banana stands for a regiment. A claim or conjecture is either true or false. If true, the banana already represents the regiment; if false it does not. Nor do I secure the representation by recommending that you now see the banana as having done this, by requesting that you imagine or make believe that the banana was doing this or by suggesting that the banana would be a very apt instrument for doing this. Imagining that the banana represents a regiment leaves it wide open whether the banana actually does so. A suggestion might lead you to take it that the banana does this, but that too is not the same as its actually doing so.

Suppose I misunderstand the representational function of the banana or want to offer a revisionary interpretation of its representational function. I claim, conjecture, recommend, or suggest that it represents a trench. That still does not get the banana to represent a trench. Again, the claim or conjecture is either true or false. If it results from a misunderstanding, it is obviously false. On the other hand, it is not appropriate to make a claim or conjecture if I mean to offer a revisionary interpretation. A suggestion or recommendation would be more appropriate and might seem a more promising vehicle of property change. However, before agreeing to this, we need to determine more precisely what is being recommended. Does it concern Phyllis's representational act? Then we merely have a recommended way of taking it. If we follow the recommendation, we will think about the act in a new way, but that does not itself imply a genuine change in what Phyllis represented with the banana. Is the recommendation that we engage in a new representational act of using the banana to represent a trench? If we follow the recommendation, the banana would now truly represent something new, but we would no longer be interpreting its representational function. We would be appropriating the banana and intending it to represent a trench! We would indeed be doing something on a par with what Phyllis did, but this is so because we would be creating a new representation, not interpreting at all.

So, on the face of it, it looks like interpretations are not on a par with intentions. If they are not, we cannot argue from the fact the properties of various items stem from intentions to the claim that they stem from interpretations.

Here is another argument against the dilemma. What is the obstacle, one might ask, to there being a predicate with the following satisfaction conditions?

For all times t, an object x satisfies the predicate "p" at t just in case there is a time t* no later than t at which p has been ascribed to x (Percival 2000: 54).

If there can be such a predicate, then a statement ascribing p to x can be true, but not independent of its being ascribed. Hence the first horn of the dilemma can be rejected.

However, there is an obstacle to there being such a predicate. Normally, when we ascribe a predicate to an object, we say something about the object. When I ascribe "is red" of a book, I say of the book that it is red. What do I say of x when I ascribe "is p" to it? The satisfaction condition at best leaves us in the dark. Suppose, by way of enlightenment, it is suggested that there is no obstacle to the predicate "represents Elizabeth II" being such a predicate. However, "represents" does not, and could not, work like that and retain anything near its normal meaning. There is a lollipop in a glass jar in my study. Suppose someone walks into my study and I say, "See that lollipop; it represents Elizabeth II." If I have done nothing else to give the lollipop a representational function, have I succeeded in getting the lollipop to represent the Queen? No. The Lollipop is doing no representational work, and so represents nothing.

It might be thought that the obstacle we have been discussing could be removed if we modified the satisfaction condition stated above, as follows: For any time t, an object x satisfies "p" at t just in case "p" has been ascribed to x at a time no later than t, and Fx. The condition removes the problem of what we are saying about x when we ascribe "p." We are saying F of x. However, there is a new problem. In saying F of x aren't we already ascribing "p" to x, and so is not the first conjunct of the condition redundant? Not necessarily. Suppose we claim that for any time t "depicts Elizabeth II" is true of x at t just in case "depicts Elizabeth II" is ascribed to x at a time no later than t, and Elizabeth II can be seen in x at t. Notice in saying of x that Elizabeth can be seen in it, we are not ascribing "depicts Elizabeth II" to x. The problem is that this is just not a good account of depiction. The fact that we are able to see the Queen in a picture of her sister Margaret combined with the fact that someone had asserted a moment before "That's the Queen" won't make it true that the picture depicts the Queen. In general, asserting that something is so, even in conjunction with something else, won't make it so.[6]

Intentional Objects

The moderate constructivist thesis is often thought to depend on the kinds of objects that are being interpreted, or alternatively, the kinds of properties possessed by such objects. The claim is that we are dealing with intentional objects which have intentional or relational properties, which require a different treatment from ordinary physical objects.[7]

> With non-intentional objects . . . the line between the properties they possess inherently and those imposed on them is *reasonably* clear. . . . But Intentional objects are *essentially* relational, in the sense that they depend for their existence on human thought processes and practices. *How they are taken* is not just incidental but determinative of their natures. (Lamarque 2000: 114; his italics)

The aim of this section is to figure out what can be meant by these claims, and whether they help the constructivist escape the dilemma.

There are a number of different things that can be meant by "intentional object." One is an object of thought. Two distinct conceptions of objects of thought (there may be others) are as follows: On one conception, it is simply an object that happens to be thought about. It is the object with whatever properties it happens to have independently of whether we assign those properties to the object in thought. This is obviously *not* what is meant by "intentional object" by those who believe that intentional objects have special properties, since it includes those nonintentional, noncultural physical objects that were distinguished from the intentional in the above quotation. Alternatively, an object of thought might be conceived as an object that exists in thought, as it is thought about, even if nothing corresponds to it in reality. Thus, I can think about unicorns, even though no unicorns exist. Unicorns will still be the intentional object of my thought. Yellowstone National Park can also be an intentional object in this sense as long as we understand this to be the park as I conceive it rather than as it exists in reality.[8] Intentional objects in this sense not only depend on human thought but on a single individual's thought. Hence, they do not have the intersubjective availability that moderate constructivists claim for the objects they are concerned with. Also, to claim that intentional objects in this sense are the objects we are interpreting is another instance of the confusion, discussed in the last chapter, which consists in taking the vehicle of thought for the object of thought. If I am to think about lions, I will need some sort of mental representation of lions – an idea or conception of lions. But this latter is not what I am thinking about, not the object of thought. It is more like what I am thinking *with*. The object of thought is the lion. Hence, objects of thought conceived in this second way also turn out *not* to be the best candidate for the intentional objects we are looking for. (See chapter 4, pp. 82–4, for further criticism of this conception of the objects of interpretation.)

A different conception of intentional object is an object that possesses intentional properties either inherently or in virtue of being produced by things with intentional properties.[9] So people are intentional objects in this sense because they have intentional states (beliefs, desires, intentions, and so on) and things made by people are intentional objects because they are produced by people. In virtue of this, they have certain intentional properties of their own, for example, being made or used with certain intentions, in order to satisfy certain desires, because of beliefs about certain means–end relationships. A subclass of these intentional objects depends for their existence not just on individual people, but on broader practices or institutions. Thus something is not a coin just because someone makes something that resembles coins or even attempts to use it as a coin. To be a coin it has to arise in the right way from the financial institution of a political state. We can call this subclass of intentional objects practice-dependent intentional objects. They are the sorts of objects that John Searle discusses in the first six chapters of *The Construction of Social Reality* (1995: 1–147). I believe that such objects are more in line with what moderate constructivists mean by "intentional objects," though I am not sure we have an exact match, in part because one wonders whether different conceptions of intentional objects might be conflated in the thought of some moderate constructivists.

It is not obvious that the existence of intentional objects in this last sense, or of the subclass of practice-dependent intentional objects, implies the truth of moderate constructivism or provides a way out of the dilemma. Such objects are not thought-dependent in the way that the second conception of objects of thought, mentioned above, are thought-dependent.

Still, even in the case of fairly straightforward practice-dependent intentional objects, we have patterns of change and stability that might provide hope for the constructivist project. Consider a £50 note issued in the UK. That it has the value of £50 sterling is an intentional property, but one fixed by its origin, not by any subsequent events. What is £50 sterling worth? This is what can change. For example it might have the same value as US$100 at one time and US$120 at another. This too will be due to various institutional cum intentional facts. An analogue of both the stability and change that moderate constructivists seem to seek is embodied in this example.

What is not clear is how this carries over, if it does, to objects of interpretation such as artworks, and whether the special intentional and practice-dependent properties they possess imply a moderate constructivist story. There are other kinds of stability and change, which might better account for the relevant facts. To accept the moderate constructivist story, we need to be pointed to the crucial meaning-changing circumstances, properties, or relations. In the following sections, I will consider a variety of candidates: salience creation, the inapplicability of bivalent logic, indeterminacy, and the nature of various historical properties.

Salience Creation as Property Change

Here is one modest suggestion for defending the claim that there is interpretation-induced property change.[10] The basic idea is that a given interpretation of an object makes certain features F salient, while a different interpretation makes other features G salient. So the property change that a given interpretation might bring about would be something like this: before interpretation i is given, the interpreted object o has F all right, but F does not have the property of being salient, while, after i is given, F is salient. On this view, what interpretations change are second order properties, that is, properties of properties.

An example or two might help us decide on the plausibility and significance of the proposal, as well as get a clearer idea of what it is. Recall the example of an ambiguous figure like the duck/rabbit or the vase/faces. When one looks at a picture that can be seen either as a vase or as profiles of two faces facing each other, it might be claimed that one interprets the picture by assigning salience to certain aspects of features (Krausz 1993: 68). An example would be taking this sharp angle as separating the fore-head from the eyes and that one as representing the nose joining the mouth.

I have two questions about this example. The first, perhaps nitpicking, question is whether what is going on here is properly described as assign-ing salience to features (or aspects of features). I am unsure what the mod-erate constructivist means by salience, but to me to assign salience is just to assign special significance, prominence, or importance to a feature. It is not to say what kind of significance we assign. All the features to which we assign significance or prominence when we interpret (or see) the picture as two faces, we would equally assign significance or prominence when inter-preting (seeing) the picture as a vase. The converse of this, however, does not happen to be true. The top line of the picture has salience when we see it as representing the top of the vase, but lacks salience if we see the picture as representing two faces. So, regarding the first question, my answer would be that some of what is going on when we interpret or see the picture in one way rather than another is a matter of assigning salience differentially, but a good deal of what is going on is simply seeing the very same salient features as representing different things.

The second, more important, question is whether the creation of sali-ence is best understood as property change? For that matter, is the fact that we can see or interpret the same features as representing different things best understood in terms of property change?

In answering this question (or questions) we can note that a trivial sort of property change spoken of earlier certainly occurs. Before seeing or in-terpreting the picture, *I* did not take the line as representing this or that, and *I* did not give it special significance or importance. It was only upon my seeing or interpreting the picture that the line acquired the property of being so understood by me.

To decide whether any more interesting property change occurs, it is useful to consider what is asserted when we offer an interpretation or con-vey what we see. With regard to the ambiguous figures under discussion, which are not artworks and whose origin in studying the psychology of perception is well enough known, what would or should be asserted is relatively straightforward, though still relative to the aim of interpretation. If the aim is to say what the picture represents, then what should be as-serted is that it represents a vase *and* it represents two faces. The evidence one would give for this claim would be twofold. First, by noticing certain features, and by taking them in certain ways (that this angle can be taken as a forehead meeting the eyes or, alternatively, as a sharp corner of a vase), we easily can see the picture as both vase and faces. Second, the figure was purposely made so that both vase and faces can easily be seen, though not easily seen in a single perceptual act. The finding of certain features as salient, and seeing certain lines as representing this or that were simply the means by which we discovered the representational facts. No more interesting property change than the one already noted (viz., the trivial sort) need occur when we see or interpret the features of the picture.

So far we have looked at fairly straightforward cases: using a banana to represent a regiment, drawings invented for the purpose of psychological investigation. It might be that things are different with artworks such as paintings, since, with them, interpretive questions do not stop once we determine what is represented, while even determining that is a far more complex and debatable matter. In connection with the thesis that the assignment of salience to features brings about a significant change in the work, consider some interpretive claims made in four different interpretations of van Gogh's *The Potato Eaters*.[11] H. P. Bremmer claims that the painting represents a close-knit family and this close-knittedness is paralleled, perhaps symbolized, by the placement of four mugs closely together. Albert Lubin, in a similar vein, claims that the glowing lights of the house speak of "warmth and happiness within," though he goes on to say that the painting is about mourning.[12] H. R. Graetz, on the other hand, sees lonely and isolated figures that represent van Gogh's relationship to his own family. The light symbolizes kindness, but as something longed for rather than possessed. Griselda Pollock sees the painting as the exploration of "otherness," hence she does not associate the painting with van Gogh and his family. An important aspect of the painting is to represent peasants without the usual romantic clichés.

It is true that these interpretive claims suggest sometimes similar, sometimes quite different, ways of thinking about (seeing) van Gogh's painting, and one of the ways they do this is by giving special significance (salience) to certain features of the painting (e.g., the arrangement of the mugs, the lamplight, the "primitive faces" of the peasants). But of course, since these are competing interpretations, one still has to decide whether the painting represents, symbolizes, or expresses the various things attributed to it in the proffered interpretations. The mere issuing of interpretive claims hardly settles which of these interpretations are true or acceptable. Such claims may indeed permanently alter the painting's reception, but this still leaves these other questions open.[13]

What these examples illustrate as they stand is that, when an interpretation changes the way we think about an object, those changes can be profound indeed. However, it does not illustrate any other kind of change that an interpretation brings about.

Nevertheless, we should consider a possibility, which we will discuss in more detail below, that the fictional world of the painting is too indeterminate to rule out any of the above interpretations, which become reasonable ways of taking the painting when certain of its features are made salient. Even if we assume that the salience of the features is a consequence of a given interpretation rather than being intrinsic to the work (which is a reasonable assumption given the stipulated fictional indeterminacy of the work), this fact offers little support for moderate (or any other form of) constructivism. Given the work's fictional indeterminacy, these interpretations provide optional if (sometimes) very worthwhile ways of taking a work. There is no reason to suppose that the meaning of the work has changed, precisely because the slants these interpretations give us are optional (any more than there is reason to say that a new object of interpretation has come into existence).[14] This optionality appears to be guaranteed by the postulated indeterminacy of the work.

Can One Escape the Dilemma by Rejecting Bivalence?

An alternative to trying to show that a horn of a dilemma is false is to show there is a way between the horns. One ingenious proposal regarding the present dilemma claims that the alternatives that the dilemma presents are not exhaustive. Interpretive statements are properly understood, it is claimed, as evaluable in a multivalued logic. Interpretations are not truth valueless, but they lack bivalent truth values (in particular, the truth value *true*). One version of this view claims that interpretive statements have *truthlike* values such as *plausible, reasonable, apt*, as well as *false* (but not *true*) (Margolis 1980, 1991, 1995a, 1995b, 1999a, 2000).

The existence of multivalued logic shows that the alternatives of the original dilemma are not exhaustive. However, this fact will help the constructivist only if two further claims can be established. First, it must be true that a bivalent logic is an inappropriate, and a multivalent logic is an appropriate, evaluative tool for interpretive statements. I have argued against this elsewhere (Stecker 1995b; also see S. Davies 1995), but will, for the moment, accept it for the sake of argument. Second, the nature of interpretive statements – the purported fact that they have multiple truthlike values – has to help explain how interpretations can change their objects. Let us call the purported fact *M*. If *M* does not help to explain how interpretations can alter the meaning of their objects, we can remake our dilemma into a trilemma and be none the worse for wear.

It is not clear how *M* explains how interpretations can accomplish this change. Consider the interpretive question whether Hamlet's hesitation in revenging his father's murder has an Oedipal explanation. Before, I said that either an interpretation that says this is true, in which case *Hamlet* (the play) already has the property of implicitly ascribing this motivation to Hamlet, or that every interpretation which says this is false, in which case the play does not have the property. In either case the interpretation changes nothing except how people perceive or think about the play. We also considered the possibility that "Hamlet has an Oedipus complex and it causes him to hesitate" has no truth value whatsoever. Now we have to take into account another possibility: that some interpretations that say this of Hamlet, though not true, are plausible, apt, or reasonable which leaves it open that other interpretations which deny this are also plausible, apt, or reasonable. Does this show, or even suggest, that such interpretations change the play or what the play represents, or anything else that might be regarded as a meaning property of the play? It does not.

In fact, it seems that the present view *precludes* the possibility of an interpretation changing its object. The latter, it might be claimed, can occur only if the following is true: before an interpretation i is given for an object o, o does not have property F, but after i is given for o, o has F. O has F if and only if it is true that o has F. But it is never true that o has F on the present proposal. Hence, on this view, an interpretation cannot change its object. The trilemma is in place. Further, if one holds both M and the view that interpretations can change their object, one holds a view that is true if and only if it is false.

In the next section we will see how a moderate constructivist could reply to the above argument.

Indeterminacy and Imputation

Most moderate constructivists would object to the discussion of the preceding section because it assumes that the representational, symbolic, and expressive properties that an interpretation assigns to a work are straightforwardly possessed by the work, either prior to or following on interpretation, or else that they are incorrectly assigned. They would claim instead that many properties are *imputed* to a work rather than simply discovered or falsely predicated. This means that there can be grounded ascriptions of properties to works without those ascriptions being strictly true or false. They go on to claim that a work changes by having new properties imputed to them. In this section I will examine the imputational conception of what is going on in (at least some) interpretations.

The chief rationale for thinking that some properties are imputed to works is the thought that works are indeterminate in one respect or another. An alternative way of putting the point is to say that there is no clear border between what is in the work and outside the work (Krausz 1993, Lamarque 2000, and Margolis 1980, 1995a, 1999b). We already took up this idea in the last chapter where it was deployed in an argument for radical constructivism and, briefly in this chapter, in the section entitled "Salience Creation as Property Change."

Such claims as these give rise to two questions. First, what grounds are there for taking works to be indeterminate, and second, what argument takes us from indeterminacy to imputation, and from imputation to moderate constructivism?

Regarding the first question, I find three reasons offered for the indeterminacy claim. First, in works that contain fictional representations, the fictional entities "represented" are always incomplete in certain respects. These gaps can be (or seem), from the interpretive point of view, trivial or important. It is of small matter that we are left in the dark about the exact length of Hamlet's fingernails at any given moment in the play. It would be more important to us if what motivates Hamlet were left, to some extent, indeterminate. Second, in works that are made to be performed, such as musical works and dramas, various details of the performance are left open by the work even after we add features of performance practice that are not written down but taken for granted. This is equally true for musical works, which do not contain fictional representations, as it is for works that do. The third reason, which is rather different from the first two, is that incompatible interpretations are often given to the same work, and, it is claimed, that this is possible, only if a work is indeterminate with respect to the interpretations.

Reflecting on these reasons shows us that none is conclusive to believe that artworks themselves are indeterminate or lacking in clear boundaries. The inevitable fact that fictional entities represented in a work are indeterminate does not show that the work itself is. In fact, for any property you like, it is compatible with fictional indeterminacy that there is a yes/no answer to whether the work has the property. For example, from the fact that the length of Hamlet's fingernails is left indeterminate by the play, it *follows* that *Hamlet* has the property of not representing the length of its protagonist's fingernails.

For similar reasons, the fact that a work allows for different performances does not entail that there is any property, such that, it is indeterminate whether the work has it or not (S. Davies, 2001). There are many purported counterexamples to this claim. Among the simplest and most easily understood in the case of musical works concern volume and tempo in-structions. "Forte" means that the music is relatively loud, "allegro" that it is relatively fast. Obviously such instructions leave room for lots of varia-tion. This means that properties of scores such as these are vague, and the musical work inherits this vagueness from the score. It is not indetermi-nate, however, but true that works and their scores have vague volume or tempo properties, and it is false, not indeterminate, that they have more precise properties. While some recent "serious" music tries to eliminate a great deal of this vagueness, it is aesthetically advantageous for most music to possess it, because it leaves room for a great variety of performance interpretations of the same work. (These, by the way, are not logically incompatible with each other, primarily because they assert nothing.) This point applies to many other properties of musical works including, in the case of many works, their expressive properties.

We can conclude that the first two reasons commonly offered for the idea that artworks are indeterminate do not establish that they are, at least if we mean by "indeterminate" that there is no fact of the matter whether a work has or lacks a given property or (to put it more loosely) that its boundaries are generally undefined. Of course, if we choose to mean by a work being indeterminate that the fictional entities it represents are incom-plete in many respects, and that many other properties of works are vague, then works are unquestionably indeterminate, in fact obviously so.

The final reason commonly offered for indeterminacy is that there are incompatible interpretations of the same work. This claim is true, but of no significance in itself. The existence of incompatible interpretations is consist-ent with perfect determinacy, if it is always true that at least one member of a pair of such interpretations is false and unacceptable, even if we cannot al-ways tell which one it is. To support indeterminacy, we need two further claims. The first is that both of a pair of incompatible interpretations can be good or acceptable interpretations of the work. (If we say this, however, we must add "but not in virtue of both being true," because logically incompat-ible statements cannot both be true.)[15] Second, what explains this situation is that an unusual logic applies to artworks and other objects of interpreta-tion such as the multivalent logic discussed in the previous section of this chapter. (Strictly speaking, in the light of this second claim, we should revise the first to say that interpretations that would be incompatible, had a biva-lent logic applied, can both be acceptable. I will ignore this refinement for ease of expression.) If the value *true* does not apply to many interpretive statements, then the properties ascribed to works by those statements won't be either clearly in or out of the works in question. Hence, works would be indeterminate with respect to many properties.

Call this the incompatibility argument. It looks like a powerful argument for a robust indeterminacy in objects of interpretation. Its success, however, hinges on the truth of the two claims just mentioned: that there are good or acceptable incompatible interpretations of a given work and that this is explained by the inapplicability of bivalent logic in this domain and the applicability of multivalent logic. The first of these claims is far more dubious than might first appear. On close scrutiny, purportedly incompatible interpretations turn out to be something else. Thus, when we have the kind of vagueness or incompleteness in the specification of fictional entities discussed above, it may be both legitimate and logically consistent for one interpreter or performer to take a work to be F and another to take a work to be non-F, for it may be true that the work can be *taken* in both ways. An interpretation that "wishes only to demonstrate that one can perceive" (Margolis 1980: 151) a work through a particular habit of thought, such as a Freudian perspective, is consistent with another interpretation that wishes to demonstrate that one can perceive a work from another perspective.[16] It is *true* that we *can* perceive a given work in both ways. In general once we see what such acceptable pairs of interpretations assert (or what they could legitimately assert), they turn out to be compatible even when we assume bivalence holds. Furthermore, the recognition that interpretations are undertaken with different aims, and that evaluation is relative to aim, also eliminates apparent inconsistencies. Hence, there is no need to turn to a multivalent logic to account for the mutual acceptability of such interpretations.[17]

(I note parenthetically that the second claim made by the incompatibility argument for indeterminacy is that bivalent logic does not apply to interpretive contexts. This already implies an imputational conception of property ascription in interpretations, since it implies that many such ascriptions are neither true nor false. Hence, it won't be possible for a proponent of this argument to use indeterminacy to argue for imputation without falling into circular reasoning.)

The conclusion we should draw is that, at least based on the usual reasons, it is far from obvious that works are indeterminate with respect to any of their actual properties. However, it is true that some are vague in many respects, and that the fictional entities represented in some of these works are (of necessity) incomplete.

Let us, however, grant that it may serve a legitimate interpretive purpose to impute to works properties they lack or to impute properties to fictional items that a work literally leaves unspecified. "Think of Hamlet's hesitation as having an Oedipal etiology," might be such an imputation. This could be legitimate because it provides an optional but artistically interesting way of filling out an aspect of the play and/or provides a basis for a compelling production (as it in fact did). Hence, the "indeterminacy" of works does indeed permit imputation, if that is regarded as certain optional but artistically worthwhile ways of taking works.

However, as noted above, thinking of imputation in this way does not provide a line of argument to moderate constructivism. The whole point of imputation as just conceived is that there is an artistically valuable payoff in looking at a work in a way that the work itself does not require. There is nothing work-changing about that.[18]

If we assume that works are indeterminate in a more robust way than we were able to establish above, would this lend greater support to moderate constructivism? By itself, it would not. As we interpreted robust indeterminacy, it is the idea that there is a set of properties about which there is no fact of the matter regarding whether or not the work has them. Suppose that *being about the costs of repression* is such a property with respect to Hawthorne's novel *The Scarlet Letter*. Then it may be extremely plausible that the novel is about these costs but not true that it is. Rather it is plausibly imputed.[19] Does this imputation change what *The Scarlet Letter* means? So far, we have no reason to believe that it does. If robust indeterminacy is correct, the imputation does not make it true that *The Scarlet Letter* is about the costs of repression. Further, for all we have been told, it may be the case that it always has been and always will be extremely plausible that this is what the novel is about. If so, the imputation changes nothing.

Suppose, however, it is denied that the properties it is plausible to impute to a work remain unchanged over time. Rather it is claimed that what is plausible changes from one historical context to another. Then the imputationalist has an argument for a constructivist conclusion. A work's interpretive meaning consists in what is plausibly imputed to it. What is plausibly imputed changes over the course of history. Therefore, a work's interpretive meaning changes over the course of history. It is plausible now that *The Scarlet Letter* is about the costs of repression. Perhaps in the future, this will no longer be plausible, or will be less plausible. Would that not be a change in the meaning of the novel?

It might be objected that, if we accept multivalence and robust indeterminacy, we are surely precluded from claiming that interpretations can change the meaning of their object. All that we would be able to say is that it is plausible, apt or reasonable to claim that interpretations can change their objects, where this claim can coexist with the claim that it is plausible, apt or reasonable that interpretations do not change their objects. On this way of thinking about the matter, nothing is, or can be, settled about moderate constructivism. However, the constructivist could reply that when such changes in plausibility occur, meaning has changed in the only available sense, and further, it would not be equally reasonable to claim that meaning has not changed.

This line of thought offers an appealing and coherent rationale for constructivism. Unfortunately, the argument turns on two unproven assumptions. The first is that works are robustly indeterminate and the best we can do, for a range of properties, is impute them to works with a greater or lesser degree of plausibility. The second is that a change in the historical context of interpreters can change either what it is plausible to impute or an imputation's degree of plausibility.

Regarding the first assumption, I have already argued against it. I see no route to supporting it that we have not already explored and found wanting.

The second assumption is a variant of historical constructivism. It is time to turn to assessment of that view.

Historical Constructivism

Recall that an artwork is historically constructed if changes that occur in a work's historical or cultural context change its meaning. Such changes can be either accretions in meaning, that is, simply add to the current meaning of a work, or they can be alterations in meaning, that is, bring it about that a work ceases to mean one thing and begins meaning something else. One way an alteration can occur is where the addition of a relevant property interacts with other properties to alter the overall artistic significance of a work. This "addition" would occur if, in virtue of a change in historical context, a work comes to have a property it never had before. Another kind of alteration occurs if one property simply replaces another. Thus, if one were to claim that changes in the meaning of the word "mill" bring it about that the occurrence of "mill" in Blake's poem *Milton* now means factories of a certain type, whereas when the poem was created it meant something else, and hence *the meaning* of the poem has undergone a change, one would be making a *historical constructivist* claim. If someone were to claim that the pervasiveness of a Freudian conception of human psychology, during a period within the twentieth century, brought it about (in combination with various events represented in the play) that, during that period, it is part of the meaning of *Hamlet* that its protagonist's behavior is caused by an Oedipus complex, that would also be a historical constructivist claim.[20] Among the things that might bring about such change, would be, on some constructivist views, an interpretation, or perhaps the wide acceptance of an interpretation. On this view, interpretation would be seen as a vehicle for meaning creation, not merely meaning discovery. Note, however, that one can be a constructivist in the sense defined here, and see all interpretation as discovery. It would be discovery not of the meaning fixed at the work's creation, but of meanings that arise afterwards according to historically shifting variables. On this alternative constructivist view, interpretations would have to be sensitive to, for example, new contexts or conventions that impinge on and change the meaning of the work, and thereby *discover* what are these changes in meaning.

On this conception of construction, what might be the identity conditions of an artwork? There is not one set of identity conditions required by historical constructivism, and the two proposals considered below are not intended to be exhaustive.

Although it may seem paradoxical, it would be perfectly coherent for a constructivist to accept the identity conditions set out in chapter 4. That is, a work could be identified with an object (material object or structural type) "produced" by an individual or individuals in a certain context. Origin would fix the identity of the work, and changes in meaning would be contingent, though not unimportant, facts about it. Identity and meaning would be two different things not essentially related. An alternative historical constructivist view would be that meaning is essential to the identity of a work. This does not imply that one gets a new work with each change in meaning. Rather, it would require that only something that goes through *that* exact sequence of meaning changes could (in the metaphysical sense) be that work. If there were a world in which there was a work just like van Gogh's *The Potato Eaters*, except that it has a slightly different meaning than the actual painting for a period of ten years (say from 1950 to 1960), it would be a different work on this view. If origin fixes identity, we would have the same work.

Unlike some versions of constructivism, such as strong radical constructivism (and moderate constructivism if it cannot escape our dilemma), the version of historical constructivism in question here is perfectly coherent and consistent with our proposed account of interpretation in chapters 3 and 4 (*sans* the account of work meaning endorsed there). Interestingly, there do seem to be "objects" that change their meaning in the fashion predicted by this kind of view. The words of a language are objects of this type. They undergo changes in meaning – both accretions and alterations – of precisely the sort we have been discussing, and do so as a result of historical contingencies.

Are artworks, like words, objects the meaning of which is historically constructed? Let us begin with some examples that suggest that developments subsequent to a work's creation alter the artistically significant properties of the work.[21]

Before looking at new examples, let me refer the reader back to the examples discussed in the "Madagascar argument" of the previous chapter. The burden of those examples was to show that a way of taking some object, which by itself does not effect a change in the object, can eventually lead to such a change by achieving wide social or cultural acceptance. I argued that we need to distinguish differences among cases here, and, in particular, the argument fails to establish either radical or historical constructivism for artworks.

One large category of new example comes from the fact of conceptual change. There are a large variety of such changes. Some of these come from the study of the history of the arts. One thing such study does is to codify or classify works of art as belonging to a period, style, form, or genre. It is often true that the artists whose work is being so categorized could not straightforwardly apply the category to their work or that of others. Nevertheless, one can certainly claim that being in sonata form, belonging to the baroque period, or exhibiting the chiascuro style are important artistic properties.

Related to art-historical categories are others that arise from an earlier work bearing a similarity to a later work or style, which makes the similarity salient or preeminent. Thus some nineteenth century works might be described as Kafkaesque, something the authors of those works would be unable to do.

Relevant conceptual change comes also from developments in disciplines not directly associated with the arts. For example, developments in psychology or psychiatry give us ways of talking about the motivation or other mental features of characters in fiction not straightforwardly available to the authors of those fictions. The standard example here is Freudian or, more broadly, psychoanalytic concepts (and this chapter has certainly made liberal reference to them). However, they are not the only categories a critic could appeal to.

A different kind of example derives from historically significant properties of works. Such properties include being original, being influential, being the culmination of a style, and so on. These are relational properties, and the relations that form their basis connect one work to the past or the future in some way. It is those properties that imply a relation to the future that provide the strongest ammunition for historical constructivism. A relation between a and b cannot obtain, one could claim, until both a and b have come into existence. I can will my fortune to my firstborn grandchild, should such a person come into existence, but there is no child now who stands in the relation of beneficiary of my will, hence no relation holding between my will and such a child. Therefore, there is also no relational property now possessed by my will in virtue of the above relation. If a work becomes influential, that can only happen after the work enters into a relation with later works, and hence only after those later works come into existence.

I will consider just one more type of example without suggesting that I have exhausted all relevant types. This sort of example is based on the idea that the properties a work possesses can change due to a change in the comparison class in which it is placed. For example, when it was first performed, Stamitz's music was heard as possessing an unusual grace. However, later on, when it could be compared to the music of Mozart, the gracefulness of Stamitz's music was considerably downgraded. The claim is that the degree of grace possessed by Stamitz's music actually changed over time.[22]

This is a bevy of examples, and they do not all deserve the same treatment. However, none deserves a treatment that would actually support historical constructivism. Most of the examples really are not cases of property change. Those that are, are not cases of a work's meaning changing due to a change in an artistically important property.

The examples based on conceptual change raise two large and interesting questions. When is a concept in the possession of an individual? When does a concept first apply to an object? Regarding the first question, consider some examples. Suppose Freud's theories about sexual development are true, and these imply that the phenomenon of the Oedipus complex is something that occurs in most or all societies. Suppose further Shakespeare had some sort of awareness of this phenomenon, and this awareness played a role in the creation of *Hamlet*. Should we say that Shakespeare possessed a concept of the Oedipus complex? One certainly might say "no" based on the thought that it is a theoretical concept in Freudian psychoanalysis, and Shakespeare certainly did not have an understanding of the concept's role in that theory. Alternatively, one might say yes, because of Shakespeare's awareness of the phenomenon the concept identifies. If one is more inclined to say no rather than yes in this case, consider another example, that of Mozart and the concept of sonata form. The specification of this form in music theory postdated Mozart's life. Did Mozart have a concept of this form? Again there may be grounds for both yes and no answers, but in this case the yes answer is overwhelmingly more plausible, because of Mozart's thorough familiarity with the ins and outs of this form, even if he could not say, "The first movement will be in sonata form." I am not saying that all cases where the question of concept possession arises deserve the same answer, but if the artist does possess the relevant concept, that should settle in the affirmative the question whether a work has a property picked out by a concept at its creation.

However, in general, we should not suppose that the question "Does a given concept apply to an object at a given time?" has the same answer as the question "Does a given individual at that time possess that concept?" Nor is the former question the same one as whether the concept is available to individuals at that time. When a concept that applies to a phenomenon comes into use (or, if you like, existence) long after the phenomenon occurs, it does not follow that the concept was not true of the phenomenon right when it was occurring. A concept of a property has that property as its content and makes it available to thought. A concept applies to an object if a statement ascribing the property (i.e., using the concept) to the object is true. In other words, a concept applies to an object if the object has the property that is the content of the concept. Hence Baroque music was Baroque in 1700 just as dinosaurs were dinosaurs in prehistoric times, since the properties that make something Baroque were possessed by musical works back in 1700 just as the properties that make things dinosaurs were possessed by those creatures while they lived. This should be distinguished from the separate issue, namely, when the property that is the content of a concept becomes available to thought. That can only happen once the concept comes into use. Hence, Baroque composers and their contemporaries could not apply the concept *Baroque* to their music. (They could, however, apply to it many of the concepts that make compositions baroque.)

Something similar is true of the claim that stories like Gogol's "The Nose" or Melville's "Bartleby, the Scrivener" are Kafkaesque. Each story has some among the galaxy of properties that we think characteristic of the work of Kafka. Gogol's story, with its detached and fancily dressed nose riding about town in a coach, realistically describes a surreal, inexplicable situation. Bartleby undergoes a metamorphosis from an extremely hardworking clerk to someone who would "prefer not to" engage in any required work or accept any option offered. When we ask ourselves what brought this metamorphosis about, a range of economic, social, and metaphysical possibilities present themselves, much as they do in Kafka. Insofar as the claim asserts that the stories possess some Kafkaesque properties, it is always true since these qualities were always possessed by these works. Perhaps the claim asserts more. One thing we might do in calling these stories Kafkaesque is to make the said qualities salient. We already know that creating salience is not to be confused with property change. We also may be pointing to a similarity between the earlier works and Kafka's. This similarity can only exist with the appearance of Kafka's writing, so here we have a property acquired long after the earlier works were created. However, it is not obviously a meaning property: it points to common qualities that the works in question always possessed.[23]

When we say that A influences B, we are also pointing to a relation that cannot exist without B existing, and so must come to hold after A is created. Even if we follow Baxandall (1985: 59) in thinking that an assertion of influence is always best rephrased in terms of a relation that has B acting on A, A still acquires in the course of time a new relational property. However, once again there is no reason to think this is a meaning property. Being similar and being influential are much alike in this respect.

Finally we turn to the gracefulness of Stamitz's music. Being graceful is an aesthetic property, and so must be considered a meaning property according to our definition.[24] If Stamitz's music actually was very graceful on first appearance, and becomes less graceful or not graceful with the appearance of Mozart's music, it does undergo a change in meaning. But is this what happened? I am inclined to think not. I find it more plausible to suppose that Stamitz's original audience miscalculated the degree of grace in his music. This is a faultless mistake. Stamitz is one of the early exponents of the classical style, and it is understandable if his contemporaries were both overly impressed with his departures from earlier music and unaware of the potential of this new style, revealed by Haydn and Mozart. There is a temptation to suppose that, had the classical style failed to develop beyond Stamitz, his music would really have a higher degree of grace than we now credit it with. We should resist the temptation to say this. The worst-case scenario is that we should never be in a position to truly assess the music because of a lack of development in the style. The much more likely course of events would be that, without further developments, classical music in general, and Stamitz in particular, would seem increasingly insignificant. This is just another route to a truer assessment of the music.

Here is what seems an analogous example. My daughter was formerly a pretty good student of ballet. When I saw her dance, I was impressed with her grace and skill, and I can even say that I was equally or more impressed with some of her fellow students toward whom I lack a natural bias. But were they graceful ballet dancers? Not in comparison to really fine professional dancers. Nevertheless, I might have said they were graceful dancers, if the comparison class were unknown to me. As it is, only a more qualified judgment is appropriate, such as that the children are graceful and accomplished for their level. I think the Stamitz case is not essentially different.

One might suppose that if accurately gauging the degree to which an item possesses a property sometimes requires making an appropriate comparison, we will be led to accept a deep skepticism about such judgments. Not so. It is true that we could be wrong in attributing some properties to works, performances, or performers, but that only shows that such judgments are corrigible. A comparison class often is available and we often have a good idea about what it is. People would have been able to offer a good assessment of the gracefulness of Stamitz's music not too long after it was written, and the situation has not changed much since.

Oeuvres

I turn now to a much more limited class of cases, those confined to the *oeuvres* of a single artist.[25] These are cases where, purportedly, what we discover in later works within the *oeuvre* of an artist changes, or rather completes, the meaning of an earlier work of that artist. It is further claimed that two conditions have to be met for meaning change (completion) to occur. The first condition is that the earlier and later works are properly seen as products (or parts) of a single, extended, artistic act. Second, the later part of this act (the later work or its creation) changes what is most reasonably construed as the intention with which the earlier work is made. These two conditions need to be seen against the background of a theory of work meaning to be properly appreciated. The theory (hypothetical intentionalism) is that the core meaning of a work, its utterance meaning, is the intention most reasonably ascribed to it by an ideal audience. Notice that the conditions on meaning change (completion) are tied to this hypothetical intentionalism. Otherwise, the fact that it is most reasonable to attribute one intention at one time, and a different intention at a later time, does not indicate a change of meaning. It simply suggests that we should revise our beliefs about a work's meaning in the light of new evidence.

Notice also that if hypothetical intentionalism were keyed to actual audiences, it would invite quite radical changes in meaning, unless we choose a single privileged actual audience. This is because actual audience members would be in varying epistemic situations regarding which intention it would be most reasonable for each of them to attribute to the creator of a work. This would vary not only from individual to individual, but from one generation to another, given the different facts that would be available to each as well as the differing conceptual and theoretical orientations of each. However, much of this variation could be assumed to be smoothed out in the case of the ideal audience.[26] Nevertheless, even an ideal audience would necessarily have to come to different conclusions at different stages of the artistic act unless we could implausibly attribute to it knowledge of the future. Hence, the meaning of the work is not fixed (an ideal audience is not in a position to judge) until the artist's most extended artistic act is complete.

Could there be other events, not part of the creative act, which occur after the work is completed, which also alter which intention it is most reasonable to ascribe (in effect contradicting the first condition mentioned above)? This question I postpone until after we have examined examples of purported *oeuvre*-related meaning change.

The first example concerns Mahler's Third and Fourth Symphonies. Here it seems quite plausible that the first condition is met, that is, that the creation of these musical works can be considered part of a single, extended artistic act. This has to do with the special circumstances of composition of the symphonies, which were closely intertwined. It is much more in doubt that the crucial second condition is met, that is, that knowledge of the second work changes the meaning of the first. Exactly how this happens turns out to be "very difficult to say. . . . Perhaps, when we have them both, then knowing that redemption comes in the succeeding symphony retrospectively frames the despair of the preceding one, tempering its sting."[27] Perhaps, but this conclusion is so optional, it is hard to say that what we have here is a change of meaning rather than one possible way of taking Mahler's Third. We can equally well take it as just different in emotional tone than the Fourth, and note with interest that this is so despite similarities in other musical respects.

I take this problem with the Mahler example to carry over to the next and last one I will consider. After looking at Mondrian's pure abstractions of 1917, "perhaps" we can see in the already highly abstract landscapes of 1914 and 1915 a teleological content of striving to isolate the structural essence of the visible world. One might see that, but one might also claim that one sees a more inchoate or ambivalent intention in the earlier paintings, or, yet again one might claim that those earlier works are sufficiently abstract that, when combined with some knowledge of Mondrian's sensibility, one can discover the striving without the help of the later paintings. The matter is too indeterminate, the choices too optional, to make a strong case for the claim that the later works alter the meaning of the earlier ones.

There is, however, another point about the Mondrian example that needs to be made, and it is that, in this case, we do not have the same convincing evidence that the first condition is met. The Mahler case is based on an appeal to biographical information about the circumstances of composition. Nothing like this is offered for the case of the Mondrian. Rather, we have similarities of form or structure. Given that being in the same *oeuvre* is not sufficient to establish a single artistic act, it is not clear that such similarities are sufficient either. The idea that there is such an extended act is unclear in these, if not in all, cases.

None of this shows that the sort of meaning change contemplated in these examples could never occur. Perhaps the best place to look would be in works that are explicitly connected such as a trilogy of novels. But the failure of the examples examined raises the question why clear cases are not easier to come by.

Light can be shed on this by returning to the question postponed above, whether condition 2 can hold without condition 1, and whether this would be sufficient for a hypothetical intentionalist to ground a claim that work meaning has been altered. One type of example that has been proposed in support of this possibility is the case in which critics are only able to discern a core artistic property of a work in the light of the preeminence of that property in the work of later writers. Thus, as we have seen above, it has been claimed that the Kafkaesque aspect of earlier writers could only be properly understood in the light of the work of Kafka, or the artistic purpose of the dense and abstruse aspects of Melville's later prose could only be understood in the light of early twentieth century writing.[28] Of course, no one is claiming that we should see the earlier and the later writers as participating in a single artistic act, but it is being claimed that the intention it is most reasonable to attribute to the earlier writer changes with the advent of the later one(s). Does that not suffice, from a hypothetical intentionalist viewpoint, to indicate a change in meaning?

The right thing to say about these cases, as we have already argued, is that, insofar as we are talking about core aspects of the meaning of the earlier works, and not merely optional ways of taking them, significance they come to have for later generations, or the greater appreciation of their artistic properties in virtue of this significance, the meaning was always there. The later works only helped us to see them. But how can a hypothetical intentionalist say this? Only by giving ideal audiences the ability to discover these properties without knowledge of the later works. Such a claim might not be implausible, because it seems to be contingencies that made actual audiences blind to them (if they were).

These considerations create a very narrow hoop through which a defender of intra-*oeuvre* meaning change (completion) would have to be able to jump. One would have to identify a core aspect of a work's meaning, not merely an optional way of taking it, a significance it has, or a greater appreciation of the work based on one or the other of these. Further, it would have to be an aspect of meaning necessarily unavailable to an ideal critic (audience) without knowledge of the artist's later work. We haven't shown that this condition could not be met, but we haven't seen it met. We haven't seen, by the way, that it could not be met in the inter-*oeuvre* case either. What we do know is that it won't be easy to meet it.

Conclusion

In this chapter we have examined many proposals in defense of the idea that the meaning of objects of interpretation change over time. Our chief examples have been artworks. We have not found convincing arguments that their meaning does change. In the next chapter we will look at different examples that are more convincing.

NOTES

1   This characterization is probably too broad, as it could be interpreted to include contextual properties such as being created by so and so at time *t* in connection with the artistic movement *m*, and historical properties, such being original or exerting influence. Both classes of properties are important for proper appreciation, but arguably not part of a work's meaning. We could attempt to refine the characterization to include only representational, symbolic, expressive, and formal properties of a work that must be taken in for proper appreciation. However, in presenting this conception of work meaning, I would rather err in the direction of being overly broad so as not to exclude any properties to which the constructivist would want to appeal. This is not, after all, my own conception of work meaning, which is traditionally historicist in character.

2   Joseph Margolis defends moderate constructivism in works too numerous to do anything but sample. Such a sample should include Margolis (1980, 1995a, 1999a). It is also defended very judiciously in Lamarque (2000).

3   Graham McFee (1980, 1992, 1995) argues for historical constructivism. For a critique of the 1980 piece as well as other constructivist proposals, see Jerrold Levinson (1990: 179–214). McFee is also criticized in Sharpe (1994). McFee's 1992 piece replies to Levinson.

4   I first presented this dilemma in Stecker (1997b).

5   In this section I respond to arguments presented in Percival (2000: 51–4).

6   In the above discussion, I have only shown that certain purported examples of what might be called ascription-dependent properties are not in fact actual examples. Is it possible to show that there could be no such properties? No. With enough stage setting, we could cook one up. Suppose I have a contest. The prize is US$100. The sole criterion for winning is my asserting of an actual person that he or she is the winner. So my asserting that Fred Adams (my former colleague) is the winner makes it true that Fred Adams is the winner. Further, being the winner is now a property of Fred. What is perfectly obvious is that we cannot make interpretations true like that or give works interesting properties this way.

Instead of talking about ascription-dependent properties, perhaps we should be thinking about the broader class of response-dependent properties. Where such properties depend on merely individual reactions, I would suggest they are of the trivial sort discussed above (p. 125). If they are nonindividualistic, they bring us to the territory covered by the "Madagascar arguments" discussed in chapter 5. I refer the reader to that discussion.

7   Margolis (1980, 1995a, 1999a, 199b) is a strong proponent of this view. It is also endorsed in Krausz (1990, 1993) and Lamarque (2000).

8   Thom (2000a: 20) clearly characterizes an intentional object as an object of thought in this second sense. Krausz (1990: 231) suggests that objects-of-interpretation are best thought of as items "as seen in a certain way under specifiable historical circumstances."

9   Margolis emphasizes that intentional objects include this class of things, though I do not know if I have captured here everything he wants to capture with the notion of the intentional.

10   Both Krausz (1993) and Lamarque (2000) endorse this conception of property change.

11   All of these examples are discussed by Krausz (1993: 70–7).

12   Lubin's interpretation, as set out by Krausz, seems to border on the incoherent, or at least the highly implausible. Not only is the happy family in mourning, but the faceless though clearly female figure in the foreground is said to represent Vincent's dead brother.

13   Krausz (1993) does not discuss the acceptability of these interpretations.

14   For an alternative view on this matter see Lamarque (2000), whose position is outlined in note 18 below.

15   There are some nonlogical notions of incompatibility. See Stecker (1997a: 129–31).

16   Margolis draws a very different conclusion than I do claiming that such considerations support indeterminacy and nonbivalence in the interpretive domain.

17   This is a complex issue and I acknowledge that these brief reflections hardly settle the matter. They merely give the gist of a more thorough treatment, and a more decisive argument that I present elsewhere. See Stecker (1992, 1997a: 119–32).

18   In a careful and well-balanced discussion of these same issues, Lamarque comes to a different conclusion, namely, (d) that assigning salience to features of a work might bring about a meaning change in the work (2000: 115). His premises are that, with respect to literary interpretation of a given work, (a) many issues are indeterminate, (b) interpretations concerning these issues should be regarded as lacking in bivalent truth values, and (c) interpretations, by making certain (determinate) features of works salient, impute other features to works with greater or lesser degrees of plausibility (2000: 119). Should we accept Lamarque's claims a–c, and do they support moderate constructivism as d suggests? Lamarque makes these claims following a discussion of Joseph Frank's interpretation of "the long standing critical crux" of the conflicting motives behind Raskolnikov's crime in *Crime and Punishment.* We should certainly accept premise a, since it is established by (mere) fictional incompleteness. Premise b may sometimes also be true, but in any given instance, it depends on what an interpretation is asserting, an issue which theorists of

interpretation attend to too little. Frank is clearly making claims about what Dostoyevsky is doing in the work, and his point in doing it. He is offering and supporting a hypothesis regarding this. If Lamarque is right about the fictional indeterminacy surrounding the issue (and I am not sure he is), then Frank's claims are literally *false*. They could be charitably reconstrued as making a claim about a reasonable way of taking the work, in which case they would be literally *true* (presumably). Premise c is certainly sometimes true, if it can be rephrased by saying that fictional entities are incomplete in literary works; and where this is so, all that can be reasonably done is to suggest (optional) ways of taking works and to argue for the merits of those ways. The main point is that premises a–c do not entail d, and hence do not provide a valid argument to moderate constructivism.

19 Carroll (1999: 43) suggests that the truth of the above interpretation of *The Scarlet Letter* is compatible with imputationalists' claim that we cannot demarcate what is inside or outside the artwork.

20 Note that there could be other reasons for saying that a Freudian interpretation applies to the play, which are not constructivist. For example, if one thinks Freudian theory is true, Shakespeare had some inkling of some of its truths, and incorporated them into his character's psychology, this would not be a constructivist account.

21 See "Artworks and the Future" in Levinson (1990) for a very thorough categorization and discussion of examples. Some of these examples are also discussed in S. Davies (1996).

22 I owe this example to Alan Goldman who presented it in his comments to my paper "Can Artworks undergo Meaning Change," at the 2000 American Philosophical Association Pacific Division Meeting.

23 One might wonder what arguments a historical constructivist might give against the present construal of the examples discussed so far. McFee (1992, 1995), in replying to similar construals by Levinson (1990) and Sharpe (1994), offers three reasons against my construal. One is that the content of a statement ascribing a property changes as the reason for the ascription changes. This challenges the account of the content of a property-concept given above. For McFee, the content is not merely the property but the reasons available for ascribing the property. Second, McFee claims that meaning requires understanding, or, in other words, the applicability of a concept at a time requires that the concept be available for use at that time. This challenges my claim that these are two different matters. Finally, he claims that ascriptions are only meaningful within a critical practice, and this changes over time. Hence meaning also changes.

As far as I can see, McFee simply asserts these three reasons, each of which strikes me as either question begging or counterintuitive or both. As Sharpe points out (1994: 170–1) the first implies that we cannot give further reasons for an ascription or that people cannot believe the same thing, but for different reasons. McFee is willing to accept this, but that does not make it plausible. The second reason seems to draw an absurd distinction between discovering that there are black swans and discovering that there are dinosaurs. We had the concept of a black swan prior to their discovery, so the applicability of the concept predates the discovery. We did not have the concept of a dinosaur prior to the discovery of dinosaurs, so, by McFee's lights, the applicability of the concept begins with the discovery. This not only makes it hard to say what was discovered, but makes essentially similar cases radically different. The last reason relativizes the meaningful application of concepts to practices. This is a claim that obviously requires argument. As McFee offers none, and as the issue of relativism will be taken up in a later chapter, I put this reason aside for now.

24   There are alternative understandings of gracefulness as an aesthetic property. According to one alternative, it has an ineliminable evaluative element. On this construal, the example is not a problem, since it is quite possible that the music is evaluated differently at different times without the music changing.

25   The argument for intra-*oeuvre* meaning change along with examples discussed below are taken from "Work and Oeuvre," in Levinson (1996: 242–73).

26   Not that there is a simple or obvious way of choosing a single ideal audience. For a discussion of the problems, see Stecker (1997a: 197–202).

27   Levinson (1996: 254–5).

28   McFee (1980) uses the Kafkaesque example. Silvers (1990) uses the Melville example. Levinson attempts to reply to the latter by claiming that what has changed is the evaluation of Melville's later prose, not the understanding of its meaning. But this seems wrong, because what came to be appreciated was the point of the convolutions, which is a matter of literary meaning.

Interpretation and Construction in the Law

I now turn to a different arena of interpretation – the law. It is a practice at least as complex as art. In the preceding chapters I have argued against various versions of a constructivist conception of art interpretation. However, as we will see, when it comes to interpreting the law, there is some truth to moderate constructivism. Sometimes interpretations of the law bring about changes in the law. They sometimes do this directly, sometimes through a gradual process of sociopolitical uptake.[1]

Consider, for example, the part of the First Amendment to the United States Constitution that says, "Congress shall make no law respecting the establishment of religion, or prohibiting the free exercise thereof." Both the phrases "respecting the establishment of religion" and "prohibiting the free exercise thereof" are vague or ambiguous. This permits them to be taken in more than one way, and so they have. For example, the latter phrase could be taken more narrowly to forbid the government from passing laws that discriminate against the practice of a religion, or, more broadly, to forbid the government from impeding some religious practices, even though not on the basis of discrimination. In 1990 the US Supreme Court had to decide a case that turned on interpreting the free exercise of language (*Oregon* v. *Smith*, 494 US 872, 878). Oregon had passed a ban on the ingestion of hallucinogenic substances, which did not exempt the religious use of peyote.[2] The law was not passed to discriminate against a particular religion, but it had as an "incidental effect" (as Justice Scalia wrote for the five-member majority of conservative and liberal justices) the impediment of a religious practice. The majority ruled that the Oregon law does not violate the free exercise clause, though even among them there was not agreement on how narrowly the clause should be interpreted. Four other members of the court (which also included conservatives and liberals) interpreted the clause in a broader way.

When courts (or lawyers and scholars) interpret a case like this, are they attempting to clarify the clause in question or are they taking something that is essentially indefinite in its implications (in this case because it is essentially vague or ambiguous) and looking for a good reason to render a determinate judgment? This chapter will argue that sometimes the latter is what is happening, and as a result, interpretations sometimes modify the law.

The constructivism in legal interpretation endorsed here is *not* thoroughgoing. Particular legal items such as statutes, constitutions, and their parts (such as articles or clauses), common law precedents, and so on are utterances and have an utterance meaning. Part of what is involved in interpreting the law is clarifying these individual items, and at least part of what is involved in clarifying these items is identifying their utterance meaning. So there are aspects, or stages, of legal interpretation that are not constructivist all. However, for various reasons having to do with the nature of the objects of legal interpretation, the aims of such interpretation, and its role in adjudication, there are other aspects or stages in the interpretation of the law and these are constructive in character. This is the main thesis the chapter will attempt to establish.

In doing so, I will proceed as follows. We first need to take note of the objects of legal interpretation, because they are more various, and in some ways more complex than the objects of art interpretation. This part of the discussion paves the way for the argument proper, which begins by examining the limitations of interpreting legal items for their utterance meaning, goes on to examine the aims of legal interpretation and the respects in which they differ from the aims of art interpretation. I have argued throughout this book that it is the special aims of a region (subdomain) of the intentional domain that determine the peculiar characteristics of interpretation within that region. The law has a complex set of aims that distinguish interpretation in the law from both art interpretation and the conversational interpretation. Hence identifying the aims of legal interpretation is a crucial part of the argument. We will also take note of two other major differences between interpretations in the two domains: the authority of certain interpreters (judges) in the domain of the law which has no counterpart in the artworld, and the practical consequences of the decisions issued by these interpreters of the law. The argument of the chapter will be that these three features: the aims, the authority, and the consequences of judicial interpretations of the law make a variety of considerations relevant to legal interpretation that imply that it continues to be constructed after its initial making.[3]

Objects of Legal Interpretation

"The law" is ambiguous. When we speak of interpreting the law, we are sometimes referring to what I will call a particular legal item: a statute, a constitutional clause or article, a common law precedent or judicial decision. We are also sometimes referring to groups of items organized along varying principles. If a court is deciding on the constitutionality of a statute, at a minimum, it has to consider the following items: the statute, the relevant part of the constitution, earlier judicial decisions (precedents) that are relevant to this decision. Each item may need interpretation, but the determination of how they collectively bear on the case is also an interpretation, in fact the interpretation that the decision consists in. The law can also refer to a body of laws within a particular legal "compartment" such as liability for emotional damages or copyright law or, for that matter, to the "code" of a legal entity such as the state of Arkansas. This variation in the reference of "the law" implies that an interpreter of the law does not have to answer just one question, but at least three: What are the relevant legal items in a particular case? How should those items be clarified? And how do they bear on (should they be applied to) the case? As will be argued below, one occasion for interpretive construction of the law occurs when answers to the first two questions leaves the answer to the third unsettled. In this case, construction makes something that was indeterminate in its implications more determinate, and so it effects a change in the law.

Before leaving the topic of the objects of legal interpretation, let me mention something that I believe some people think is yet another referent of "the law" (Dworkin 1986), though I doubt that it is. This purported referent can be understood roughly on the model of a genuine ambiguity in the word "morality." We can refer to my moral beliefs as my morality or to society's moral code as the morality of the society. However, we can also ask whether my beliefs or a society's code are *really* part of morality, where the latter use of "morality" refers not merely to what someone *takes* to be right or wrong, but what *is* right or wrong. What is right or wrong might be cashed out in terms of what one would be most justified in asserting to be so or as what conforms to a set of norms it would be most rational to accept. Similarly, with regard to "law," one might hold that in addition to its sometimes referring to legal items or bodies of such items, it sometimes refers to norms or principles implied by the best justified interpretations of those items. I will discuss this view later in this chapter in the section called " An Alternative View: Dworkin's Constructivism," but for now I mention it just to indicate that I am not initially including such (ideal) norms or principles among the objects of legal interpretation.

Utterance Model of Legal Interpretation

If we use the model of artwork meaning set out in earlier chapters, it tells us to think of a statute, a precedent-setting decision, or a constitution as an utterance, or rather, it tells us that they are utterances. In the case of linguistic utterances, the meaning of an utterance is not identical to the linguistic meaning of the sentences that compose it (word sequence meaning). It is not necessarily identical to the intention with which it is uttered (utterer's meaning), because things can get said that are not intended. According to the unified view (see chapter 2, p. 42), the meaning of an utterance is determined by what is successfully intended, conventions in place at the time the utterance is made, and other features of context. There are alternative conceptions of utterance meaning such as hypothetical intentionalism.

On the above model, the meaning of a statute or precedent is its utterance meaning. This implies that its meaning can conceivably diverge from both literal word sequence meaning and intended meaning. There is nothing wrong in thinking of individual legal items as utterances, and this implies that they have an utterance meaning. However, neither art interpretation nor legal interpretation is exclusively concerned with identifying utterance (work) meaning, but this fact plays out very differently in art and the law. In the case of art, it permits a variety of different kinds of interpretation, guided by different aims, of the same work. This is because having a variety of perspectives on the same work is widely believed to enhance the possibilities for appreciating the work. In the case of law, because, for reasons set out below, a single best interpretation is the most desirable outcome, the various aims of adjudication, and the considerations they give rise to, have to be blended together in the same interpretation.

The literature on the interpretation of the law provides an affirmation of this point. I find few endorsements of the idea that the aim of legal interpretation is exclusively to identify utterance meaning. The "textualist" position – the idea that the only thing to be considered in legal interpretation, is what the text of a legal item explicitly says – comes closest to such an endorsement. However, I know of few current theorists who argue for strict textualism, and, even if it is sometimes *endorsed* (Scalia 1997), I doubt that it is now (if it was ever) *practiced.* Some current views are intentionalist (Bork 1984, Alexander 1996, 1998), thinking of law as a species of communication. The many who reject this do not appear to opt for an utterance model either. If a satisfactory model of legal interpretation should take into account everything a judge considers in adjudicating a case, then it is obvious that many other considerations are relevant.

Although there are many "canons" or rules of legal interpretation, there seem to be four main considerations to which interpreters (e.g., judges) appeal.[4] Theories of legal interpretation often place greatest emphasis on one or two of these, though they typically find ways of accommodating the others. Two such considerations have already been mentioned. First, in interpreting the law, one wants to be faithful to the text of a statute or constitution, or, more accurately, to its utterance meaning. I take it this requires attempting to figure out what the legal item actually and explicitly says rather than simply pointing to words on a page, or at least something it could mean when understood fairly literally in its historical/legal context. Second, one wants to be faithful to the law that the authors of a legal text *intended* to promulgate. Third, one wants to be aware of and take into account a law's reception in the courts or the reception of other laws that might have a bearing on the interpretation of the one in question. That is, *precedents* and legal doctrines based on precedents to some extent refine the meaning of existing laws, and these refinements are in fact taken into account. Precedents have variable authority depending on the court they issue from and the customary legal practice of a given society. However, there is no question that precedent adds to the law in some way, and this is taken into account in adjudication. Fourth, there are a variety of considerations that I will call *considerations of prudence, justice and morality*, though they vary greatly in their generality. More will be said about these below.

Any of these considerations might be challenged in a given legal theory, which, after all, is concerned with the question of what considerations *ought* to be appealed to. However, a theory that can explain how these various considerations are all acceptable and hang together seems on the face of it preferable if only because considerations deeply embedded in a practice has at least a prima facie advantage. Unfortunately, while it is patent that all of these considerations are appealed to, it is not at all clear how they hang together.

At this point, it is crucial to think about the aims of legal interpretation if we are to reach a more plausible position or legal interpretation.

How the Law Is Different from Art

I begin to do this by suggesting some ways that the aims of legal interpretation differ from those of art interpretation. We bring a variety of purposes to the interpretation of the law, but these purposes are shaped by different values and circumstances than hold in the case of art interpretation.

Here are two important circumstances (there are no doubt others)[5] in which law is interpreted that set it apart from art interpretation. One is that, among the interpreters of the law are judges, and their interpretations occur in the course of reaching legal decisions. Others who interpret the law, such as lawyers and academics, present interpretations that are by no means divorced from the context of judicial interpretation. This circumstance has several important consequences. First, judges, unlike critics of art and literature, not only make assertions about what the law is, but their rulings have authority in determining the law (however hard people try to distinguish "merely" interpreting the law and making it). As a general rule, the higher the court, the greater the authority. Second, legal interpretations have grave practical consequences that art interpretations usually lack. This rules out inquiry concerning what something (e.g., a statute) could mean as a form of interpretive play valued for its own sake. If it is asked what a statute *could* mean, this is a stage in a larger inquiry concerning (depending on one's view of the aim of such interpretation) what the statute does mean, or what it was intended to mean or how it *should be* taken. Finally, this circumstance also suggests something prima facie unsatisfactory about the view that there is a plurality of equally good interpretations of the law. It certainly does not sound satisfactory for a judge to rule, "According to one impeccable interpretation of the law, your company is liable for damages, but according to an equally good interpretation, you are not liable at all. Since both interpretations are equally good, and I prefer to find you liable, I do so." This is not to say it is impossible for the law to be indeterminate regarding which of two interpretations of it is better. Rather, it is to say that the ideal is to eliminate this indeterminacy, and we should expect legal interpretations to permit procedures that minimize it.[6]

The other circumstance is that legal interpretation often seems to be separable into several stages that do not have an obvious counterpart in the critical interpretation of art. One stage consists in identifying the relevant body of legal items that bear on a case. Since this may not happen all at once, it is a bit misleading to call this a (discrete) stage. As interpretation proceeds, the body of law deemed relevant may expand or contract. (Dworkin [1986: 245–54] gives a nice example of this.) Nothing like this happens in art interpretation.

Another stage is determining what the law is or says. This is the stage I called clarificatory above. It in part consists in identifying the utterance meaning of individual legal items. However, just as we balance an interest in utterance meaning with an interest in intended or speaker's meaning when interpreting some conversational utterances, we also do this when we attempt to clarify laws. To illustrate this clarificatory stage, as well as the interest within it to balance what is said with what is intended, consider a law passed by the Arkansas legislature that contained the language: "all laws . . . are hereby repealed" (Alexander 1996: 377). One issue of clarification is whether the law actually says what it seems to, namely, the all of the Arkansas code is repealed. However, if the Arkansas legislature really did use language that would repeal the entire state legal code, and it did so inadvertently, then the above-mentioned interest in the intention of the legislature comes into play and would, in this case, no doubt override what the statute actually says.

If one may not refer to actual (or perhaps hypothetical) intentions of lawmakers,[7] as well as other aspects of the context in which the law arose, the clarificatory enterprise is bound to be minimal, prior to the consideration of precedent. Once one identifies how words were used in the legal environment at the time the legal item came into existence, the clarificatory enterprise would be over, and law that seems vague or ambiguous would almost invariably remain just that. This is a reason why identifying original context and intent (if possible) of a legal item should be part of clarification. It enhances our chances of identifying laws with a content that is more determinate in its implications prior to the intervention of the judicial process. This is not to say that considerations of text, context, and intention will always render laws determinate. Sometimes even omniscience about intention and context would not do that because the intentions themselves can be vague or ambiguous, and have imperfect application to future cases. In addition, we are not omniscient and the needed information is not always available to us.

The final stage consists in applying the law to a new situation where what the law says (or seems to say under the proposed clarificatory interpretation) leaves it unclear how a judge should rule (hard cases).[8] The difference between this and the other stages can be illustrated as follows. While language quoted above from a law passed by the Arkansas legislature raises an issue of what the law is, not how it applies to a particular case, the famous case of *Riggs* v. *Palmer* seems to raise an issue of application. Here the law appears to be silent about whether a murderer who would otherwise be the legal heir to the person murdered remains in that position after being convicted of the murder. The legislators who crafted the relevant inheritance law do not appear to have considered such a situation, and the law contained no language that addresses it. The courts had to apply the inheritance law to a circumstance about which it is silent, or at least not explicit. The majority of the appeals court that made the final decision in the case found the murderer did not have the right to inherit under the law.

Oregon v. *Smith* (1990) is an example of the distinction at the constitutional level.[9] A part of Justice Scalia's interpretation in this case is clarificatory, as it is based on an examination of original context. However, that part of the argument simply leads to the conclusion that the narrow reading of the free exercise clause is "permissible." The crucial part of the remainder of the argument that is intended to take us from a permissible reading of the clause to a correct or required reading hinged on the proper understanding, the weight, and especially the relevance, to be given to conflicting precedents. Here, unfortunately, there was no consensus, even among the majority. While it is arguable that one side got the precedents wrong, clarification of the clause itself will not be decisive in choosing between the narrow or broad reading. Further considerations are needed to apply the law to the case in question.[10]

The distinction between clarifying and applying or making more determinate might seem to be eliminated by adopting any number of views about how one should settle what a law is. There is the literalist or textualist view, sometimes adopted by a dissenting judge in *Riggs*, that if a law contains no explicit language regarding the circumstance in question, the circumstance makes no difference to the application of the law. Hence the murderer remains the legal heir in virtue of the law explicitly saying nothing to the contrary. (However, that judge also reasoned that to deprive the murderer of the inheritance would be to punish him twice for the same crime, a consideration that goes beyond the inheritance law itself, though one that, it might be argued, appeals to other relevant law prohibiting such punishment.)

Alternatively, there are various strategies for understanding statutes so that they have implicit content. These would make, at least many and perhaps all, questions of application matters of what a statute implicitly says. What remains true is that there is no way of exhaustively identifying what the law implicitly contains, and the impetus for extending what we currently think it contains comes from questions about its application to real or hypothetical new circumstances. So unless we adopt the literalist view, something like the several stages of legal interpretation remains intact, though it might be redescribed as extending the implicit content of a statute by asking how it should be applied to a case containing new circumstances.

Digression: Indeterminacy in Art and the Law

A reader may feel a worry at this point, and we should digress for a moment to address it. Chapter 6 contained an extended argument that artworks are *not* indeterminate in their properties and hence, one could not appeal to a premise asserting such indeterminacy in an argument for a moderate constructivism in art interpretation. In the present chapter, I appear to be arguing that laws are indeterminate, and this fact can be used to argue for moderate constructivism in legal interpretation. This may give rise to the suspicion that there is an inconsistency or double standard in play that undermines the argument in one or the other chapter. However, there is no such inconsistency and no double standard.

This can be seen if we take care in noticing to what "indeterminacy" is being applied in the two cases, or putting it another way, the sense of "indeterminacy" in question. In the last chapter I was concerned with the view that artworks have an ontological peculiarity, namely, there is no fact of matter whether they have or lack certain properties. Call this ontological indeterminacy. This is what I opposed in chapter 6, and I am *not* claiming in the present chapter that laws are ontologically indeterminate. If someone were to claim this, the same arguments deployed earlier could be used again. What I am claiming for laws is indeterminacy in their implications or applications to cases. This derives from their being vague or ambiguous in certain respects, inexplicit in others, and so on. There is nothing ontologically peculiar about this. Rather, it is a thoroughly predictable feature of the use of language in complex situations.

It is perfectly true that artworks possess something analogous to indeterminacy in application, which I also discussed in chapter 6. For example, the instructions scores give to performers do not determine every aspect of a performance. So neither artworks nor laws are ontologically indeterminate, and both are capable of indeterminacy in application. The different implications this has for the fate of moderate constructivism in art and legal interpretation is not a consequence in differences in indeterminacy, but, as I have already mentioned, in differences in the aims and authority of interpreters, and the consequences of interpretations, in the two domains.

Aims of Legal Interpretation and Conceptions of the Law

Let me summarize the several aims of legal interpretation that my discussion has suggested. One is to clarify the explicit content of an individual legal item such as a statute (section of a statute), an article of a constitution (or a clause within it), and so on. Interpretation is not always needed here, because it may be perfectly clear what the content of such an item is – what the law is. When it is not clear, one job of interpretation is to make it clear.

Second, interpretation is concerned with bringing the law, not necessarily one legal item but the total relevant law, to bear on a case to reach a decision. This is a different matter than the clarification of an individual item, for a number of reasons. Even if the relevant law is restricted to a single item such as a single statute, the item may not be explicit about the law in the case in question as it was not in *Riggs* v. *Palmer*. However, often a number of different legal items are relevant to a case. Just which items these are may be a controversial matter, and resolvable only in the light of interpretation. This was precisely the case in *Oregon* v. *Smith*. In addition to legal items not being explicit about what the law is, they may have to be weighed up against each other if they point in different legal directions.

Where the law, even after it is clarified, is not explicit about how the case should be decided, aims beyond the seeking of clarity about explicit content come to the fore. One such aim is making the law as determinate in application as possible. The law is determinate in a case if one decision in the case is made preferable over the alternatives. A second aim, which derives from the great practical consequences of legal judgments, is to reach decisions that are morally acceptable or just.[11]

Different conceptions of the law and its interpretation treat these aims and the interpretive desiderata they bring forward differently.

One conception sharply distinguishes between interpreting the law and other desiderata that ought or are permitted to enter into reaching a judicial decision (Alexander 1996, 1998, Coleman and Leiter 1996, Hart 1961). Interpreting the law is determining what it says, explicitly or implicitly. Proponents of this view, of course, may differ about the criteria for deciding what the law says. However, what the law says may turn out to be unclear; it may be clear but fail to determine a decision in a given case; it may be patently unjust so that its authority comes into question. In some or all of these cases, other desiderata are legitimately brought to bear in reaching a legal decision. (There is a further controversy whether reasoning with these further desiderata is legal reasoning or goes beyond legal reasoning without it being an inappropriate reasoning for judges to engage in. This controversy will not concern us. For discussion, see Postema 1996.)

An alternative conception of legal interpretation simply sees all reasoning relating to a decision as part of interpreting the law (Dworkin 1986, Moore 1996, Sunstein 1989, Waldron 1996). There is no distinction to be

drawn, on this view between figuring out what the law is (says) and bringing further desiderata to bear. All desiderata that count toward a determination of the law are relevant to an interpretation of it. (There is an ambiguity
in the phrase "a determination of what the law is." When a court, especially
the highest court such as the US Supreme Court, issues a ruling, it is law,
hence the ruling determines the law, and all the reasoning that the majority
engages in went into determining that law. However, a different sense of
"determination" is at work than when we speak of what an interpretation
determines. The ruling of a high court *makes* something law; an interpretation *asserts* that something is law.)

There is an intermediate view. It agrees with the first conception in claiming that we can distinguish between reasoning that aims to identify what
the law is (prior to a particular judicial decision) and other reasoning, for
example, reasoning that aims to make a determinate decision where the law
is indeterminate, or reasoning that aims to remedy an injustice in current
law. However, it agrees with the second conception in claiming that both
kinds of reasoning are part of interpreting the law.

The differences between these conceptions raise important issues in the
philosophy of law, especially concerning how the law should be conceived.
(My own opinion aligns with the intermediate view.) However, it seems to
be agreed on all hands that there are a number of distinct kinds of inquiry
potentially relevant to reaching a legal decision. If it can be agreed what
these are, and when it is appropriate for a given consideration to kick in
(though about this, there may not be general agreement), it is not terribly
important whether or not we call what is going on "interpretation." On
the other hand, "interpretation" is used broadly enough these days to make
that appellation appropriate. So for the purpose of setting out a theory of
legal interpretation, the distinctions made by these different views is more
semantic than substantive.

Precedent and Judicial Authority

Precedents are earlier judicial decisions that carry some sort of authority,
though the degree of authority varies. When we are concerned with the
interpretation of law that originally comes into existence independently
of precedent-setting legal decisions, such as law established by a written
constitution or by statutes passed by a legislature, precedent plays a com-
plicating role. A precedent relevant to a given case contains an interpretation either of the very legal item we are attempting to interpret or of
related law. Thus it makes an assertion about what the law says or about

its permissible or required application. It is always possible to look at the grounds of this assertion and reevaluate it. However, precedents have a standing, in virtue of whatever authority they possess, which marks them off from mere interpretative claims such as those made by critics in interpreting an artwork, by lawyers in a courtroom, or by academics in a law review article. The authority of a precedent may give added weight to a view of how a law is to be clarified, or, alternatively, on how a law, which initially was or seemed indeterminate for a range of cases, should be made more determinate. (In clarifying the Arkansas law mentioned above, the courts found that it did not repeal that state's legal code; *Riggs* seems to have accomplished the latter feat of rendering the inheritance law more determinate.)

In keeping with the idea that the authority of a precedent is a factor in determining what the law is independently of its persuasiveness as an interpretive assertion, there are some precedents that have played such a fundamental role in shaping later legal opinion and expectations, that they make law whether or not they were initially good interpretations of existing law. For example, Robert Bork, in the course of his confirmation hearings, mentions a number of precedents he says *cannot* be overturned whether or not they were correct interpretations of the US constitution at the time they were issued. He says that the commerce clause cases cannot be overruled and the way the court has applied this clause to overturn state law cannot cut back. He makes the same claim for equal protection cases. Bork also says that the incorporation doctrine by which the Bill of Rights is applied to the states is thoroughly established (Patterson 1996: 141). The point in mentioning Bork's opinion here is that it supports the idea that precedent plays a role in shaping what the law is in virtue of its authority, and independently, to some extent, of its persuasiveness as an interpretive assertion.

The degree of authority, possessed by precedent, is not permanent. In weighing the role a precedent should play in determining a new decision, a court can attempt to diminish the authority of a precedent (as the current US Supreme court is doing in the case of some of the items Bork appeared to regard as virtually sacrosanct, such as the commerce and equal protections clauses).

These considerations suggest that the role of precedent in interpreting (adjudicating) the sort of written law mentioned above is not uniform. It can simply make existing law clearer, it can make it more determinate, and it is conceivable that it can virtually make new law by its subsequent social uptake even if the interpretative claims it originally made were false or not adequately established.

Considerations of Prudence, Morality, and Justice: Judicial Liberty

Considerations of this type were already broached in the discussion of precedent. When a precedent or a legal doctrine derived from precedent becomes widely accepted so that it provides a basis for many subsequent legal decisions, when it gives rise to social or political institutions, then the consequences of overturning it can be very bad, and the dashing of expectations thereby created can be unjust. This would be especially true if the precedent-setting decision and its subsequent effects corrected what has become widely acknowledged to be an injustice. This is part of the explanation of the authority of such precedents.

It is not, however, the only situation where it is permissible for seemingly extra-legal consideration to play a role in adjudication. The majority in *Riggs* appears to refer to such consideration, for, when quoting Blackstone, they assert, "'When some collateral matter arises out of general words, and happens to be unreasonable, then the judges are in decency to conclude that the consequence was not foreseen by the parliament, and, therefore, they are at liberty to expound the statute by equity . . .'" (quoted from Patterson 1996: 173). That is, instead of taking silence in the law of inheritance about the rights of murderers to inherit from their victims, to mean there is such a right, since granting such a right would be unreasonable (i.e., patently unjust, not to say unwise), a judge should conclude that the statute is indeterminate (i.e., the legislature in passing the law failed to address the issue) which can be permissibly rendered determinate in the reasonable (just and wise) way using the "*liberty* to expound the statute by equity."

It is not necessary here to attempt to figure out the extent of this liberty (judicial discretion), nor am I competent to do so, but it seems to be widely recognized that it exists. It is mentioned in legal decisions and by writers on legal interpretation from many different theoretical stances on the subject, though not all are willing to call the use of this liberty "interpretation" (Alexander 1996: 1998).

A Constructivist Conception of Legal Interpretation

These considerations provide an argument that a moderate constructivist conception of interpretation, much like the one rejected in chapter 6 for literature and other arts, holds in the case of the law. The law is gradually

constructed by the acts of makers of constitutions, legislation, judicial decisions, and the reaction of other branches of government to these decisions.
The reason for the constructivist character of the law and its interpretation
has to do with its aims, the authority of judicial interpreters, and the social
consequences of the interpretations. These create quite different circumstances than hold in the case of art interpretation.

Some of the aims of legal interpretation seem to push us in different
directions. On the one hand, we value the rule of law, that is, the idea that
the rules we collectively are expected to obey cannot be altered simply
because an individual believes it would be better to have a different rule in
force. To bring about the desired alteration would typically require a legislative process. For this reason we value clarificatory interpretive aims in the
hope of fixing the law as much as possible at the point that legal items such
as constitutions and especially statutes were first confirmed or passed. On
the other hand, as Richard Posner has pointed out, "a statute is necessarily
drafted in advance of, and with imperfect application for the problems that
will be encountered in, its application" (quoted from Patterson 1996: 175).
This means that sometimes a legal item even after clarification, will not
determine a single preferred judicial decision. However, because of the
practical consequences of such decisions it is undesirable that the law in a
given case be open to several equally good interpretations, since that will
make the inevitable decision look, and in fact be, arbitrary. So as to minimize (though not eliminate) this, the law is open to further construction
by precedent and judicial liberty.

While these different aims may seem to pull in different directions, they
are in fact combinable. They are unfortunately combinable in more than
one way. They can be regarded as creating a set of lexically ordered considerations so that, say, if the law as it exists at its origin is clear and determinate for a given case, that settles the matter, but if not, other considerations
may kick in. On the other hand, one could think that one has to weigh all
relevant considerations on a case by case basis. The former view is too
simple, because, once a law has a rich judicial history, it may have already
undergone a change in its legal properties. So, after *Riggs* the inheritance
law had undergone such a change that should not be ignored in later decisions. Perhaps some extra weight can be built into the textual and, to the
extent that they can be clearly identified, intentional, considerations.

If these claims are plausible, it would follow that as with interpretation
of the arts, there is not one interpretive question to be asked about the law,
but several. Certainly the question "What is the law?"/"What is law *L*
(what does *L* say?)" is asked of a particular legal item, but this question
should be time-indexed in recognition of the fact that different answers

might be correct at different times. The question might be supplemented by the further question "What has the law become?" Then there is the additional question, which will sometimes arise, of how the law should be extended, applied, made determinate in this (these) case(s). What these questions show is how the aims of legal interpretation inevitably lead to the construction of the law even while maintaining respect for the law as it was originally written and intended.

Part of the explanation of the constructivist character of legal interpretation lies in its aims, but part lies in the authority of some of those who interpret the law. I won't dwell on this now since it was already mentioned in the discussion of precedent. The point is that, besides making claims about the law, judicial interpretations of the law have a degree of authority that is not necessarily proportional to the plausibility of the arguments for the interpretive claims. When the Supreme Court in the US, for example, issues a decision overturning a law passed by Congress, or limiting (extending) its application, that decision has the effect of law until further events occur (if they do) that supersede the decision. This is true, independent of whether there is consensus about the persuasiveness of the Court's arguments for the decision.

Finally, the social consequence of judicial legal interpretations, in the form of expectations, institutions, subsequent legal decisions, and so on is the third factor that renders legal interpretation constructive. These consequences give the interpretations from which they result added authority, once again not necessarily proportional to the plausibility of the interpretations considered as truth claims.

A moderate constructivist view of legal interpretation implies that interpretations of the law (or more specifically, judicial interpretation) bring about changes in the law. But exactly what changes? Is it always a particular legal item that changes? Or, alternatively, can the *addition* of a precedent change a body of law without changing any individual legal item? If and when individual legal items do change, what properties of these items change? Answering these questions will help clarify the constructivist view proposed here.

I take it, and I am certainly ready to stand corrected, that here there is a significant difference between common law and statutory law. In the case of the former, the mere *addition* of a new precedent can change a particular body of law by doing such things as extending it to cases it had not previously addressed. Such is what appears to have happened in the *McLoughlin* case, where emotional injury liability was extended to cases where the injury occurred away from the scene of an accident, and where prior emotional injury rulings do not dictate this outcome (Dworkin 1986:

240–54). This happened without the legal properties of earlier precedents changing, but rather because a new precedent was made.

Regarding statutory law, two different views are possible. On one view, which I favor, the most common case is that constructive, as opposed to purely clarificatory, interpretations bring about changes in particular legal items. I suspect this is also true in the case of constitutional law. An alternative view is that such interpretations make additions to a relevant body of law, thereby changing the law of (say) inheritance or equal protection without changing the legal properties of a particular legal item previously in existence. On this view *Riggs* does not change the legal properties of the New York State inheritance statute. It simply adds to the inheritance law. The problem with this latter view is to explain how an *interpretation of the statute* results in a state of affairs in which inheritance law changes, but the statute is left untouched. Just as clarificatory interpretations of a legal item discover properties possessed by the item, constructive interpretations of the item alter its legal properties.

If the US Supreme Court restricts the application of a statute, as it did recently with the Americans with Disabilities Act, ruling out the option of individuals suing states under the act (Board of Trustees of the *University of Alabama* v. *Garrett* no. 99–1240), then, by this decision the court made the statute more determinate in virtue of ruling out that it could have this application, assuming that prior to this decision, the exact scope of the statute was indeterminate. This case, in fact, contains an interesting mix of clarificatory and constructive interpretation. Regarding the former, the court noted that the Americans with Disabilities Act (ADA) says and was intended to say that states could be sued for violations of the act. However, in finding that Congress does not have the power to make states liable in such cases, was the Court engaged in constructive or clarificatory interpretation of the Constitution? This is obviously a controversial matter, but I suspect one would be hard put to find either clear language (i.e., something the relevant clauses of the constitution clearly say), a clearly identifiable intention, or even a clear set of precedents that decisively support the Court's interpretation, which makes a twofold claim about the Constitution. First, that the Constitution does not permit Congress to place a burden on states beyond conformity with the Constitution, and second that the Constitution is not necessarily violated when a state engages in discrimination against a disabled person. (The dissenting opinion in the case disagreed with both claims and appealed to the same precedents.)

If in reaching this interpretation, the Court gives greater determinacy to clauses of the constitution than they had prior to the ruling, then those clauses acquire legal properties that they did not have prior to the ruling (while also altering the legal properties of the statute under consideration, the ADA). One can appeal to just those properties to justify further rulings.

Similarly, in *Oregon* v. *Smith* (1990), the Court examined what is certainly an ambiguous clause of the Constitution, the free exercise clause of the First Amendment. In deciding that the clause should be understood more narrowly to prohibit laws intended to discriminate against the practice of a religion, not laws that impede some religious practices, but not on the basis of discrimination, it made it more determinate by narrowing down just what the clause prohibits. The clause seems to acquire, in virtue of the decision, a more precise legal property regarding the legislation it rules in or out.

An interesting question arises in the case of decisions that are (or at least many think are) clearly mistaken, such as the *Lochner* decision, and come to be recognized as mistaken (or at least are superseded) at a later date. Here we seem to have a case where the legal properties of a constitutional clause (the Due Process clause) change as a result of the decision, and then change again when the decision is superseded (in the case of *Lochner*, roughly thirty years later). Further, this change does not actually require indeterminacy in the relevant legal item, for, if the decision is mistaken, it claims an interpretation is permissible, when in fact it is not. This mistake may be made with respect to an item that either has determinate application to the case in hand (but not perceived as such) or does not have determinate application to the case. Where such a mistake occurs, do we really have a change in the legal properties of the item that we seem to have? We do. Though the *Lochner* decision made a mistaken interpretive claim, it still made law, and in doing so gave the Due Process clause legal properties for approximately thirty years. Just as may happen to other precedents good and bad, it lost authority after that point, which, as should be no surprise, brought about a further change in the legal properties of the clause.

Although a rationale for constructive interpretation in the law is to remove inevitable indeterminacies in the application of the law to actual cases, indeterminate application is not required for construction to occur, as already illustrated by *Lochner*. It is also illustrated, with special clarity, by the way certain parts of the constitution are now construed. Consider the Eleventh Amendment. It says, in so many words, that "the judicial power of the United States shall not be construed to extend to any suit . . . commenced or prosecuted against one of the United States, by a citizen of *another* state, or by a citizen or subject of any *foreign* state" (my italics). The utterance meaning of the amendment could not be clearer in saying that a state cannot be sued by a citizen of another state or a foreign country. It is equally clear that it does *not* say that a citizen of a state cannot sue that state. Nevertheless, precedent (established by the exercise of judicial liberty) has extended the legal force of the amendment to include the latter prohibition (though without making the prohibition absolute). All, including those justices and theorists who think of themselves as textualists or strict constructionists, recognize this extension.

The features that render legal interpretation constructive also set it apart from art interpretation. Art interpretations have neither the same aims, the same authority, nor the same social consequences as do some legal interpretations. Art interpretations are claims, conjectures, or suggestions about what artworks could or do or are intended to mean, or their significance to some group. Claims of this sort can offer new ways of taking a work, but are incapable of changing its fundamental artistic properties. In looking at constructivists' arguments about art interpretation, we saw that they failed because they failed to identify anything interpreters of art do, or an authority they have, that is capable of being meaning changing (or creating). The case is quite different with some legal interpretation.

Michael Krausz has pointed out that constructivism is compatible with both monism and pluralism (1993, 2000). That is, one can be a constructivist about interpretation in some domain, while believing either that there is a single correct interpretation for a given item or, alternatively that there are several acceptable interpretations of it. I pointed out in chapter 2 that monism and pluralism are not themselves always incompatible. However, constructivists in the arts usually favor pluralism (or relativism) and oppose monism. With regard to legal interpretation, the rationale for constructivism is to make the law more determinate. Ideally, one hopes that a single best interpretation can be reached. This is not to say that this ideal interpretation is always available, much less actually achieved. It is also not to say that construction only occurs in the face of such indeterminacy or that it always effectively removes it.

An Alternative View: Dworkin's Constructivism

In the enormously important *Law's Empire* (1986), Ronald Dworkin also offers a constructivist conception of the law and legal interpretation. My view bears some similarities to his. However, there are some very important differences. I should explain why my version of constructivism is preferable to Dworkin's in the sense of offering a better account of legal interpretation. The first task at hand is to sketch the main elements of his view.

Dworkin calls his approach "Law as Integrity," which ascribes an overarching aim to the interpretation of the law: making it the best it can be. (He ascribes a similar aim to art interpretation, and for that reason believes it to be constructive as well.) Dworkin thinks of his understanding of legal interpretation as constructive because it is tied to this aim. He also calls it "creative" interpretation (1986: 50–1). When we interpret, we are not simply trying to identify what someone meant, for example, when a piece of legislation was passed. If we were, we would be involved in "conversational" interpretation, which Dworkin regards as a poor model for legal interpretation.[12]

Because Dworkin endorses the above-mentioned overarching aim, some have taken him to be committed to the position that legal interpretation is virtually unconstrained by what laws actually say, and how they have been interpreted in the past (Alexander 1996: 400). However, this would be a misunderstanding of the view Dworkin advances in *Law's Empire*. The pursuit of making law "the best it can be" is undertaken via two subsidiary aims: fit and justification. "Fit" serves as a constraint on interpretation that requires close examination of what laws say and earlier judicial opinions.

When a judge formulates an interpretation, for Dworkin, what is formulated is a *principle* regarding people's rights and duties that ideally covers the case at hand, the law as written (in the case of written law) and past precedent, and that shows "the community's structure of institutions and decisions" in the best light "from the standpoint of political morality" (1986: 254). In easy cases, for example, where a statute, such as the speed limit law, creates a clear duty that is not overly burdensome, serves a clear public interest, and is not in conflict with other parts of the law, fit does all the work. Dworkin would say that a judge is still interpreting the law in such cases, while others would not say this (Patterson 1996), but Dworkin would not deny that the correct interpretation is obvious. Hard cases occur when more than one interpretation – more than one principle regarding rights and duties – survive the threshold test of fit. Issues of fit are still relevant and may be decisive. For example, suppose that a judge is trying an emotional injury case, and more than one principle fits this case and past precedent quite well.[13] However, when we expand consideration to personal injury cases more generally, or to other compartments of the law, one principle may provide an overall better, if not perfect, fit. This is a consideration in its favor, quite possibly a decisive one.

There will be times when considerations of fit fail to be decisive. These are occasions that I described earlier in terms of the indeterminacy of the law in which judges have no choice but to exercise judicial liberty. Dworkin describes these occasions as ones where a judge has to decide on a principle based on considerations of "substantive political morality" (1986: 248).

This is what Dworkin has in mind when he speaks of the (second subsidiary) aim of justification. Even here there are two different considerations that may potentially diverge: consideration of abstract justice and considerations of fairness by which Dworkin means conformity to the moral consensus (where such exists) in society at large.

Where does Dworkin's conception of legal interpretation differ from the one I have proposed? The guiding question for an interpreter of the law for Dworkin is: What principle makes the legal material at hand the best it can be (given the subsidiary aims of fit and justification)?

My alternative is more piecemeal. When it comes to written law such as statutes, one wants to know what the law says (roughly its utterance meaning) and (to the extent possible) what it is intended to say and how it is intended to be applied (its utterer's or speaker's meaning). The weight these two items have varies in different, even in very similar, political entities,[14] but it is likely that both need to be taken into consideration to some extent for the purpose of determining what the law is, if only because they can diverge, and when they do, we have to decide which to give more weight. To the extent that legal interpretation is confined to these items, it is not constructive at all. However, the law can change as a result of its interpretation in the courts, and the law can be indeterminate, that is, its application may be left open even after we determine its sense and intent (including precedent-determined sense). It is within the authority of courts to create precedents, and in the exercise of judicial liberty that legal interpretation becomes constructive.

Why shouldn't we prefer Dworkin's more unified, and for that reason more elegant, conception of legal interpretation? There are two problems with Dworkin's theory. First, it is essential that he have a plausible account of "fit," which distinguishes it from "justification." Without such a distinction, he is far more exposed to the criticism cited above that legal interpretation in his hands becomes unconstrained by what laws say. Yet, his account of "fit" always has something tenuous about it. Dworkin denies that we are ever engaged in "conversational" interpretation or the identification of "speaker meaning" when interpreting the law. Yet he recognizes that it is standard practice to consider legislative intent when interpreting statutes, and in some political states (such as the United States) somewhat formal procedures have been developed to identify this via committee reports and the statements of sponsors or managers of bills. When it comes to identifying "legislative intent" the question that needs to be asked is: What did the legislative body intend or what intention does the legislative record reveal? This looks like an attempt to identify speaker's or utterer's meaning, but such an understanding is ruled out by Dworkin's approach. The question

Dworkin (1986: 336) tells us to ask is: What convictions would *justify* what a legislature has done consistent with the legislative record? Even if one rejects intentionalist interpretation in the law, a similar problem arises for Dworkin when it comes to reading statutes, to textual interpretation or the identification of utterance meaning. The question that needs to be asked is: What does the statute say, but the question Dworkin tells us we should ask is: What "*justification* fits and flows through that statute, and if possible is consistent with other legislation in force" (338; my italics). The aim of justification tends to swallow up the aim of fit, although Dworkin needs some distinction between them for reasons just cited.

The second problem concerns the identification of the law at a given moment in the history of a political entity. This is obviously a tricky matter. The issue is whether Dworkin's position helps to clarify this difficult issue. One of the things that motivates Dworkin to develop his theory is his disagreement with a number of legal theories, but especially legal positivism, that imply that in hard cases (which require the exercise of what I called judicial liberty) there is no law, until a judicial decision has been made. Dworkin is certainly not obviously wrong in opposing this view, but how does he answer the question "What is the content of the law in such cases?"

One possible answer mentioned earlier, is that the content of the law includes not just what is explicitly stated in a statute, for example, but what is implicitly stated there. Some develop this point by referring the actual and hypothetical intentions of legislators (how they would fashion the law had they thought about the specific application at hand), but this approach obviously would not be acceptable to Dworkin. An alternative that might be more appealing is to say that the law is what an ideal interpreter, who accepts Law as Integrity, would decide in the case at hand. Dworkin believes that in most, if not all cases, there is such a best interpretation, and that is his ground for believing that the law is more determinate than is sometimes claimed.

However, the question that now needs asking is: Should the law be *identified* with this best interpretation, assuming for argument's sake that it exists. It seems obvious that the answer is *no*. For suppose the actual decision in the case is different from the ideally best decision; suppose even that it is arrived at through rather shoddy reasoning. Under the right circumstances, nevertheless, the actual decision will have the force of law, that is, be law. Further, the courts may never reach the "best interpretation," so it never comes to have the force of law. Dworkin might say that the actual decision is not law, because it *shouldn't* be treated as a precedent, though it may eventually solidify into law if it becomes an integral part of the legal/political institutions of the state.[15] However, whether the decision is law really depends on how it is treated, not on how it should be treated. *Lochner* made law, mistaken though it was.

Law as integrity does not provide a satisfactory answer to the question "What is the law?" It either incorrectly identifies what law is, or it is silent about how interpretation constructs the law (when it does).

One can summarize the preceding discussion as follows. One can think of Dworkin's theory of legal interpretation as having two main aims: first, to give an account of what is (and ought to be) going on when the law is interpreted, and second, to provide a theory of what the law is, derived from the theory of legal interpretation. The first problem noted above challenges Dworkin's success in meeting the first aim. The second challenges his success in achieving the second.[16] It is because Dworkin's theory fails in achieving its chief aims that it should not be preferred to the theory offered here.

The Relevance of Intention: Con and Pro

There are many theories of legal interpretation other than Dworkin's. I have referred to some of these in notes and attempted there to indicate how some of these are oriented with respect to my own view. However, detailed examination of these theories is beyond the scope of this chapter. In the remainder of the chapter I want examine two objections to the theory of legal interpretation endorsed here. Both concern the place of intention in legal interpretation. I focus on intention because it seems to be the most contentious element among the various considerations that I claim to be relevant in interpreting the law. Even very conservative theorists find ways of taking precedent and even judicial discretion or liberty into account, while arguing that interpretation strictly speaking is a matter of identifying original intent (Alexander 1996, 1998, Bork 1984). More liberal theorists leave room for textual interpretation even when claiming intention is out of bounds (Waldron 1996).

Anti-intentionalists argue that there is no place for the identification of actual, historical intentions in the correct theory of legal interpretation (Dworkin 1986, Moore 1996, Waldron 1996). They would fault me for attempting to give it one. Some intentionalists argue that it is incoherent to attempt to give anything else a place. They would fault me for attempting to do so. I consider first the anti-intentionalist's argument.

One caveat before I proceed further. Although I believe the actual (shared) intention of lawmakers is relevant to legal interpretation, if it turned out, for whatever reason (and there are several possible ones), that I am wrong about this, it would not effect my overall position. This is because I recognize that there are situations where intention plays no role in determining utterance meaning (see chapter 2, p. 48). If intention is irrelevant to legal interpretation, then the clarificatory part of legal interpretation would consist of the determination of utterance meaning by looking at context and convention at the time a legal item is created.

Arguments against the relevance of intentions

One problem for identifying original intent in the context of legal interpretation is that we are normally concerned with the acts of a public body composed of many individuals. We are concerned with a group or shared intention, rather than an intention of an individual. How does one identify this shared intention, and is it even plausible to suppose that such an intention exists as opposed to the many, conceivably divergent intentions of individual lawmakers? If it does exist, beyond looking at the text of the legal item (e.g., the statute), how does one identify this intention? There is the legislative record in the case of statutes, but how does one decide if something in the record identifies the group or shared intention or if it merely identifies an individual intention?

There are two different anti-intentionalist conclusions that these considerations might be used to support. One is that one should not regard legislative acts as intentional at all. The second does not deny that they are intentional but claims that the actual intentions with which laws are made are not relevant, or should not be considered, in their interpretation. If any intention is relevant, it is one that interpreters *construct* from the historical facts.

The argument for the first conclusion (Waldron 1996), that much legislation is not to be regarded as intentional at all, derives from a combination of empirical facts about the modern legislature, and hypothetical voting procedures, which attempt to distance individual intentions to vote a certain way from the aggregate result. The empirical facts emphasized are two: first, that legislators are a "diverse body of people drawn from different groups in a heterogeneous and multi-cultural society" who are not "transparent to each other" (1996: 333). Second, that because of the "large part played by compromise, logrolling and last minute amendment in contemporary legislation" its product is not analogous to "one person's coherent intention" (1996: 337). Abstracting from these particulars, Waldron points out that even ordinary voting procedures can result in legislation that corresponds to nobody's (initial) preference.

However, even if the resulting law corresponds to no legislator's first choice, it does normally correspond to the will of the majority, taking into account what is politically possible given everyone's views. This, however, is claimed to be a contingent fact of current voting procedures. We can imagine a different procedure in which there is a preliminary discussion during which all issues likely to provoke division are identified, followed by general debate. Members would then feed their votes on various issues into a machine (the legislation machine), which would produce a statute in its final form and promulgate it automatically to judges, officials, and the general population (1996: 336). The point of this procedure is that there is no statute formulated in advance that ever receives an up or down vote, and so it is harder to claim that there is a group intention to make such a statute law or that it is intended to be understood one way rather than another.

How do these various considerations add up to an argument that legislation is not to be regarded as intended at all? We can reconstruct the argument as follows:

1. We can conceive of a procedure, via the legislation machine, in which legislation is produced without its being intended.
2. Because of the composition of modern legislatures, the nature of their procedures, and the complexity of the legislation produced, laws are actually produced in a way more like the legislation machine process than like the expression of a coherent intention.
3. Therefore, legislation is best understood as legislation without intention.

Are the premises of this argument true, and does the conclusion follow?

The conclusion does not strictly follow. The reason for this is that we have been given no idea when a bunch of individual intentions yields a group or shared intention. It is both implausible and unnecessary to claim that there are never group intentions (nor does the argument claim this). If the management at a corporation decides to hide a damaging fact about a product, then it is not just the individuals who are responsible for this, but the corporation as well, and the guilty intentions include a shared intention to deceive. Where at least two people engage in a common action that requires *a degree of coordination, mutual commitments, meshing subplans and common knowledge of these*, it becomes plausible to speak of a group or shared intention. There are theories available that make more precise the conditions for their being such an intention and for identifying it (Bratman 1999, Gilbert 1989, 2000). Since premise 2 is, of necessity, cast in terms of degrees of similarity, it still might be that actual (and all likely) legislative circumstances satisfy these conditions.[17]

Even in the case of a voting process using the legislation machine, it is plausible that some shared intentions are in play, for example, to decide on legislation regarding particular issues. However, what is not in play is the crucial shared intention when it comes to matters of interpretation: to decide on a bill with a specific content mutually understood as having that content (or at least having a content which may or may not perfectly match the actual content). In the case of actual legislation considered by modern legislators, are such shared intentions in play? If so, is it merely a contingent fact that they are? The answers to these questions are, respectively, yes and no. These answers show that premise 2 of the above argument is false.

In modern legislatures there may be many forces that shape the legislation that is actually voted on, but such legislation is carefully formulated and revised at each stage of the process before being voted on. The purpose of this process is to have something with a specific content up for vote, and a mutual understanding of what this is. Nor is this a mere accident. It reflects a standing desire for legislation that is maximally coherent in its own right and consistent with the rest of the law, and also to hold legislatures collectively responsible for the laws they pass or fail to pass. These goals are promoted by our actual practices and undermined by the legislation machine procedures. This suggests that the concept of shared intentions with respect to items with a mutually understood content is crucial to an acceptable legislative process. This in turn suggests a crucial dissimilarity with the voting machine process, and hence the falsity of premise 2.

Let us suppose that there is or can be such a thing as legislative intent with regard to a statute, a shared intention regarding its meaning and application. The second argument to be considered acknowledges this, but claims that this shared intention cannot be identified simply as a matter of historical fact. It must be constructed with the use of normative considerations of political morality.

In order to identify the shared intention of a legislature, the argument claims, three questions have to be answered: (1) Who are the authors of the statute? (2) How do their individual intentions combine to form a shared intention? (3) Which mental state (e.g., beliefs, hopes, expectation) constitutes their intentions (Dworkin 1986: 316)? There are no uniquely correct answers to these questions, it is claimed. For example, regarding the second question, the remarks of various legislators may suggest different understandings of the same bill. We might look for a *representative view* – something like a common denominator shared by the various opinions, or a *majority view* – an intention shared by enough people to pass the bill even if no one else voted for it, or a *plurality view* – the intention of the largest single group, even if the other groups combined together amount to more people overall. In order to arrive at one answer among the various possible ones, one has to decide which among the three views just mentioned constitutes the shared intention of the legislature, and this will involve a judgment of political morality about how such issues should be decided. So while we can speak of legislative intention, it has to be constructed using considerations about how to make the law the best it can be.

Dworkin is not wrong in claiming that there might be different ways of identifying shared intention among legislators, just as there might be different procedures for assigning authorship. Nevertheless, we can approach the issue of shared intention from a more historical perspective – asking how much common ground there was in the legislature regarding the meaning and application of a bill, or alternatively, from Dworkin's preferred perspective, asking what assignment of intention would best *justify* the outcome. Dworkin's argument does not preclude the possibility of distinguishing these perspectives, and pursuing the former rather than the latter. If, for example, there is virtually unanimous agreement that proposed legislation has application A but widespread disagreement about application B, then interpreting the legislation as having application A has the support of legislative intent at the time of passage. Interpreting it as having application B does not, or at least, it has less support. For example, in *Garrett* (discussed above) it was not a controversial issue whether Congress intended to let individuals sue states under the ADA, because it was patently clear that it did. (As we know, intent at the time of passage is not the only interpretive consideration, so it would be jumping to a conclusion to infer that this is the correct interpretation of the statute.) How the identification of a historical shared intention should be made may have to be determined on a case by case basis. I suggest that there is a default assumption that intent and the best literal assignments of meaning to a statute are identical, unless there is reason to think otherwise. When such a literal reading yields a result that a legislature is unlikely to intend (as in the Arkansas statute mentioned above), we have one type of case where there is not only a divergence, but intention trumps textual meaning. Where there are inconsistencies, vagueness, ambiguity, uncertain application, it makes sense to look to see if there is an intention to guide us. There needn't always be.

Aware perhaps of both the importance and the difficulties in identifying the shared intent of a legislature, sometimes conventions for identification come into force that help to avoid some, if not all, problems. I have already mentioned above the convention for identifying intent for legislation passed by the US Congress by placing great emphasis on statements of sponsors and managers of bills, and those found in formal committee reports. A different convention was in force, at least until recently, in the UK, where debate in Parliament was excluded from consideration for the purpose of determining intent. Regarding the former convention, some have suggested that the privileged statements have simply become part of the legislation, and so their interpretation is of a piece with the identification of textual meaning (Waldron 1996: 356). However, this is to give such statements, not just interpretive privilege, but the force of law, which overestimates their authority (Dworkin 1986: 346).

So far we have examined and rejected two arguments against the relevance of actual historical shared intentions to interpret the law. Before moving on, it is worth noting another anti-intentionalist position. This would claim that even if such an intention could be clearly identified it would be irrelevant to the interpretation of the law. In the realm of literary interpretation, this is, if anything, the standard anti-intentionalist view. It is the substance of the so-called intentional fallacy. This form of anti-intentionalism seems much less predominant among writers on legal interpretation. It is certainly not Waldron's view since he admits that there are circumstances (such as single-author legislation) where intention is determinative of meaning. It is closer to Dworkin's official view, except that his anti-intentionalist arguments always veer off into ones like that just considered, arguing for a rather different conclusion. Furthermore, his appeal to fit would be more convincing if we could identify historical intentions. Perhaps this suggests that legal interpreters are hard put to deny the relevance of shared intention, if they can only convince themselves that they exist and can sometimes be identified.

Arguments against the relevance of anything except intention

At the other extreme in the spectrum of views about legal interpretation are those who claim that intentions are what interpretations are *all* about (Alexander 1996, 1998). Sometimes this is made a semantic point. If we bring in a consideration other than one concerning intent in thinking about the law, we may be engaged in legal reasoning, even legitimate legal reasoning, but not interpretation. Interpretation, by definition, it is claimed, is trying to figure out what someone meant (or would have meant if he or she had thought about it). Such semantic arguments are not very interesting. Even ignoring that they are out of step with what everyone else means by interpretation, we could grant the stipulation and carry on the debate under a different name.

A different, more interesting argument, claims that there is some sort of incoherence in combining different considerations in interpretation:

> The practical reason approach suggests that in interpreting statutes, one should look to the words' meaning, the authors' purposes, norms regarding consti-tutional relationships, rule-of-law virtues, social norms, efficiency, and jus-tice. . . . The "practical reason" approach is pure conflationism. The questions of what the authorities intended by a statute and what authority that intent should possess are run together into one question of statutory interpretation that is supposed to give "weight" to both factors. However, the two factors, one factual, the other normative cannot be "weighed" on the same scale. (Alexander 1996: 395)

The practical reason approach claims that a variety of different "factors" needs to be weighed up in determining how to apply the law in a given case. Interpreting the law is just figuring out its correct application. Alex-ander's objection to this approach is that it asks us to weigh factual and normative considerations on the same "scale" and that there is something incoherent about this. To decide whether he is right, it is best to imagine how the reasoning prescribed by the approach under consideration would go. There are two models that might be invoked. On one, the practical reason approach envisions a number of different norms of interpretation, that is, it says that a number of different factors *ought* to be considered. So it might say that you ought to consider intent, plain meaning, but also widely held social norms, and considerations of basic justice. Such norms of interpretation would license attending to certain facts: evidence of in-tent, the words of the statute, evidence for the existence of a widely held social norm, evidence of injustice (e.g., that a piece of legislation creates unequal treatment before the law). We then need to determine which in-terpretive conclusions the evidence for each consideration supports, assign "strengths" to the considerations, and weigh accordingly. There is nothing incoherent about such reasoning. The other model, the one Alexander actually seems to have in mind is that factual and normative considerations have to be weighed directly against each other. The fact that the legislature intended application A has to be weighed against the (assumed) injustice of A. Even here there is no obvious incoherence. For example, one can imagine the majority in *Riggs* reasoning this way: If the legislature had clearly expressed the intention that murderers should not be prohibited from inheriting from their victims, then that would be the law no matter the apparent injustice of allowing it, but as no clear intention is expressed on this matter, and as many other laws recognize the injustice of allowing

murderers to profit from their crimes, this consideration of justice is decisive here too.[18] Whether or not this is good reasoning, it is certainly coherent reasoning. So we can conclude that the charge of incoherence is not
well founded.

Conclusion

It is a good thing that the practical reason approach, on either of the two
readings just considered, turns out to be coherent because the theory of
legal interpretation proposed here is a version of it. It is a version that
admits that interpretations in the right setting can sometimes change the
law, not just discover what it is. This sort of construction is possible because of the peculiar aims of legal interpretation, the authority of some
interpreters of it, and the sociopolitical consequences of their interpretations.

NOTES

1   What I am calling "constructivism," which implies that interpretation changes
    the law and, to that extent, makes law, is obviously a quite different position
    than, and should not be confused with, the doctrine of strict construction.
    The latter view is that when we interpret what I call below legal items, such as
    a statute or an article of a constitution, our interpretation should be confined
    to identifying what the item says or what it was originally intended to say.
    Strict constructionists would say that if judges confined themselves to strictly
    constructing legal items, as they ought, their interpretations would *not* change
    the law.

2   The prohibition on Congress's restricting the free exercise of religion was ex-
    tended to the states by the Fourteenth Amendment, or, at least, it is standardly
    interpreted as doing so.

3   My view is that it is primarily judicial interpretations that construct law. This
    raises the question about what is going on in nonjudicial interpretations of the
    law such as one finds in law journals. Such interpretations do not actually
    construct – bring about changes in – the law, but they needn't be just con-
    cerned with clarifying the law either. They might, for example, argue for ways
    of extending the law to bring about a determinate application of it to cases
    where the mere clarification of the law leaves its application to these cases
    indeterminate. Such arguments might create an intellectual atmosphere that
    makes this interpretive extension much more likely. Such academic interpreta-
    tions of the law might make the same assertions about the law as judicial inter-
    pretations, and these assertions are not merely clarificatory, but the former
    interpreters lack the right forum and the right authority to bring about the
    changes in law they are arguing for.
        There is a related question: How do academic and judicial interpreters of

the law stand to authors and critics of literary works? If academic interpreters are similar to literary critics (in their capacity as interpreters of works), are judges similar to authors in virtue of the fact that some judicial decisions make law? Judges occupy a role different from both authors and critics, but bearing some similarity to each. Judges are not authors, because authors create their works not via interpretations of them (not by making claims about them), but from scratch, as it were. Judges operate by interpreting, by making claims about legal items and bodies of law already in existence. But they do not merely make claims. Sometimes their claims, in the context of a legal decision that sets precedent, makes law. Their difference from critics consists in their being in a position to do something beyond the making of claims in interpreting the items about which those claims are made.

4   Dennis Patterson is perhaps most explicit in claiming legal interpretation is guided by the four considerations cited below (Patterson 1996: 169–79). Also see Raz (1998) on constitutional interpretation. However, many other theorists incorporate them into their views of legal interpretation in one way or the other. See, for example, Dworkin's discussion of the interpretation of common law and of statutes (1986: 238–58, 337–54, where all four considerations are invoked though reinterpreted in ways to fit his theory of interpretation). Alexander, though a thoroughgoing intentionalist, accommodates the other considerations either as a step in the determination of intention (textual interpretation, 1996: 363–6) or as (what he takes to be) extra-interpretive reasoning about whether we should change the meaning of laws (moral and prudential considerations [1996: 386–91]).

5   Shiner (1987) discusses additional differences.

6   Coleman and Leiter (1996: 240) point out that there is some indeterminacy in the law, but claim that, while the decision in such cases is arbitrary, it need not be unjustified. It would be justified if the system of formal dispute resolution were better overall than the alternatives. Such a system requires that someone has to win and someone else loses. Even if their justification is acceptable, it remains obvious that it would be better if such decisions were never arbitrary.

7   In this context a hypothetical intention is an intention an individual or group would have had, if they thought about an issue such as the application of vague language or the resolution of a legal conflict. It is to be distinguished from what hypothetical intentionalists in the realm of art and literary interpretation are talking about.

8   Perry (1998) rejects the distinction in the terms I have framed it ("understanding the law"/"applying the law" [118]), but endorses the idea that the interpretation of the law involves two steps, which he describes as (1) identifying the norm a legal text represents, and (2) deciding what shape to give an indeterminate norm in a particular context (118–19). I think that we are both pointing to the same thing using different language.

9   Some people think that this requires a different interpretive principle than do statutes. For example, Joseph Raz endorses a form of intentionalism in interpreting statutes (1996). However, when it comes to interpreting constitutions, there are a variety of relevant considerations, which roughly divide into "conserving reasons," that attempt to elucidate the law as it is and "merit reasons" that are developed to remove shortcomings in the law (1998: 177).

10   Perry discusses this case and some of the preceding and subsequent legal history (1998: 108–10). I am following his view that, because of the ambiguity of the language of the clause (and probably the underlying intentions as well), clarification will only take us so far in resolving the legal issue in this case.

11   The proponents of this view include Alexander (1996), Dworkin (1986), Horowitz (2000), Moore (1996), Raz (1998), and Sunstein (1989).

12   Others who agree with Dworkin about this are Moore (1996) and Waldron (1996).

13   Dworkin's discussion of *McLoughlin* (1986: 238–54) is a good example of the use he makes of considerations of fit and justification.

14   Legislative intent seems to be given more weight in the US than in the UK. Different conventions that suggest this are discussed below.

15   I am grateful to Jonathan Neufeld for suggesting this reply.

16   Others who criticize Dworkin include Alexander and Kress (1996), Fallon (1992), Patterson (1996: 71–98), Postema (1987), and Raz (1986).

17   For Gilbert, there is a group or shared intention to do A when there is a shared commitment to do A. "Shared commitment" is a technical notion which requires explication, but the upshot of Gilbert's analysis is that a body of legislators would have various shared commitments, therefore group intentions, when considering and voting on bills. Of course, they do not have a shared intention to *pass* a bill, but there is such an intention to decide on a bill. Bratman would require a degree of coordination among legislators, meshing subplans and a common knowledge of these. Normally a shared intention would concern a proposed statute that eventually emerges with a mutually understood content. In the case of the legislation machine, this mutually understood content is absent. One problem with importing Gilbert's or Bratman's analyses to the legislative context is that here we are dealing not just with cooperative activity, but, at the same time, the activity of rivals and antagonists

18   This reasoning should not be confused with the following: Since the legislators would have been breaking with normal practice by allowing murderers to profit, and since they did not explicitly state they were allowing murderers to inherit, we can assume they did not intend this. This is purely intentional reasoning. It may be good reasoning, but it is different from the reasoning given above and does not imply that the above reasoning is incoherent.

Relativism versus Pluralism

In earlier chapters I have defended various kinds of pluralism about interpretation. I have argued that there are several different but perfectly legitimate questions an interpreter can be asking and several different aims with
which interpretations are made. In the realm of art interpretation it is
legitimate to pursue one aim rather than another. In the realm of legal
interpretation, although here too there are different aims, it is not legitimate to simply ignore one aim because one takes an interest in another. A
good interpretation of the law is expected to pursue the several aims of
legal interpretation insofar as this is possible. However, since the pursuit of
these aims may push an interpreter of the law in different directions, it is
not always possible to satisfy all aims equally.

I have also defended another kind of pluralism – critical pluralism. This
is the idea that there can be more than one, sometimes many, equally acceptable, noncombinable interpretations of a given item. I argued for critical pluralism especially with regard to art interpretation, where it not only
holds, but is desirable that it holds. The case of the law is different. It is
certainly possible that there can be equally acceptable interpretations of the
law in some cases, but this is not a desirable outcome, since it will render
some judicial decisions arbitrary. Critical monism provides the ideal in the
case of legal interpretation, though one not always attainable.

Finally, I have argued that the truth of critical pluralism is primarily,
though not only, due to the truth of the first kind of plurality just mentioned – the plurality of interpretive questions and aims. In the case of art
interpretation, critical pluralism is also true because some interpretive aims
(especially aims derived from "could mean" and significance seeking questions) themselves invite a plurality of acceptable interpretations.

Neither variety of pluralism should be confused with relativism. In this
chapter I evaluate relativism about interpretation and its relation to plural-

ism and constructivism. I also revisit the constructivist's dilemma advanced against moderate constructivism in chapter 6. The status of the dilemma needs to be reconsidered in the light of the defense of moderate constructivism in the domain of legal interpretation. If moderate constructivism ever holds, the dilemma cannot, strictly speaking, be sound. Nevertheless, valuable lessons can be learned from it.

Relativist Claims

Works of art are not only apt to be interpreted over and over again, but, over the course of time, different forms of interpretation become dominant only to be superseded by others as critical schools rise or fall. Though the phenomenon is by no means confined to them, works from the relatively distant past are often recipients of this treatment, which is facilitated by the obscurity of their origin. An example of such a work is Jan van Eyck's *The Arnolfini Marriage*. To a modern eye the painting cries out for interpretation. From the hornlike hairdo of the bride and the demeanor and dress of the groom, to the various everyday objects that populate the room, the painting presents a fascinating but puzzling scene. Early interpretations of the painting attempted to understand all this simply in terms of naturalism. Later, without denying the naturalistic aspect of the painting, interpreters claimed that a full understanding of the work required seeing the objects arrayed in the representation as symbols referring to such things as the sacrament of marriage. Still later interpreters supplemented or replaced religious symbols with psychoanalytic ones.

Is there a single truth about this painting that these different interpretations are attempting to identify? Are they perhaps noticing different aspects of this truth? Or can we only assess the acceptability of an interpretation from within the framework of a critical school, conceptual scheme, or some other similar reference point? The relativist holds this last position.

Relativists standardly make two claims. First, with regard to some subject matter, they claim that there is no universal standard for understanding or evaluating it. Second, they claim that the correctness of an understanding or evaluation always depends on something local such as a conceptual scheme, conventions or norms shared within a community, or the reactions of a group or an individual.

One can be a relativist about the *truth* of these judgments, by claiming that this varies with a variation in conceptual scheme, in community norms or conventions, or simply in the actual or hypothetical reactions of individuals or groups. Such a relativism implies that these judgments are true or false, but not true or false *simpliciter*. Rather, their truth value is relative to scheme, convention, or individual or group reaction. Hence not all conjunctions of (nonrelativized) true judgment preserve truth.

One might instead be a relativist about the *justification* of such judgments, claiming that what would justify them for one group differs from what would justify them for another, depending again on variation in scheme, convention/norm, reaction, or alternatively, differences in histories or practices. A relativist regarding justification *may* not be one regarding truth. This might be because one believes these judgments lack truth value or because one believes their truth value is nonrelative.

Finally (for the purposes of this survey), one may be a relativist about the very *meaning* of such judgments. Thus if one believes that one's procedures of justification enter into the meaning of one's interpretive claims (as does McFee 1992, 1995), and these procedures vary from group to group, then the meaning of these judgments would also vary from group to group. Two individuals from different groups might say, "*The Arnolfini Marriage* has many symbolic elements," but they would be making different statements. An individual from a third group might at first appearance deny the first two judgments by claiming that the painting does not make use of symbolism. But if her standards of justification were different in nature than those of the others, and the assumption holds that these standards enter into the meaning of her judgment, then she says something different, but not strictly inconsistent with, the others.

Relativism and Constructivism

There appears to be a mutual "attraction" between relativism and some form of constructivism. What is the basis of this attraction? It is not that constructivism entails relativism. There is no such entailment. Suppose that it is true that novel interpretations alter their objects. So suppose that, because of ways it is interpreted, it is true (apt) that a work is F (allegorical) at one time but not F at another earlier time. This in itself does not imply the truths in question are relative to something, such as the consensus of critics, any more than does the fact that someone is bald at one time and not bald at an earlier time imply that baldness is a relative notion. Or suppose that novel interpretations actually create a new object of interpretation. This has in itself no relativistic implications any more than does the fact that novel uses of the same words create different utterances.

What is true is that if one is a relativist it will be hard to impossible to avoid being a constructivist. Whether it is impossible or merely hard to avoid this depends on the exact nature of the relativism and constructivism in question. Suppose one thinks that *the truth* of any interpretation is relative to something, say consensus among critics at a given time; if consensus changes, the truth of interpretations changes as well. If, due to a changing consensus, it is true at one time that a painting is allegorical, whereas this is not true at an earlier time, it follows that the painting is allegorical at the later time, but not at the earlier time. That *implies* that interpretations alter their objects, at least when they are part of a changing consensus. Or suppose the very meaning of our interpretive claims is relative to critical consensus. Then, as consensus changes, different things are meant by "*Guernica*" or the "*The Arnolfini Marriage*." That strongly *suggests*, at least, that interpretations, when they are part of a new consensus, create new objects, new *Guernicas* and *Arnolfini Marriages*. (It *implies* that such interpretations refer to different objects, but it is logically compatible with this claim that all of these objects always existed, but were never before noticed.)

Constructivist claims are puzzling. How can thought or discourse about something change it? How can thought or discourse, initially directed toward one object, create a subsequent object? Relativism seems to offer an explanation of this. For example, if truth is relative to critical consensus, we can understand how truth can change as the consensus changes.

So relativism is one route to constructivism that also seems to explain away some of its puzzling features. This explains the mutual attraction between relativism and constructivism. If one is a relativist, it will be hard to impossible not be a constructivist. If one is a constructivist, one need not be a relativist, but relativism may provide a good explanation of the (purported) truth of constructivism.

This will be so, however, only if there are good, independent reasons to accept relativism, good reasons to suppose that truth is relative to such things as critical consensus. Are there?

Motivations for Relativism

What makes a relativistic position attractive? One of the strongest and most widespread reasons for embracing relativism is the existence of seemingly irresolvable disagreements. Such disputes appear to continue without closure, and often without mutual agreement on the evidence or considerations that would produce closure. This motivation is epistemic in nature, based on a problem of establishing to everyone's satisfaction the interpretive claims that we make.

A second reason to accept some form of relativism derives from a sociological or political conception of the origin of interpretive claims. It is some-times suggested that these claims have their basis in supporting the he-gemony or legitimacy of a particular class, or group, whether that be a large social class such as the bourgeoisie or a small academic subdiscipline. Given such a view, it might seem plausible to suppose that such judgments only have validity within the relevant group. If, as the preceding paragraph suggested, there really were no generally accepted evidential criteria for accepting or rejecting the statements in question, that fact might bolster this view of them.

Third, there is a way of conceiving of the world that also can provide a reason to accept relativism. There is no easy way to state this conception, but a simple rendering would be that the world is in part constructed by human cognitive activity (by perceiving, conceiving, theorizing, and inter-preting). What is meant is not merely that among the things that exist are artifacts, which are in part the result of the aforementioned cognitive activ-ity of their makers. What is meant is that even "natural objects" are at least in part constructed, and artifacts reconstructed, by our ways of thinking about them. Add now to this idea that this construction of the world varies according to historical period, tradition, society and culture, language or conceptual scheme, and one has a basis for believing that the truth, justifi-cation, even the meaning of our statements, would also vary and be rela-tive. Notice, however, that the basis of this relativism is itself a kind of ontological relativism that would be in need of independent justification. (See chapters 5 and 6 for a detailed discussion of the constructivist view.)

A final motivation is based on an understanding of the appreciation ap-propriate to art and the role of interpretation in bringing about this appre-ciation. We appreciate many works of art by interpreting them, and if we can come to interpret them in more than one way, perhaps in many ways, then the possibilities and opportunities for appreciation are enhanced. Hence, the practice of interpretation ought to, and in fact does, allow for multiple interpretations of artworks, even interpretations that often seem to clash. This has suggested to many that some sort of relativism is required by the very nature of art or the very point of art appreciation to explain how clashing interpretations can all be acceptable. Let us examine in more de-tail why this is so.

Relativism and Pluralism

The doctrine that there are acceptable, clashing or noncombinable inter-pretations of the same work is known as critical pluralism. Critical pluralism is widely, though not universally, accepted. Relativism provides one explanation for the truth of critical pluralism (just as it would provide an explanation for constructivism, if constructivism were true). The standard relativist explanation is that the correctness of an interpretation is not determined simply by its adequacy to the work under interpretation, but by the conventions, assumptions, or norms of a community of interpreters. Correctness is relative to such a community. The correctness of interpretation i of a work w in community c_1 does not imply correctness in any other interpretive community, and hence there is no valid inference from the fact that i is correct in c_1, and j is correct in c_2 to the conclusion that the conjunction of i and j gives a correct interpretation of w. Since this implies that there are acceptable, noncombinable interpretations of w, the truth of critical pluralism is secured by this route.

Some of the clearest examples of this standard version of relativism in contemporary thought are provided by the writings of David Carrier (1991) and of Stanley Fish (1980, 1989).[1] Carrier and Fish not only hold that interpretations of a given work are true only relative to the assumptions of an interpretive community, but that this is so because works acquire meaning only when these assumptions are applied to them. Hence the very meaning works possess and the justification for ascribing such meaning to them are also relative to such communities.

Carrier is impressed by a number of features of art-critical and art-historical writing, including some items already mentioned above as motivators of relativism. One feature is that there seems to be no end to the interpretations that can be offered for a given painting, such as Piero della Francesca's *The Baptism of Christ* or van Eyck's *The Arnolfini Marriage*. A second feature is that it is not the work alone that dictates the character of these interpretations. In different periods, properties will be found in works that were not even conceived of in earlier periods. For example, prior to Panofsky, *The Arnolfini Marriage* was conceived of as a work of pure naturalism. Following Panofsky, the work is understood in a new way: one that combines naturalism and allegory based on the symbolic, iconographic significance of various represented objects in the painting. Still later critics might introduce psychoanalytic concepts into their interpretations. It is plausible that it is not only the work being interpreted but something about the context of the interpreter that determines the concepts through which interpretations are offered. Third, it is not only the properties found in the work, but norms of adequacy or methodology that change from period to period or from critical school to critical school. When *The Arnolfini Marriage* is regarded as a purely naturalistic work, it is not necessary to explain why it has just such a combination of represented objects scattered about its periphery: a dog, shoes, oranges. To make a work naturalistic, such objects are needed, but the choice of objects is not that important. Once it is regarded as an allegory, each of these objects is bound to have symbolic significance, and a norm of adequacy in such an interpretation is to find meanings for all of the details that cohere together and with the action of the painting's main figures. Finally, the last feature that impresses Carrier is that these stages in the development of interpretations of a given work do not lead to a final agreement or convergence about how it should be interpreted. Instead there seems to be endless disagreement.

Carrier believes that these features all point to a relativistic conclusion. An interpretation's truth "is measured by the consensus among professional art historians. This consensus determines the implicit rules governing art-historical discourse" (1991: 237). As just noted, this consensus changes over time, and perhaps, at a given time, the consensus is different in different schools of criticism or art history. The claim that "truth is measured by consensus" and the fact that consensus changes from time to time and school to school implies relativism about interpretive truth.

An alternative view is advanced by Joseph Margolis (1980, 1995a, 1999a) under the label "robust relativism." Margolis rejects the standard relativist approach of indexing the truth or warrant of an interpretation, or the meaning of an object of interpretation, to something such as consensus within a community. His alternative is to claim that interpretive claims are to be understood within a many-valued logic. On such a logic, interpretive claims can be false, but are never true. Instead they are affirmed by "truthlike" predicates such as "plausible," "reasonable," and "apt." According to Margolis, this view permits us to affirm (as plausible, reasonable, or apt) interpretations that would be logically inconsistent, that is, incapable of being true together, in a bivalent logic. Such interpretations nevertheless remain "nonconverging" even within the many-valued logical framework. If Margolis is right about all of this, then he offers an alternate route to critical pluralism, since on his view too there are acceptable, noncombinable interpretations.

Robust relativism resembles standard relativism in asserting that the appearance of logical inconsistency, between interpretive statements that we accept, is illusory, *because*, when properly understood, such statements make true (or truthlike) claims, which nevertheless cannot be conjoined (since that would imply convergence). Hence, while they offer different routes to critical pluralism, they are routes that share a somewhat similar strategy.

Both sorts of relativism hold that, prior to being interpreted, it is indeterminate whether objects have certain properties that can only be attributed by means of interpretation. The difference is that standard relativism claims that agreement (consensus) within a relevant community actually makes certain interpretive statements true ("*The Arnolfini Marriage* is allegorical") at least relative to the community, and hence actually makes it the case that, relative to the community, the object under interpretation has the properties predicated of the object in the interpretation. Robust relativism claims, in contrast, that such properties are imputed to works in interpretations, and while such imputations can be plausible, apt, or reasonable, it never becomes true that the object under interpretation has the property. If we were to accept the point of agreement shared by both these views, that prior to interpretation it is indeterminate whether the object has the property, then robust relativism is the more plausible position on this issue. It is not creditable that mere consensus can make it true that something is allegorical, when prior to that consensus it is not. It is somewhat more creditable that such a consensus might select, among the possible views one might hold about a work, a set that is more reasonable or plausible than others. This would especially be so on the assumption that properties are imputed to works rather than simply possessed by them.

Evaluation of Relativism about Interpretation

Should we accept any of these reasons in support of relativism? Sometimes "relativism" is a term used to dismiss a view as beyond the pale of reason. A universal relativism (e.g., the view that all truth is relative) is sometimes said to be self-refuting, since its very assertion implies that at least one truth is not relative (viz., that *all* is relative). However, the relativisms we have been examining – about the interpretation of artworks and other objects in the intentional domain – are local rather than universal, and so could not be criticized in this way.

A limited relativism is not an intrinsically unreasonable doctrine. The question we should ask is whether the motives for adopting relativism provide *sufficient* reason to accept it.

Here it has to be said that the motivations discussed above for a relativism about interpretation fail to do this.

One motivation for relativism is the view that interpretive claims have an underlying social or political basis. Whether or not such a view has plausibility, it supplies the weakest reason to accept relativism – a view about the truth, justification, or meaning of interpretive claims. A political basis for such claims – such as a tendency to help sustain the power of a group – tells us nothing about the meaning of those claims or whether they are true or justified even within a particular group. Hence, they do not provide a good reason to accept relativism.

Another reason to accept a relativism about interpretive claims derived from an ontological relativism: the idea that what exists is constructed by human cognitive activity and the practices and institutions in which this activity is embedded. This view itself is not an easy one to understand, and hence its implications are far from clear. One way to understand it is to suppose that it implies that groups with different institutions and practices are interpreting different *Guernicas* and different *Hamlets*, which are, in part at least, constructed by the cognitive activity of individuals within the respective groups. It would then be true that they would be interpreting objects with different meanings, which would make appropriate different truth claims, but this would be no more surprising than that *Hamlet* and *Twelfth Night* or *Guernica* and *The Man with a Violin* (1912) have different meanings.

An alternative metaphysical view is to suppose that though constructed in different ways in the course of its history, via the imputation of different properties, reference to a single object is somehow secured, albeit one in constant flux. Such an object of interpretation fits the model provided by robust relativism.

These metaphysical views embody a far more sweeping relativism than the interpretive relativism we are attempting to evaluate. I believe, but will not try to show here, that even these more sweeping views can be formulated coherently. It is not surprising that a more modest relativism follows from the sweeping views, just as it follows from the fact that all A's are B that some A's are B. However, what does not look consistent with general metaphysical relativism is giving a positive argument for it. Such an argument either holds relative to some framework or holds independently of one. The latter possibility violates relativism. The former leaves open that outside a certain framework relativism is false. If one doubts that relativism holds in all frameworks, we could doubt we are in the framework in which it holds.

Without such an argument, metaphysical relativism is a philosophical bet.[2] As such it will not persuade those who are not already inclined to accept interpretive relativism to do so. So it is better to focus on more down to earth arguments for the latter.

A third reason for accepting relativism, of the more down to earth variety, is that nature of artistic appreciation encourages us, perhaps requires us, to accept multiple interpretations of artworks. That, however, merely points to the truth of critical pluralism. There are nonrelativistic ways of establishing pluralism. One is to take matters a step further than Margolis and deny that interpretations make claims that are true, false or even truthlike. On this view, an interpretation's acceptability is determined in other ways, such as its ability to heighten appreciation of a work. Clearly, there can be interpretations that are acceptable because they accomplish this, but are noncombinable because, when yoked together, they fail to enhance appreciation.

There are more conservative strategies that suffice to establish critical pluralism. Suppose we hold the view that interpretations of a work are to be constrained by the conventions in place when it is created (not conventions in place when it is being interpreted, as relativists tend to hold) and only by such conventions. Such a constraint provides a standard of acceptability that applies to all interpretations, but may permit several noncombinable interpretations of the same work.[3] Or suppose one holds the view that interpretations of a work are acceptable if we are highly justified in believing they were intended by the creator of the work (whether or not they were really so intended).[4] Again several different interpretations may satisfy this requirement.

Finally, one can arrive at critical pluralism by recognizing that we interpret with different aims. Sometimes we aim at understanding a work as the product of the historically situated artist. Sometimes we merely look for *an* understanding of a work, one that makes sense of it in a way that promotes appreciation. Sometimes we aim at maximizing the aesthetic value or intelligibility of a work. Sometimes we are trying to make a work relevant to a particular audience by finding a significance in the work especially appropriate to that group. In the process of pursuing these different aims we will sometimes offer interpretations that genuinely contradict each other, and, hence, both of which cannot be true. Even in this case both may be acceptable relative to the evidence on hand, which is insufficient to eliminate one of the interpretations. However, given the different aims with which we interpret, it will often happen that apparently inconsistent interpretations are really logically compatible. The assertion that a work *can* be understood as representing an F is compatible with the assertion that it *can* be understood as representing not F, but G. (Grant Wood's *American Gothic* is usually understood as representing a man and his wife, though there is some evidence that it was meant to represent a man and his daughter. It is at least true that it can also be understood in this way.) While such interpretations are strictly compatible, there may be no point in combining interpretation pursued with different aims (or sometimes the same aim, as in the case just cited).

A last reason to accept relativism is the apparent irresolvability of interpretive disagreements. Standard relativism explains some of this irresolvability by claiming that many of the disagreements are not real when relativized to different communities. Irresolvability results from the different standards underlying the apparently conflicting interpretive claims. However, proponents of this view fail to show us that real disagreements within an interpretive community are any more resolvable – as they should be – than merely apparent disagreements among different communities. Robust relativists would claim that interpretations are evaluated as more or less plausible, apt, or reasonable. This process would eliminate some interpretations, while leaving a plurality of others in the field. What a robust relativist is not so clear about is why disagreements should persist beyond this point.

There are other approaches that offer as good, or better, explanations of interpretive disagreement. The approach that claims that we interpret with different aims would suggest that a certain amount of apparent disagreement arises through confusion about interpretive aims, through talking at cross-purposes as it were. The remaining real disagreements have to be handled piecemeal, for resolvability turns on what is actually asserted by an interpretation, and this will vary with aim. Once again the problem does not require a relativist solution.

We can conclude that none of the motives for accepting relativism about interpretive claims gives us compelling reasons to do so. At least the highly schematic versions of arguments for relativism that we have looked at so far do not accomplish this.

However, perhaps the implausibility of the arguments considered so far is due to the highly abstract and schematic versions we have looked at. Possibly a more compelling case can be made if we look at the detailed positions of actual proponents of relativism. To this end, I return to the views of Carrier and Margolis as representatives of standard and robust relativism respectively.

Carrier was impressed with four features of art interpretation. Two of these – interpretive pluralism and the unresolved disagreement among interpreters – I have already discussed. However, the other two are yet to be considered. These concern the questions we ask (the properties we look for) on the one hand, and the methodological norms we follow on the other. With respect to both, Carrier points out that these change with time and do so while the object of interpretation remains constant. However, these facts do not settle anything. At different times and in different schools different interests will hold, and different concepts will be salient, and so different questions will be asked. As different questions are asked, different kinds of evidence will be needed. All this is consistent with both relativism and nonrelativism.

Ironically, it is the degree of disagreement among art historians and critics, which Carrier identifies better than almost anyone, that is the undoing of his view. Remember that the nerve of his relativism is that consensus is the measure of truth. But with regard to substantive interpretations consensus does not exist even at a given time or within a given school. Even within the iconographic school of Panofsky there is little agreement about the allegory to be found in *The Arnolfini Marriage*.[5] There are some who even doubt that there are sufficient methodological constraints on the identification of allegory for the claim to be critically respectable.[6] There is, if anything, as much or more agreement across schools as within them. For example, most agree that van Eyk's painting is naturalistic, even when it is denied that its naturalism can explain all of its artistically significant features. Within a school or period, consensus encompasses more the question we should ask than the answers we should give. Hence if consensus is the measure of truth, there is little truth to be found in art history or criticism. Rather, we have many nonconverging interpretations of varying degrees of plausibility. Standard relativism with consensus as the measure of truth devolves into robust relativism.

However, it is not clear that robust relativism can ultimately succeed in satisfying two conditions any genuine relativism must meet. First, it has to be able to identify pairs of interpretations that would be logically incompatible were a bivalent logic to apply to them and assign to them positive truthlike values. Second, the two interpretations must remain nonconverging even after their nonbivalent logical status is correctly understood. It is not clear that robust relativism ultimately meets either condition.

Beginning with the latter condition, that the interpretations remain nonconverging, consider two plausible allegorical interpretations of *The Arnolfini Marriage*. On one, the dog in the picture is a symbol of "marital faith, the burning candle stands for the wisdom of an all seeing God, and the fruit on the window sill for innocence before the Fall" (Panofsky 1966: 203). Alternatively, the dog denotes both fertility and carnality, and the oranges symbolize the expectation that the woman will produce an heir (Harbison 1984: 602). Assuming these claims about what the painting symbolizes to be mutually exclusive (i.e., there is an implicit denial that the alternative symbol is present) and that both are plausible, what does the robust relativist say about them? It asserts that it is plausible that the oranges symbolize innocence, and it is plausible that they symbolize the hope that the marriage will produce an heir. However, if both really are plausible, what is the barrier in conjoining them into the view that each of the claims is plausible (as just done above). Such a claim is comparable to saying of an ambiguous figure that it can be seen as a duck and it can also be seen as a rabbit (except that both these claims are not merely plausible but true). Just as recognizing that an ambiguous figure can be seen in more than one way is a more adequate perspective on it than one that merely gives us one way of seeing it, so a perspective noting several plausible ways of taking the allegory to be found in *The Arnolfini Marriage* is also a more adequate one. This claim could be challenged, if there were a truth to be discovered about the painting's allegorical nature beyond the plausibility of the above claims. This, however, is what the robust relativist denies.

If we ask, "What allows the two interpretations of the *Arnofini Marriage* to converge in the way specified above?" one answer is that the evidence underdetermines any one interpretation. As Carrier notes (1991: 86), no clear evidence from van Eyck's time directly supports the claim that the painting is allegorical. (Also see Roskill [1989: 62–85].) Rather, such interpretations belong in what I called earlier the "could mean" category. That is, they answer the question "What could the details in the painting mean?" by offering "visually convincing" answers to these questions. These answers are based on an assumption that the details need an explanation that tells us why the painting has just these features rather than others, and does so by giving them a coherent set of symbolic meanings. While I deny that it is reasonable to string together all the different ways a painting could be taken, a working critic would approach a painting like *The Arnolfini Marriage* with just the sort of conjunction mentioned in the previous paragraph: that *a* and *b* are plausible ways of taking the painting as allegory, whereas *c* is less plausible and *d* is not plausible at all.

This reveals that the first condition mentioned above, for a successful robust relativism, is also not met. We have not identified pairs of interpretations, which are incompatible under a bivalent logic, but nevertheless are acceptable in virtue of their plausibility. It is *true* that each allegorical interpretation of *The Arnolfini Marriage* is plausible. It is *true* that each specifies something the painting "could mean." Such claims are not incompatible in a bivalent logic. It may even be true that the painting (considered in terms of what its artist does in his historical context) does mean something identified in one of these interpretations, although the claim that it does would not be fully supported by the available evidence. The fact that we are limited to plausibility claims (or "could mean" claims) in this case hardly drives us into the arms of the robust relativist. Pluralism gives us everything we need to handle the case.

Margolis would deny that pluralism is adequate to handle such cases, in part because he would not accept the diagnosis just considered of the problem of choosing among allegorical interpretations of *The Arnolfini Marriage*. Following Carrier, I described this as a problem of insufficient evidence. Margolis would say, rather, the problem derives from the nature of "Intentional objects." Such objects lack a clear boundary between properties had and not had when it comes to the sorts of properties ascribed in interpretations. Hence some properties are necessarily imputed. Of imputed properties, it is never *true* that their objects have them; it is only plausible, apt, or reasonable. It is misleading, on this picture, to say that there happens to be insufficient evidence for a certain interpretation. Rather, there could not be conclusive evidence for its truth, since there is no such truth for which evidence might have been available.

Fortunately, I have already taken up, and rejected, this conception of a work's properties in chapter 6. It may be true that some properties of works are vague, in the way the property of being bald seems to be vague, and that the fictional worlds of works are incomplete or indeterminate in that there are no answers to some questions we might ask about those worlds, but it does not follow that the works themselves are indeterminate. In fact, there is reason to deny this (see chapter 6, p. 137). So, if rejecting bivalence derives from accepting the imputational model of a work's properties, we do not have good reason to reject bivalence.

If we have no good reason to give up bivalence, we have no reason to accept robust relativism. Recall, however, that we were led to robust relativism as a way out of the problems faced by standard relativism. So we are now in a position to reject both versions of relativism.

The Constructivist's Dilemma Revisited

Relativism offers an explanation for the truth, where it exists, of constructivism. However, I have just rejected that explanation. The reader is owed an alternative explanation, especially in light of the fact that in chapter 6 an argument was offered that seemed to show that moderate constructivism could not be true, while chapter 7 argued that it is sometimes true, namely, in the case of legal interpretation. That apparent inconsistency also needs to be ironed out.

The argument against moderate constructivism is the constructivist's dilemma. It claims that interpretations are either truth valued or not. If they are, then when an interpretation is true, the object in question already has the property it is asserted to have; when it is false, it lacks the property. On the other hand, if an interpretation lacks truth value, while it can change the way individuals think of the object, it cannot change the object.

If we remind ourselves of our conclusion about legal interpretation, we can see there must be something wrong with this reasoning. A judicial interpretation of a legal item can change the legal properties of that item, but not in virtue of its truth or falsity, though it may be truth evaluable. The interpretation can change the item primarily because, besides being an interpretation, it is also a judicial *decision*, which has legal authority. (If one can somehow distinguish the decision from the interpretation, one can deny that this is a counterexample to the constructivist's dilemma.) Just as a justice of the peace can change your legal status from unmarried to married, a judge in the appropriate courtroom, in the right circumstances, can change the content of a legal item, by attaching a certain interpretation to the item.

This implies that some speech acts can change the items they are about, not just the way people think of those items. That challenges the second horn of the dilemma. Further, even where someone uses speech that can be evaluated for truth or falsity, they may, at the same time, be doing something else that can change the object, not just the way we think about the object.

Does this mean we should revise our conclusions about art interpretation to permit the construction of what artworks mean by interpretations of those works? It does not. Before turning to artworks, consider conversational utterances. The meanings of utterances are not apt items for construction. This is because, as almost everyone agrees, their meaning is fixed at the time of utterance by context, convention, and intention. While certain properties of utterances can change, subsequent to their making, meaning properties are not among these. Interpretations of the meaning of utterances are typically truth evaluable claims about that meaning. Since the meaning in question depends wholly on what the utterer does (says) in context on the occasion of utterance against the background of certain conventions, the first horn of the constructivist's dilemma describes perfectly the situation of the interpreter of utterance meaning. In interpreting an utterance in order to identify its meaning, no speech act other than a statement-making one like assertion or conjecture comes into play. Since the assertion or conjecture is about a meaning the utterance already has at the time of interpretation, there is no occasion for the construction of meaning; there is only occasion for its discovery.

I have argued, in chapters 2 and 3, that the meaning of artworks is much like that of utterances. In chapters 5 and 6 I examined and rejected many arguments for the claim that interpretations construct artwork meanings. So the construction of work meaning does not occur in this domain. The constructivist's dilemma should be regarded as a heuristic device for helping us to understand this situation, but it is not the most accurate statement of the argument why art interpretation is not constructive of a work's meaning.

From the conclusion that art interpretation does not construct work meaning it should not be inferred that no construction at all is to be found in the domain of art. First, artworks come in many varieties. The ones that are most immune to meaning change are those "uttered" by an identifiable artist or group of artists.[7] Where works are anonymous, where they belong to an oral tradition in which their origin is at best murky and in which they can undergo constant modification, they are less utterance-like because their meanings are less tied to a particular historical act of production. However, even in the case of artworks like these, critical interpretation is not the appropriate vehicle of meaning change. It is not critics, but those responsible for re-presenting these works, for presenting new versions of them, that accomplish this. No doubt they will be influenced by their own interpretations of earlier versions, but, as usual, mere (critical) interpretation will not do the trick.

The second qualification to the claim that meanings are not constructed in the domain of art interpretation should by now be *very* familiar. Identifying work meaning is not the only aim of art interpretation. Interpretations of the "could mean" and significance seeking varieties are not only permitted but encouraged for artworks. That is, it is perfectly all right to offer interpretations that enable audiences to perceive works from perspectives *other than* those that reveal what the artist, in his or her historical context, does in the work. The reason this is permitted and even encouraged is that it adds to the artistically valuable encounters between audiences and the works. However, because these interpretations give us optional ways of perceiving works, they do not add to or alter the meaning of those works.

An Acceptable Relativism?

Although I find no compelling reason to accept either standard or robust relativism about interpretation, there is a another sort of relativism that does strike me as extremely compelling. This relativism derives from the view, just mentioned and discussed frequently above, that we interpret works of art with different aims. When we evaluate interpretations, it is plausible that we should bring different standards of acceptability to interpretations with different aims. Thus it would be wrong to apply the same standard to an interpretation that attempts to recover the intention of the artist and an interpretation that attempts to find significance in a work that would make it relevant to a particular contemporary audience. Success in these two cases involves very different things.

Hence, it is at least true that the acceptability of an interpretation is relative to its aim. This is one of the main conclusions of this book. The others are as follows:

1. In the intentional domain, there are several different basic interpretive questions.
2. "What is the meaning of x?" is just one of these, but one that is capable of a monistic answer.
3. Monism about meaning is compatible with pluralism about interpretation.
4. Whether such pluralism is desirable depends on the interpretive aims within a given subdomain of the intentional domain.
5. We need not and should not accept either constructivism or (standard or robust) relativism to explain the truth of critical pluralism in art and literary interpretation.
6. Legal interpretation is, in part, constructive, just because it aims to avoid a plurality of equally good interpretations in order to arrive at nonarbitrary judicial decisions based on such interpretations.

NOTES

1 I have discussed Fish's work elsewhere (Stecker 1990, 1997a: 231–41), so I focus here on Carrier.
2 The expression "philosophical bet" comes from Margolis. Margolis (1999b) is a good account of which among his views should be so characterized. See especially 339–40.
3 This approach is endorsed by S. Davies (1991).
4 This approach is endorsed by some hypothetical intentionalists, especially Levinson (1996: 175–213).
5 See the comparison of Panofsky and Harbison in the next paragraph. Regarding the convex mirror in the painting, it is variously interpreted as a symbol of the terrestrial world, of the Virgin, of painting as a reflection of the visible world, and, alternatively, not as a symbol, but as a means of making the whole room visible.
6 Gombrich (1972: 15–16).
7 It is not surprising that one strategy for promoting a constructivist view of art interpretation proclaims the death of the author.

References

Alexander, Larry. 1996. "All or Nothing at All? The Intentions of Authorities and the Authority of Intentions." In *Law and Interpretation: Essays in Legal Theory*, edited by Andrei Marmor. Oxford: Oxford University Press, 357–404.

——. 1998. "Introduction." In *Constitutionalism: Philosophical Foundations*, edited by Larry Alexander. Cambridge: Cambridge University Press, 1–15.

Alexander, Larry, and Ken Kress. 1996. "Against Legal Principles." In *Law and Interpretation: Essays in Legal Theory*, edited by Andrei Marmor. Oxford: Oxford University Press, 279–327.

Auden, W. H. 1968. *The Dyer's Hand and Other Essays*. New York: Vintage Books.

Bach, Kent. 2001. "You Don't Say." *Synthese*, 128:15–44.

Barnes, Annette. 1988. *On Interpretation*. Oxford: Basil Blackwell.

Barthes, Roland. 1974. *S/Z*, translated by Richard Miller. New York: Hill and Wang.

Baxandall, Michael. 1985. *Patterns of Intention: On the Historical Explanation of Pictures*. New Haven: Yale University Press.

Beardsley, Monroe. 1958. *Aesthetics: Problems in the Theory of Criticism*. New York: Harcourt, Brace and World.

——. 1970. *The Possibility of Criticism*. Detroit: Wayne State University Press.

——. 1982. "Intention and Interpretation: A Fallacy Revisited." *In the Aesthetic Point of View*, edited by Michael Wreen and Donald Callen. Ithaca, N.Y.: Cornell University Press, 188–207.

Blake, William. 1968. *Poetry and Prose of William Blake*, edited by David. V. Erdman. New York: Doubleday.

Bloom, Harold. 1975. *A Map of Misreading*. Oxford: Oxford University Press.

Bork, Robert. 1984. *Morality and Tradition in Constitutional Law*. Washington, D.C.: American Enterprise Institute for Public Policy.

Bratman, Michael. 1999. *Faces of Intention: Selected Essays on Intention and Agency*. Cambridge: Cambridge University Press.

Carrier, David. 1991. *Principles of Art History*. University Park, Pa.: Pennsylvania State University Press.

Carroll, Noël. 1986. "Art and Interaction." *Journal of Aesthetics and Art Criticism*, 45:57–68.

——. 1992. "Art, Intention, Conversation." In *Intention and Interpretation*, edited by Gary Iseminger. Philadelphia: Temple University Press, 97–131.

——. 1993. "Anglo-American Aesthetics and Contemporary Criticism: Intention and the Hermeneutics of Suspicion." *Journal of Aesthetics and Art Criticism,* 51:245–52.

——. 1998. *Interpreting the Moving Image.* Cambridge: Cambridge University Press.

——. 1999. "Myth and the Logic of Interpretation." In *Interpretation, Relativism, and the Metaphysics of Culture,* edited by Michael Krausz and Richard Shusterman. Amherst, N.Y.: Humanity Books, 40–60.

——. 2000. "Interpretation and Intention." *Metaphilosophy* 31:75–95.

Coleman, Jules, and Brian Leiter. 1996. "Determinacy, Objectivity, and Authority." In *Law and Interpretation: Essays in Legal Theory,* edited by Andrei Marmor. Oxford: Oxford University Press, 203–77.

Collingwood, R. G. 1938. *Principles of Art.* Oxford: Oxford University Press.

Currie, Gregory. 1989. *An Ontology of Art.* London: St. Martin's Press.

——. 1993. "Interpretation and Objectivity." *Mind,* 102:413–28.

Danto, Arthur. 1981. *The Transfiguration of the Commonplace.* Cambridge, Mass.: Harvard University Press.

Davidson, Donald. 1986 "A Nice Derangement of Epitaphs." In *Actions and Events: Essays on the Philosophy of Donald Davidson,* Ernest Lepore and Brian McLaughlin. Oxford: Basil Blackwell, 433–46.

Davies, David. 1996. "Interpretive Pluralism and the Ontology of Art." *Revue Internationale de Philosophie,* 50:577–92.

——. 1999. "Artistic Intentions and the Ontology of Art." *British Journal of Aesthetics,* 39:148–62.

Davies, Stephen. 1982. "The Relevance of Painters' and Writers' Intentions." *Journal of Aesthetics and Art Criticism,* 41:65–76.

——. 1988. "True Interpretations," *Philosophy and Literature,* 12:290–7.

——. 1991. *Definitions of Art.* Ithaca, N.Y.: Cornell University Press.

——. 1995. "Relativism in Interpretation." *Journal of Aesthetics and Art Criticism,* 53:8–13.

——. 1996. "Interpreting Contextualities." *Philosophy and Literature,* 20:20–38.

——. 2001. *Musical Works and Performances: A Philosophical Exploration.* Oxford: Oxford University Press.

Dickie, George. 1988. *Evaluating Art.* Phildelphia: Temple University Press.

Dickie, George, and Kent Wilson. 1995. "The Intentional Fallacy: Defending Beardsley." *Journal of Aesthetics and Art Criticism,* 53:233–50.

Dodd, Julian. 2000. "Musical Works as Eternal Types." *British Journal of Aesthetics,* 40:424–40.

Dummett, Michael. 1986. "Comments on Davidson and Hacking." In *Actions and Events: Essays on the Philosophy of Donald Davidson,* edited by Ernest Lepore and Brian Mclaughlin. Oxford: Basil Blackwell, 459–76.

Dworkin, Ronald. 1986. *Law's Empire.* Cambridge, Mass.: Harvard University Press.

Evans, Gareth. 1982. *Varieties of Reference.* Oxford: Oxford University Press.

Fallon, Richard, H. 1992. "Reflections on Dworkin and the Two faces of the Law." *Notre Dame Law Review,* 67:553–85.

Fish, Stanley. 1980. *Is There a Text in This Class? The Authority of Interpretive Communities.* Cambridge, Mass.: Harvard University Press.

——. 1989. *Doing What Comes Naturally.* Durham, N.C.: Duke University Press.

——. 1993. "How Come You Do Me Like You Do: A Response to Dennis Patterson." *Texas Law Review,* 72:57–65.

Gilbert, Margaret. 1989. *On Social Facts*. London: Routledge.

——. 2000. *Sociality and Responsibility: New Essays on Plural Subject Theory*. Lanham, Md.: Rowman and Littlefield.

Gilmore, Jonathan. 1995. "David Carrier's Art History." *Journal of Aesthetics and Art Criticicism*, 53:39–47.

Goldman, Alan. 1990. "Interpreting Art and Literature." *Journal of Aesthetics and Art Criticism*, 48:205–14.

——. 1995. *Aesthetic Value*. Boulder, Col.: Westview Press.

Gombrich, Ernst. 1972. *Symbolic Images: Studies in the Art of the Renaissance*. London: Phaedon.

Goodman, Nelson. 1978. *Ways of Worldmaking*. Indianapolis: Hackett.

Goodman, Nelson, and Catherine Elgin. 1988. *Reconceptions in Philosophy*. Indianapolis: Hackett.

Gracia, Jorge. 2000. "Relativism and the Interpretation of Texts." *Metaphilosophy*, 31:43–62.

Grice, H. P. 1957. "Meaning." *Philosophical Review*, 66:377–88.

——. 1969. "Utterer's Meaning and Intentions." *Philosophical Review*, 78:147–77.

Hacking, Ian. 1999. *The Social Construction of What*. Cambridge, Mass.: Harvard University Press.

Haigwood, Laura. 1996. "Blake's *Vision's of the Daughters of Albion*: Revising an Interpretive Tradition." In *William Blake*, edited by David Punter. New York: St. Martin's Press, 94–107.

Harbison, Craig. 1984. "Realism and Symbolism in Early Flemish Painting." *Art Bulletin*, 61:588–602.

Harris, Wendell. 1988. *Interpretive Acts: In Search of Meaning*. Oxford: Oxford University Press.

Hart, H. L. A. 1961. *The Concept of the Law*. Oxford: Oxford University Press.

Hirsch, E. D. 1967. *Validity in Interpretation*. New Haven: Yale University Press.

——. 1984. "Meaning and Significance Reinterpreted." *Critical Inquiry*, 11:202–24.

Horowitz, Amir. 2000. "Legal Interpretation, Morality, and Semantic Fetishism." *American Philosophical Quarterly*, 37:335–57.

Howell, Robert. 2002a. "Ontology and the Nature of the Literary Work." *Journal of Aesthetics and Art Criticism*, 60: 67–79.

——. 2002b. "Types: Indicated and Initiated." *British Journal of Aesthetics*, 42: 105–27.

Iseminger, Gary. 1992. "An Intentional Demonstration." In *Intention and Interpretation*, edited by Gary Iseminger. Philadelphia: Temple University Press, 76–96.

——. 1996. "Actual Intentionalism vs. Hypothetical Intentionalism." *Journal of Aesthetics and Art Criticism*, 54:319–26.

Juhl, P. D. 1980. *Interpretation: An Essay in the Philosophy of Literary Criticism*. Princeton: Princeton University Press.

Kieran, Matthew. 1996. "In Defence of Critical Pluralism." *British Journal of Aesthetics*, 36:339–51.

Kivy, Peter. 1993. *The Fine Art of Repetition*. Cambridge: Cambridge University Press.

Knapp, Steven, and Walter Benn Michaels. 1985. "Against Theory." In *Against*

Theory, edited by W. J. T. Mitchell, 11–30. Chicago: University of Chicago Press.

Krausz, Michael. 1990. "Interpretation and its Art Objects: Two Views." *Monist*, 73:222–32.

——. 1993. *Rightness and Reasons: Interpretation in Cultural Practices*. Ithaca, N.Y.: Cornell University Press.

——. 2000. *Limits of Rightness*. Lanham, Md.: Rowman and Littlefield.

Lamarque, Peter. 2000. "Objects of Interpretation." *Metaphilosophy*, 31:96–124.

——. 2002. "Appreciation and Literary Interpretation." In *Is There the Single Right Interpretation?*, edited by Michael Krausz. University Park, Pa.: Pennsylvania State University Press.

Lamarque, Peter, and Stein Haugom Olsen. 1994. *Truth, Fiction and Literature*. Oxford: Oxford University Press.

Lawrence, D. H. 1962. "The Scarlet Letter." In *Perspectives on Modern Literature*, edited by Frederick J. Hoffman, 42–55. Evanston, Ill.: Row, Peterson.

Levinson, Jerrold. 1990. *Music, Art, and Metaphysics*. Ithaca, N.Y.: Cornell University Press.

——. 1996. *The Pleasures of Aesthetics*. Ithaca, N.Y.: Cornell University Press.

——. 1999. "Two Notions of Interpretation." In *Interpretation and its Boundaries*, edited by Arto Haapala and Ossi Naukarinnen. Helsinki: Helsinki University Press, 8–27.

Livingston, Paisley. 1996. "Arguing over Intentions." *Revue Internationale de Philosophie*, 50:615–33.

——. 1998. "Intentionalism in Aesthetics." *New Literary History*, 29:831–46.

Margolis, Joseph. 1980. *Art and Philosophy*. Brighton: Harvester Press.

——. 1991. *The Truth about Relativism*. Oxford: Basil Blackwell.

——. 1995a. *Interpretation Radical but not Unruly: The New Puzzle of the Arts and History*. Berkeley: University of California Press.

——. 1995b. Plain Talk about Interpretation on the Relativistic Model." *Journal of Aesthetics and Art Criticism*, 53:1–7.

——. 1999a. *What, After All, is a Work of Art*. University Park, Pa.: Pennsylvania State University Press.

——. 1999b. "Replies in Search of Self-Discovery." In *Interpretation, Relativism and the Metaphysics of Culture*, edited by Michael Krausz and Richard Shusterman. Amherst, N.Y.: Humanity Books, 337–408.

——. 2000. "Relativism and Interpretive Objectivity." *Metaphilosophy*, 31:200–26.

Marmor, Andrei, ed. 1996. *Law and Interpretation: Essays in Legal Theory*. Oxford: Oxford University Press.

McFee, Graham. 1980. "The Historicity of Art." *Journal of Aesthetics and Art Criticism*, 38:302–24.

——. 1992. "The Historical Character of Art: A Reappraisal." *British Journal of Aesthetics*, 32:307–19.

——. 1995. "Back to the Future: A reply to Sharpe." *British Journal of Aesthetics*, 35:278–83.

Mee, John. 1998. "The 'Insidious Poison of Secret Influence': A New Historical Context for Blake's 'The Sick Rose.'" *Eighteenth Century Life*, 22:111–22.

Moore, Michael, S. 1996. "Interpreting Interpretation." In *Law and Interpretation: Essays in Legal Theory*, edited by Andrei Marmor. Oxford: Oxford University Press, 1–29.

Nagel, Thomas. 1986. *The View from Nowhere*. Oxford: Oxford University Press.

Nathan, Daniel. 1992. "Irony, Metaphor, and the Problem of Intention." In *Intention and Interpretation*, edited by Gary Iseminger. Philadelphia: Temple University Press, 183–202.

Nehamas, Alexander. 1981. "The Postulated Author: Critical Monism as a Regulative Ideal." *Critical Inquiry*, 8:133–49.

——. 1987. "Writer, Work, Text, Author." In *Literature and the Question of Philosophy*, edited by Anthony J. Cascardi. Baltimore: Johns Hopkins University Press, 267–91.

Olsen, Stein Haugom. 1982. "The Meaning of a Literary Work." *New Literary History*, 14:13–32.

Panofsky, Erwin. 1966. *Early Netherlandish Painting*. Cambridge, Mass.: Harvard University Press.

Patterson, Dennis. 1996. *Law and Truth*. Oxford: Oxford University Press.

Percival, Philip. 2000. "Stecker's Dilemma: A Constructive Response." *Journal of Aesthetics and Art Criticism*, 58:51–60.

——. 2002a. "Is the Constructivist Dilemma Floored?" *Journal of Aesthetics and Art Criticism*, 60:82–6.

——. 2002b. "Can Novel Critical Interpretations Create Artworks Distinct from Themselves?" In *Is There the Single Right Interpretation?*, edited by Michael Krausz. University Park, Pa.: Pennsylvania State University Press.

Perry, Michael, J. 1998. "What is 'the Constitution'? (and Other Fundamental Questions)." In *Constitutionalism: Philosophical Foundations*, edited by Larry Alexander. Cambridge: Cambridge University Press, 99–151.

Pinsky, Robert. 1984. "Song of Reasons." *Antaeus*, 52:35–6.

Postema, Gerald. 1987. "'Protestant' Interpretation and Social Practice." *Law and Philosophy*, 6:283–319.

——. 1996. "Law's Autonomy and Public Practical Reason." In *The Autonomy of the Law*, edited by Robert P. George. Oxford: Oxford University Press, 79–118.

Predelli, Stefano. 2001. "Musical Ontology and the Argument from Creation." *British Journal of Aesthetics*, 41:279–92.

Punter, David. 1996. *William Blake*. New York: St. Martin's Press.

Putnam, Hilary, 1990. *Realism with a Human Face*, edited by James Conant. Cambridge, Mass.: Harvard University Press.

Raz, Joseph. 1986. "Dworkin: A New Link in the Chain." *California Law Review*, 74:1103–19.

——. 1996. "Intention in Interpretation." In *The Autonomy of the Law*, edited by Robert P. George. Oxford: Oxford University Press, 249–86.

——. 1998. "On the Authority and Interpretation of Constitutions: Some Preliminaries." In *Constitutionalism: Philosophical Foundations*, edited by Larry Alexander. Cambridge: Cambridge University Press, 152–93.

Recanati, Francois. 2001. "What is Said." *Synthese*, 128:25–91.

Roskill, Mark. 1989. *The Interpretation of Pictures*. Amherst: University of Massachusetts Press.

Savile, Anthony. 1996. "Instrumentalism and the Interpretation of Narrative." *Mind*, 105:553–76.

Scalia, Antonin. 1997. *A Matter of Interpretation: Federal Courts and the Law*. Princeton: Princeton University Press.

Searle, John. 1995. *The Construction of Social Reality*. New York: Free Press.

Sharpe, R. A. 1994. "Making the Past: McFee's Forward Retroactivism." *British*

Journal of Aesthetics, 34:170–3.

Shiner, Roger. 1987. "The Hermeneutics of Adjudication." In *Anti-Foundationalism and Practical Reasoning*, edited by Evan Simpson, 233–46.

Shusterman, Richard. 1988a. *T. S. Eliot and the Philosophy of Criticism*. New York: Columbia University Press.

———. 1988b. "Interpretation, Intention, Truth." *Journal of Aesthetics and Art Criticism*, 45:399–411.

Silvers, Anita. 1990. "Politics and the Production of Narrative Identities." *Philosophy and Literature*, 14:99–107.

Simpson, David. 1996. "Reading Blake and Derrida – Our Ceasers neither Praised nor Buried." In *William Blake*, edited by David Punter. New York: St. Martin's Press, 149–64.

Stecker, Robert. 1990. "Fish's Argument for the Relativity of Interpretive Truth." *Journal of Aesthetics and Art Criticism*, 48:22–30.

———. 1992. "Incompatible Interpretations." *Journal of Aesthetics and Art Criticism*, 50:291–8.

———. 1993. "The Role of Intention and Convention in Interpreting Artworks." *Southern Journal of Philosophy*, 31:471–89.

———. 1994. "Art Interpretation." *Journal of Aesthetics and Art Criticism*, 52:193–206.

———. 1995a. "Objectivity and Interpretation." *Philosophy and Literature*, 19:48–59.

———. 1995b. "Relativism about Interpretation." *Journal of Aesthetics and Art Criticism*, 53:14–18.

———. 1997a. *Artworks: Definition, Meaning, Value*. University Park, Pa.: Pennsylvania State University Press.

———. 1997b. "The Constructivist's Dilemma." *Journal of Aesthetics and Art Criticism*, 55:43–51.

———. 1997c. "Two Conceptions of Artistic Value." *Iyyun: The Jerusalem Philosophical Quarterly*, 46:51–62.

———. Forthcoming. "Artistic Value." In *The Oxford Handbook of Aesthetics*, edited by Jerrold Levinson. Oxford: Oxford University Press.

Stout, Jeffrey. 1982. "What is the Meaning of a Text." *New Literary History*, 14:1–12.

Sunstein, Cass. 1989. "Interpreting Statutes in the Regulatory State." *Harvard Law Review*, 103:405–508.

Thom, Paul. 1997. Review of *Rightness and Reasons*, by Michael Krausz, *Interpretation Radical but not Unruly*, by Joseph Margolis, and "The Constructivist's Dilemma," by Robert Stecker. *Literature and Aesthetics*, October, 181–5.

———. 2000a. *Making Sense*. Lanham, Md.: Rowman and Littlefield.

———. 2000b. "On Changing the Subject." *Metaphilosophy*, 31:63–74.

Thomasson, Amie. 1999. *Fiction and Metaphysics*. Cambridge: Cambridge University Press.

Tolhurst, William. 1979. "On What a Text is and How it Means." *British Journal of Aesthetics*, 19:3–14.

Waldron, Jeremy. 1996. Legislators' Intentions and Unintentional Legislation." In *Law and Interpretation: Essays in Legal Theory*, edited by Andrei Marmor. Oxford: Oxford University Press, 329–56.

Webster, Brenda. 1996. "Blake, Women and Sexuality." In *William Blake*, edited by David Punter. New York: St. Martin's Press, 188–206.

Wiggins, David. 1980. *Sameness and Substance.* Oxford: Basil Blackwell.

Williams, Bernard. 1966. "Imagination and The Self." *Proceedings of the British Academy.*

Wollheim, Richard. 1980. *Art and its Objects.* 2nd ed. Cambridge: Cambridge University Press.

Wolterstorff, Nicholas. 1980. *Works and Worlds of Art.* Oxford: Clarendon Press.

Index